CYBERBULLYING AT UNIVERSITY IN INTERNATIONAL CONTEXTS

Cyberbullying is a problem that is being increasingly investigated by researchers; however, much of the cyberbullying research literature to date has focused on children and youth. *Cyberbullying at University in International Contexts* fills the gap in the research literature by examining the nature, extent, impacts, proposed solutions, and policy and practice considerations of bullying in the cyber-world at post-secondary institutions, where reports of serious cyberbullying incidents have become more prevalent.

This book brings together cutting-edge research from around the world to examine the issue of cyberbullying through a multi-disciplinary lens, offering an array of approaches, interpretations, and solutions. It is not solely focused on cyberbullying by and against students, but also includes cyberbullying by and against faculty members, and permutations involving both students and faculty, as well as institutional staff, presenting perspectives from students, faculty, practitioners, and senior university policymakers. It draws on research from education, criminology, psychology, sociology, communications, law, health sciences, social work, humanities, labour studies and is valuable reading for graduate students in these fields. It is also essential reading for policymakers, practitioners, and university administrators who recognize their responsibility to provide a healthy workplace for their staff, as well as a safe and respectful environment for their students.

Dr. Wanda Cassidy (Associate Professor, Faculty of Education), Dr. Chantal Faucher (Post-doctoral fellow, Centre for Education, Law & Society), and Dr. Margaret Jackson (Professor Emerita, School of Criminology) from Simon Fraser University, Canada, have been researching cyberbullying among youth and young adults for many years. They have published a range of academic articles, research reports, and policy papers on this topic locally, nationally, and internationally.

CYBERBULLYING AT UNIVERSITY IN INTERNATIONAL CONTEXTS

Edited by
Wanda Cassidy,
Chantal Faucher, and
Margaret Jackson

Routledge
Taylor & Francis Group
LONDON AND NEW YORK

First published 2019
by Routledge
711 Third Avenue, New York, NY 10017

and by Routledge
2 Park Square, Milton Park, Abingdon, Oxon, OX14 4RN

Routledge is an imprint of the Taylor & Francis Group, an informa business

Library of Congress Cataloging-in-Publication Data
A catalog record for this Book has been requested

ISBN: 978-1-138-73039-7 (hbk)
ISBN: 978-1-138-73044-1 (pbk)
ISBN: 978-1-315-18940-6 (ebk)

Typeset in Bembo
by Apex CoVantage, LLC

MIX
Paper from responsible sources
FSC™ C013985

Printed in the United Kingdom
by Henry Ling Limited

CONTENTS

TABLES

FOREWORD

The study of traditional, or offline, bullying has a history of some 40 years. Thousands of publications have come from what has developed, over that period, into a very vigorous research program. This has gone along with increased public awareness of the prevalence of bullying; the harm it can cause both in the short and long term; and the steps that can be taken to reduce the prevalence and the harm. Progress is only partial. The temptation to abuse power, and attempt to get status or material advantage, by bullying others, is likely to be present in human groups, and especially those from which the victim cannot easily depart – families, schools, colleges, the workplace. It would be foolhardy to imagine that we can 'eliminate' bullying. But it is not foolhardy to imagine that we can do a great deal to diminish the extent to which it occurs and the harm it brings about. Actions can include improving the climate of human groups, dealing with bullying incidents promptly, empowering bystanders, and supporting victims effectively. There are indications that rates of traditional bullying are declining – not in all countries and contexts, but in many. If widely substantiated, this would suggest that the extensive body of research knowledge has helped feed into awareness and action, and improved many people's well-being as a result.

Cyberbullying, or online bullying, has a much shorter history. Although the phenomenon may go back around 20 years, it is only in the last 10 years that it has been a noticeable topic of research. However, the flow of publications in the area has expanded rapidly, with hundreds of articles appearing in the last few years. Although much of this research has extended methods and concepts from offline bullying, cyberbullying brings its own particular features and challenges. These include the possible anonymity of the perpetrator, the 24/7 nature of the phenomenon, and the extent to which criteria for traditional bullying, notably repetition and imbalance of power, are useful in the cyber domain. At the time of this writing, there is also considerable debate about whether cyberbullying is much less frequent than traditional bullying, and has little extra impact; or by contrast, whether it is increasing more than traditional bullying, and has as much or more negative impact on victims. Another debate concerns whether interventions against cyberbullying should mainly follow methods used for traditional bullying, or should use more specific interventions, or both. Not only is research moving fast in the area, but so also is the phenomenon itself, as new forms of information and communication technology (ICT) develop, wider age ranges become familiar with them, and specific laws and policies come into effect.

As with traditional bullying, much of the research in cyberbullying has been on young people, still at school. The mid-adolescent period generally shows peaks in bullying and also in involvement with mobile phones and the internet. However, this may change as the 'digital natives' get older and move into early adulthood, as is happening now. This volume is thus very timely in bringing together a strong and varied collection of research, on cyberbullying in young adults, usually those at college or university. Interestingly, this can often also involve faculty, sometimes at the receiving end of anonymous abuse from students, as well as abuse from colleagues, the latter being an example of workplace cyberbullying. There are contributions from a number of different countries and indeed continents. Both quantitative, qualitative, and mixed-methods studies are represented. There are descriptive studies, including some discussing risk factors such as gender, and LGBTQ status. There are chapters demonstrating the negative impact of cyberbullying. And, there are a good number of contributions on policy issues and possible solutions, or at least ways of tackling cyberbullying effectively. The research presented in these chapters is both a challenge to all concerned to improve cyber safety in these domains, and also a valuable source of knowledge and practical actions to help us to do so.

Peter K. Smith
Professor Emeritus
Goldsmiths, University of London, UK

PREFACE

A few years ago, when we (two of the editors) were researching cyberbullying at the K–12 level, we experienced cyberbullying from undergraduate students taking courses with us through distance education. At the same time, during our presentations at conferences, audience members were telling us their stories of being cyberbullied in the academy, or stories they knew of, encouraging us to extend our research from schools to the post-secondary environment.

These experiences prompted us to secure funding from the Social Sciences and Humanities Research Council of Canada to investigate the extent to which cyberbullying was occurring at Canadian university campuses; the impact on students and faculty; whether policies, intervention, and prevention practices were in place to counter cyberbullying; and ways to more effectively address the problems as identified. We were curious whether the motivation to cyberbully at the post-secondary level was similar to the reasons younger students gave for targeting a friend, acquaintance, or stranger, and what the impacts might be on adults and the wider university culture.

We have since reported on the findings from this research at conferences and in academic journals (some of which are also included in Chapters 5, 8, and 16 of this volume). Furthermore, in 2014, we co-organized a symposium titled *Cyberbullying at Canadian Universities: Linking Research, Policy, and Practice*, where we shared preliminary findings with various university stakeholders including faculty, students, staff, and administrators/policymakers gathered for a day of dialogue on this issue. Participants clearly indicated the need to increase awareness of the nature and extent of this problem at the university level and for concrete information about applicable policies and solutions.

Interestingly, scholars in several other jurisdictions were also curious about the phenomenon and were undertaking similar research. Many of these scholars, along with several of the participants from the symposium, are contributors to this book, adding valuable insights to the discussion, and providing an international and applied perspective. What is clear is that cyberbullying at the post-secondary level among students, and towards and among faculty members, is not restricted to one country; rather, it appears to be a global problem. Higher education environments are not immune to the online bullying problems identified at the primary and secondary school levels, nor can they be seen as separate from workplace cyberbullying.

The aim of this book is to begin to fill that gap in the research literature by discussing the nature, extent, impacts, proposed solutions, and policy and practice considerations of bullying in the cyber-world at post-secondary. It is our hope that the range of international and multi-disciplinary perspectives brought together in this book will serve to raise awareness regarding this problem and offer insights into approaches for addressing it in a meaningful way.

ACKNOWLEDGEMENTS

We are hugely indebted to the thousands of research participants around the world who took the time and made the effort to share their experiences with the authors of the various chapters in this book. The wealth of knowledge that has accrued from their willingness to share their thoughts will contribute to a better understanding of this phenomenon and, hopefully, a safer and healthier online environment for all concerned.

We also wish to express our gratitude to Lucy Kennedy, our editor at Routledge, for her efforts at bringing this book to life, as well as to the two anonymous reviewers whose feedback helped to shape the book's final form.

Additionally, we extend our sincere thanks to Alyson Kissner and Cristina Serverius for their diligent text and copyediting work prior to submission of the manuscript to Routledge.

The research reported in the three chapters written by the editors was supported by Social Sciences and Humanities Research Council grant #410–2011–1800.

We also wish to acknowledge the funding provided by the Simon Fraser University Publication Fund towards text and copyediting prior to submission to the publisher.

CONTRIBUTORS

Ikuko Aoyama (PhD, Baylor University) is specially appointed Associate Professor of Shizuoka University. Her research interests are bullying, cyberbullying, and prevention, as well as social emotional learning and resilience. She is principal investigator in a cross-cultural Japan Society for the Promotion of Science (JSPS)-funded study on bullying and cyberbullying and is co-Principal Investigator on several other projects.

Tara Black was, at the time of the writing of her chapter, an Associate Director of a health promotion program at Simon Fraser University, Canada. She co-chaired an international group that led to the development of the *Okanagan Charter: An International Charter for Health Promoting Universities and Colleges*.

Catherine Blaya is Professor in Education Sciences at the Teachers' University in Lausanne and Chair of the International Observatory of Violence in Schools. She has dedicated her academic career to researching issues that might affect young people, such as dropping out of school, bullying, and cyberbullying.

Lida Blizard completed her doctorate degree in Educational Leadership from Simon Fraser University in 2014, where she studied post-secondary faculty members' experiences of cyberbullying by students and the impact on targeted individuals. She is currently employed as a full-time faculty member at Kwantlen Polytechnic University in Canada.

Wanda Cassidy is Associate Professor in the Faculty of Education and Director of the Centre for Education, Law and Society at Simon Fraser University. She researches and writes in the areas of social justice and law-related education, the ethic of care, marginalized youth, and cyberbullying at K–12 and post-secondary.

Rayén Condeza (PhD, Université de Montréal) is Associate Professor, Faculty of Communication (Department of Applied Communication) and Director of Communication and got her Education Master's degree at Pontificia Universidad Católica de Chile. Her research interests are children and youth experience using new technologies and Communication and Education studies.

Iain Coyne is Senior Lecturer in Organizational Psychology in the School of Business and Economics, Loughborough University. Iain has written numerous peer-reviewed journal articles and book chapters on workplace bullying/cyberbullying and previously led a working group on a European COST Action researching Cyber-bullying in Educational Contexts (2008–2012).

Jon Driver is Professor in the Department of Archaeology at Simon Fraser University, Canada. At the time of the writing of his chapter, he was Vice-President Academic and Provost, with many years of administrative experience within the university.

Samuel Farley is Lecturer in Organizational Psychology at the University of Leeds Business School. He is particularly interested in the 'dark side' of workplace behaviour, including bullying, cyberbullying, and incivility. Within this field, his interests include the measurement of bullying and how targets attribute blame for their experiences.

Chantal Faucher (PhD, Criminology, Simon Fraser University) is a postdoctoral fellow with the Centre for Education, Law and Society at Simon Fraser University, Canada. She is involved in research projects on cyberbullying at the post-secondary level and teaches criminal justice at Langara College, Vancouver, BC.

Gonzalo Gallardo (Master's, Educational Psychology) is Assistant Professor at the School of Psychology at the Pontificia Universidad Católica de Chile and in the Faculty of Psychology at the Universidad Alberto Hurtado. He is the Research Coordinator at the Observatorio de la Juventud Universitaria in the Student Affairs Office.

Mark Giancaspro (PhD, University of Adelaide) is Lecturer at the University of Adelaide Law School. Mark practices and researches primarily in the fields of contract law, commercial law, operational commercial law, and sports law, and his teaching philosophy centres upon student engagement and well-being.

Margaret Jackson is Professor Emerita in the School of Criminology at Simon Fraser University, Director of FREDA, an SFU research centre focusing upon violence against women, and past Director of the School of Criminology. In addition to bullying/cyberbullying issues, other research areas include justice policy and family/criminal law case decision-making.

Kenichi Kanayama (PhD) is Professor of Department of Childhood Education, Faculty of Human Development and Education, Kobe Shinwa Women's University. He specializes in clinical and school psychology.

Tomoyuki Kanetsuna (PhD, Goldsmiths, University of London) is Associate Professor of Kagawa University. He was a research assistant for the Unit for School and Family Studies, Goldsmiths, mainly involved in research on school bullying. He is leading a JSPS-funded research project regarding the relationships between online self-presentation and online misbehaviour.

Loraleigh Keashly is a Professor in the Department of Communication, Wayne State University, Detroit. Her research and consulting work focus on the quality of work relationships, particularly the amelioration of uncivil, hostile, and bullying behaviours. She has recently focused her attention on problematic behaviours in academic environments, helping universities address these issues.

Shinji Kurihara (PhD) is Professor of the Department of Learning Science, Graduate School of Education, Hiroshima University, Japan. He is the President of the Japanese Association of School Counselling and Guidance.

Colette Langos (PhD, University of South Australia) is a Senior Lecturer at the University of Adelaide Law School. Colette researches primarily in the areas of law, technology, and commercial law in a military context. Colette is an international expert on the regulation and management of negative online behaviours.

Elisa Larrañaga is a faculty member in the Department of Psychology, University of Castilla-La Mancha, Faculty of Social Work. Areas of research include sexism and behavioural problems, gender, and reading practices.

Raúl Navarro is a faculty member in the Department of Psychology, University of Castilla-La Mancha, Faculty of Education. Area of research include gender differences in aggressive behaviour, social factors associated with bullying, cyberbullying, and ghosting.

Anastasio Ovejero is a faculty member in the Department of Psychology, University of Valladolid, Faculty of Work Sciences. Area of research include cooperative learning, workplace violence, critical social psychology, bullying, and cyberbullying.

Aynsley Pescitelli is a PhD Candidate in the School of Criminology at Simon Fraser University. Her research interests include sexual violence at post-secondary institutions, sexual violence policy, media representations of crime and criminal justice, victimology, cybervictimization, gender and crime, minorities and the criminal justice system, hate crime, and feminist criminology.

Pablo Reyes Pérez (PhD, Psychoanalysis, Université Paris VIII Vincennes-Saint Denis) studied Psychology at Pontificia Universidad Católica de Chile. He is Assistant Professor at the Department of Psychology, Universidad de Chile, and in the School of Psychology, Pontificia Universidad Católica de Chile. His research interests are identity, violence, and psychoanalysis.

Dov Schafer is a PhD student in Educational Technology and Learning Design at Simon Fraser University. Dov grew up as a citizen of online game worlds; he views interactive games as tools for enhancing learning and motivation. His work is focused on leveraging the power of Augmented Reality for instruction and assessment.

Natalie Sharpe, B.A. (Hon), M.A., has been a practicing ombudsperson at the University of Alberta for over three decades and is President of the Association of Canadian College and University Ombudspersons. She has presented nationally and internationally at ombuds professional conferences and contributed to ombuds journals.

Yuichi Toda (PhD, University of Tokyo) is Professor of Osaka Kyoiku University. He was a visiting fellow at Goldsmiths College, University of London and a short-time visiting professor at University of Vienna. His research with Dr Dagmar Strohmeier received den Hauptpreis des Bank Austria Preises zur Förderung innovativer Forschungsprojekte 2008 (Bank Austria Prize for the Promotion of Innovative Research Projects 2008).

Santiago Yubero is a faculty member in the Department of Psychology, University of Castilla-La Mancha, Faculty of Education and Humanities. His areas of research include bullying and workplace violence, gender, and reading practices.

INTRODUCTION

Context, framework, and perspective

Wanda Cassidy, Chantal Faucher, and Margaret Jackson

For well over a decade now, cyberbullying has been recognized as an issue similar to, and yet also quite distinct from, traditional forms of bullying that were documented well before the proliferation of technology in everyday life. The topic of cyberbullying has increasingly been researched throughout the world, and a better understanding of the nature, extent, impacts, coping strategies, solutions, policy, and practice has begun to emerge with respect to cyberbullying among students at the elementary, middle, and secondary education levels (Cassidy, Faucher, & Jackson, 2013; Navarro, Yubero, & Larrañaga, 2016; Smith & Steffgen, 2013).

However, cyberbullying is no longer viewed just as a problem faced by the young. In recent years, the media has highlighted several serious cases of cyberbullying between students on university campuses that have resulted in suicide. As technology increasingly becomes the vehicle of communication on campuses, faculty members, too, are being subjected to online harassment and demands, from students, as well as from colleagues. University administrators recognize their responsibility to provide a healthy workplace for their staff, as well as a safe and respectful environment for their students.

While no clear consensus exists as far as the definition of cyberbullying, many researchers have tended to extrapolate some of the defining features from the accepted definition of bullying: repeated aggressive behaviours, intent to cause harm, and power imbalance between victim and bully (Olweus, 1993). However, the way in which those features manifest in the online context has been a source of interest among researchers. For instance, the self-perpetuating nature of online posts that can be re-visited and re-circulated transforms the meaning of repetition in the cyber context (Dooley, Pyżalski, & Cross, 2009; Kowalski, Limber, & Agatston, 2012; Menesini, 2012). Also, the disinhibition and deindividuation associated with online exchanges, and particularly anonymity in those communications, and the wider potential audience that characterize the cyber-world redefine the common notion of power imbalance (Davis & Nixon, 2012; Hinduja & Patchin, 2012; Lyu & Zhang, 2017; Suler, 2004).

Cyberbullying is carried out using electronic devices through text messaging, email, websites (such as rating websites and course websites, in particular, for the university context), blogs, chats, various online platforms such as Twitter, Snapchat, Instagram, Facebook, WhatsApp, and other social networking sites, game servers, YouTube and other video-sharing websites, Skype, and many more. It can include a wide range of behaviours such as using language or images that can defame, threaten, harass, bully, exclude, discriminate, demean, humiliate, stalk, or disclose personal information without consent, or that are offensive, vulgar, or derogatory. It can also be understood to include online incivility, mobbing, and online harassment. Some of these behaviours may also extend into criminal offences, depending on the jurisdiction as well as the extent and intent of the behaviours.

Relatively little research attention, however, has been paid to the nature, extent, and impact of cyberbullying among adults, including what is occurring at the post-secondary level. Some researchers have suggested that bullying and cyberbullying behaviours exist on a continuum from childhood into adulthood (Cowie & Myers, 2016; Faucher, Cassidy, & Jackson, 2015). Recent research has begun to document an increase in uncivil online discourse at the university (Clark, Werth, & Ahten, 2012; Lampman, 2012; Wildermuth & Davis, 2012) as well as the prevalence, negative effects, coping strategies, and policy and practice implications of cyberbullying among undergraduate students and faculty members (Blaya, Kaur, Sandhu, & Sundaram, 2018; Blizard, 2016; Cassidy, Faucher, & Jackson, 2014; Faucher et al., 2015; McKay, Arnold, Fratzl, & Thomas, 2008; Orel, Campbell, Wozencraft, Leong, & Kimpton, 2017; Vance, 2010; Wright, 2016; Yubero, Navarro, Elche, Larrañaga, & Ovejero, 2017).

The aim of this book is to begin to fill that gap in the research literature by discussing the nature, extent, impacts, proposed solutions, and policy and practice considerations of bullying in the cyber-world at post-secondary. The research findings that are discussed in this book have policy and practice implications for university decision-makers who are increasingly faced with the growing problems and impacts of cyberbullying on campuses.

This edited volume draws on recent research on cyberbullying at the post-secondary level conducted by scholars from North America, South America, the United Kingdom, Europe, Asia, and Australia. Since the editors, as well as the participating chapter authors, are rooted in a variety of scholarly perspectives (education, criminology, psychology, sociology, communications, law, health sciences, social work, humanities, labour studies), the book reflects a multi-disciplinary lens and array of approaches, interpretations, and solutions.

The book is divided into four main parts. In the first part, six contributions examine the nature and extent of cyberbullying in the post-secondary context. In Chapter 1, Catherine Blaya discusses her findings from two studies (surveys and interviews) of French university students. These studies examined the prevalence and consequences of cyberviolence and cyberbullying in light of variables such as gender, nationality, and year of study. In Chapter 2, Tomoyuki Kanetsuna, Ikuko Aoyama, and Yuichi Toda review what is known to date about the nature and extent of cyberbullying among post-secondary students in Japan. In particular, they examine how beliefs about online anonymity contribute to moral disengagement and social withdrawal. In Chapter 3, Rayén Condeza, Gonzalo Gallardo, and Pablo Reyes Pérez present their findings from an exploratory study of cyberbullying among post-secondary students in Chile. The vast extent of exposure to cyberbullying among students either as bullies, victims, and/or bystanders is revealed, as are certain beliefs normalizing cyberbullying behaviours among this population. In Chapter 4, Aynsley Pescitelli from Canada delves into the homophobic and transphobic online experiences of lesbian, gay, bisexual, transgender, queer, and/or questioning (LGBTQ) post-secondary students. In Chapter 5, Chantal Faucher, Wanda Cassidy, and Margaret Jackson provide an overview of their research examining the cyberbullying experiences of students and faculty members at four Canadian universities. These findings advance a gendered interpretation of vulnerability to cyberbullying, which is closely tied to power imbalances among members of the university community. In Chapter 6, Iain Coyne and Samuel Farley, from the UK, examine the international research literature on workplace cyberbullying more broadly and its potential implications for understanding cyberbullying in universities as workplaces and its impacts on individual and organizational well-being.

The second part of the book brings together three contributions discussing the impacts of cyberbullying on post-secondary students and faculty. In Chapter 7, Elisa Larrañaga, Santiago Yubero, Raúl Navarro, and Anastasio Ovejero examine a range of research on risk factors for cyberbullying victimization among post-secondary students and the protective or buffering role social support may play in mitigating the impacts of cyberbullying. The chapter also reports on the authors' recent study of Spanish university students in a teacher education program, describing their victimization experiences and the coping strategies they perceive to be most useful. In Chapter 8, Wanda Cassidy, Chantal Faucher, and Margaret Jackson discuss the mental and physical health, relational, self-esteem, and work-related impacts experienced by students and faculty members who had been cyberbullied at the four Canadian universities they studied. Participants also reported frustration with inadequate reporting and problem-solving mechanisms, which further negatively affected their health and well-being. In Chapter 9, Lida Blizard discusses the findings from her surveys and interviews with Canadian faculty members who have been cyberbullied by students. The extent of detrimental effects reported by the research participants in this study is long-lasting and wide-ranging.

The third part of the book turns to solutions to the problem of cyberbullying, with a decidedly practical slant among the five contributions. In Chapter 10,

Loraleigh Keashly from the United States examines the role of cyber-bystanders and how to prepare members of the campus community to intervene when they witness cyberbullying. The chapter explores the unique opportunities and challenges associated with decision-making processes available for cyber-bystander engagement. In Chapter 11, Natalie Sharpe, ombudsperson at the University of Alberta, Canada, describes the role of the university ombudsperson in not only responding to cyberbullying incidents on campus but also preventing such incidents through education initiatives as well as policy and protocol development. In Chapter 12, Tara Black discusses inscribing approaches to cyberbullying within a campus-wide "healthy campus" initiative led by the student services department, and in particular the health and counselling services at Simon Fraser University, Canada. In Chapter 13, Kenichi Kanayama and Shinji Kurihara discuss one Japanese university's approach to the prevention of cyberbullying, combining different levels of support for students, including peer support, mental health screening, media literacy education, teamwork among professionals at the university, counselling services, and medical referrals. This comprehensive student support approach has proven successful. In Chapter 14, Samuel Farley and Iain Coyne provide insight for post-secondary institutions' administrators and human resource personnel looking to limit workplace cyberbullying in universities. They suggest evidence-based practices for interventions, drawing from the youth cyberbullying and traditional workplace bullying intervention literatures.

Finally, the fourth part of the book adopts a policy lens for approaching the problem of cyberbullying. In Chapter 15, Colette Langos and Mark Giancaspro discuss the notion of harm and the ways in which it relates to the legal and policy contexts of universities in Australia. Survey findings reported in this chapter suggest that not all forms of cyberbullying are perceived to be equally harmful, and respondents have relatively little knowledge about the laws and policies governing cyberbullying behaviour. In Chapter 16, Margaret Jackson, Chantal Faucher, and Wanda Cassidy, review the evolution of Canadian post-secondary cyberbullying policies along with their intents and values. Arguments from differing perspectives and geographic locations are explored for a rights-based policy framework. In Chapter 17, Jon Driver provides his own observations of how best to handle faculty members who engage in cyberbullying behaviours based on his years of experience in the office of provost and other administrative positions within the university. In Chapter 18, Dov Schafer uses his own experience as a student who was anonymously cyberbullied to reflect on methods of eliminating anonymity from cyber-exchanges, such as user reporting and distributed ledger technologies, in order to reduce some types of cyberbullying such as those he endured.

The concluding chapter summarizes the dominant themes discussed in each of the chapters, including the nature, extent, and rationale for cyberbullying at the post-secondary level, the role of gender as a factor, identified impacts on the health and well-being of student and faculty victims, participants' frustrations with the lack of redress, recommended solutions including practical approaches that are being implemented, the need for appropriate policy and policy values to guide the development and implementation of those solutions, as well as areas for further research. The editors conclude with a call to action for universities to make cyberbullying prevention and intervention a priority and to work collaboratively with stakeholders to develop research-based, creative solutions to address the identified problems.

References

Blaya, C., Kaur, K., Sandhu, D., & Sundaram, S. (2018). Cyberbullying in higher education in India and France: An empirical investigation. In P. K. Smith, S. Sundaram, B. Spears, C. Blaya, M. Schäfer, & D. Sandhu (Eds.), *Bullying, cyberbullying and student well-being in schools: Comparing European, Australian and Indian perspectives* (pp. 107–129). Cambridge, UK: Cambridge University Press.

Blizard, L. M. (2016). Faculty members' experiences of cyberbullying by students at one Canadian university: Impact and recommendations. *International Research in Higher Education, 1*(1), 107–124. doi:10.5430/irhe.v1n1p107

Cassidy, W., Faucher, C., & Jackson, M. (2013). Cyberbullying among youth: A comprehensive review of current international research and its implications and application to policy and practice. By invitation, in special international issue of *School Psychology International, 34*(6), 575–612. doi:10.1177/0143034313479697

Cassidy, W., Faucher, C., & Jackson, M. (2014). The dark side of the ivory tower: Cyberbullying of university faculty and teaching personnel. *Alberta Journal of Educational Research, 60*(2), 279–299.

Clark, C. M., Werth, L., & Ahten, S. (2012). Cyber-bullying and incivility in the online learning environment, Part 1: Addressing faculty and student perceptions. *Nurse Educator, 37*(4), 150–156.

Cowie, H., & Myers, C. A. (Eds.). (2016). *Bullying among university students: Cross-national perspectives* (pp. 3–14). London: Routledge.

Davis, S., & Nixon, C. (2012). Empowering bystanders. In J. W. Patchin & S. Hinduja (Eds.), *Cyberbullying prevention and response: Expert perspectives* (pp. 93–109). New York: Routledge.

Dooley, J. J., Pyżalski, J., & Cross, D. (2009). Cyberbullying versus face-to-face bullying: A theoretical and conceptual review. *Journal of Psychology, 217*(4), 182–188.

Faucher, C., Cassidy, W., & Jackson, M. (2015). From the sandbox to the inbox: Comparing the acts, impacts, and solutions of bullying in K-12, higher education, and the workplace. *Journal of Education and Training Studies, 3*(6), 111–125. doi:10.11114/jets.v3i6.1033

Hinduja, S., & Patchin, J. W. (2012). *School climate 2.0: Preventing cyberbullying and sexting one classroom at a time.* Thousand Oaks, CA: Corwin Press.

Kowalski, R. M., Limber, S. P., & Agatston, P. W. (2012). *Cyberbullying: Bullying in the digital age* (2nd ed.). Malden, MA: Wiley-Blackwell.

Lampman, C. (2012). Women faculty at risk: U.S. professors report on their experiences with student incivility, bullying, aggression, and sexual attention. *NAPSA Journal About Women in Higher Education, 5*(2) 184–208.

Lyu, W., & Zhang, J. (2017). The influence of childhood psychological maltreatment on Mainland China college students' cyberbullying: The mediating effect of moral disengagement and the moderating effect of moral identity. *Eurasia Journal of Mathematics, Science and Technology Education, 13*(11), 7581–7590.

McKay, R., Arnold, D. H., Fratzl, J., & Thomas, R. (2008). Workplace bullying in academia: A Canadian study. *Employee Responsibility and Rights Journal, 20*, 77–100. doi:10.1007/s10672-008-9073-3

Menesini, E. (2012). Cyberbullying: The right value of the phenomenon. Comments on the paper "Cyberbullying: An overrated phenomenon?" *European Journal of developmental Psychology, 9*(5), 544–552.

Navarro, R., Yubero, S., & Larrañaga, E. (Eds.). (2016). *Cyberbullying across the globe: Gender, family, and mental health*. Basel, Switzerland: Springer.

Olweus, D. (1993). *Bullying at school: What we know and what we can do*. New York: Blackwell.

Orel, A., Campbell, M., Wozencraft, K., Leong, E., & Kimpton, M. (2017). Exploring university students' coping strategy intentions for cyberbullying. *Journal of Interpersonal Violence, 32*(3), 446–462.

Smith, P. K., & Steffgen, G. (Eds.). (2013). *Cyberbullying through the new media: Findings from an international network*. London: Psychology Press.

Suler, J. (2004). The online disinhibition effect. *CyberPsychology & Behavior, 7*(3), 321–326.

Vance, J. W. (2010). *Cyber-harassment in higher education: Online learning environments*. Ed.D. dissertation, University of Southern California.

Wildermuth, S., & Davis, C. B. (2012). Flaming the faculty: Exploring root causes, consequences, and potential remedies to the problem of instructor-focused uncivil online student discourse in higher education. In L. A. Wankel & C. Wankel (Eds.), *Misbehavior online in higher education: Cutting-edge technologies in higher education* (pp. 379–404). Bingley: Emerald.

Wright, M. (2016). Cyber victimization on college campuses: Longitudinal associations with suicidal ideation, depression, and anxiety. *Criminal Justice Review, 41*(2), 190–203.

Yubero, S., Navarro, R., Elche, M., Larrañaga, E., & Ovejero, A. (2017). Cyberbullying victimization in higher education: An exploratory analysis of its association with social and emotional factors among Spanish students. *Computers in Human Behavior, 75*, 439–449.

PART I

Nature and extent

1

CYBERBULLYING AMONG UNIVERSITY STUDENTS IN FRANCE

Prevalence, consequences, coping, and intervention strategies

Catherine Blaya

Introduction

In France, as in many countries, concern about cyberbullying has become a societal issue. Although research in the past focused primarily on teenagers' use of the internet and their negative online experiences, it is shifting now towards the university setting, since recent research in Europe and North America indicates young adults are also involved (Chapell et al., 2004; Molluzzo & Lawler, 2012; Smith & Yoon, 2013). Kowalski, Giumetti, Schroeder, and Reese (2012) found that one out of three college students experienced cyberbullying for the first time while at college, and that for six out of ten students who had been previously cyberbullied, the major part of their negative experience occurred when they attended university. These findings strengthen the necessity for researching and understanding cyberbullying during post-secondary education.

The main reported types of victimization towards students in post-secondary education are insults, threats and harassment (Molluzzo & Lawler, 2012) but also obscene content and grooming (Kennedy & Taylor, 2010; Vance, 2010). Females are more likely than males to be victims and are at a higher risk of distress (Bauman & Newman, 2013). The most used technologies for cyberbullying are social networks (Walker et al., 2011). Studies examining the characteristics of perpetrators (Doane, Pearson, & Kelley, 2014; Gibb & Devereux, 2016) highlight that as for traditional bullying, cyberbullies show low levels of empathy for the victims and favourable attitudes towards cyberbullying.

In terms of negative consequences, victims experience anxiety and/or depression, tend to consume alcohol and drugs, and their social life is reduced (Kowalski & Limber, 2013; Kraft & Wang, 2010). Victimization also impacts negatively on victims' academic achievement. The vast majority of university students need support for developing coping strategies as they do not know how to handle the situation themselves or where to seek help (Adams, Lawrence, & Schenck, 2008). The most heavily victimized individuals tend to think the solution lies with seeking legal action and intervention from the university authorities (Crosslin & Crosslin, 2014).

Recently in France, more scholarly attention has been given to cyberviolence[1] and cyberbullying. In this chapter, we present the findings from two research projects: a written questionnaire survey that was completed at two universities in the South and East of France (Berthaud & Blaya, 2014, 2015), and a qualitative study involving face-to-face student interviews completed in the South of France.

Research on cyberbullying at university in France

Measures and sample: first study (survey)

The first study aimed to assess the involvement of higher education students in acts of cyberviolence as victims and/or aggressors, the consequences of victimization, and subsequent coping strategies. We followed a convenience sampling strategy, and students were asked if they wished to participate. We collected 1,153 paper surveys (1,125 were valid; 28 were void due to missing values). Seventy percent of the respondents were female. Just over half of the sample (53%) were aged 17–20, 39% were aged 21–24, and 8% were 25 or older. Students were from various faculty departments: Social sciences (44%), Sciences, Technology and Health (24%), Law, Economics and Management (21%), and Arts, Letters and Foreign Languages (11%). Forty-five percent of the participants were undergraduates, 35% were Master's students, and 1% were doctoral students. The gender imbalance noted here is consistent with other studies, with more females participating (Faucher, Jackson, & Cassidy, 2014).

The survey used the Smith et al. (2008) and the Blaya (2013) self-report questionnaires on cyberbullying. These measures were adapted to the university and French context. The survey included questions on the sociodemographic characteristics of the respondents such as age, gender, ethnicity (born in France or not), their digital practices (time spent online, equipment), and if they were victims or authors of cyberviolence. It also asked questions about the reasons for victimization. Students answered a behaviour checklist based on the previous 12 months. They were asked the extent to which they had: received/sent nasty, hurtful, intimidating messages; received/sent humiliating, unpleasant photographs of sexual content; were victims or authors of happy slapping, hacking, impersonation, or rumours. This behaviour checklist was justified on the basis that it was deemed more reliable than asking students if they had been victims of cyberviolence or cyberbullying since these two terms may be open to interpretation. Respondents were also asked about the support they received: through SMS (short message service), emails, cell phone calls, on a social network, a blog, a forum, or by chat.

Students completed the survey at the end of their academic year. Using a Likert-type scale, participants were asked for the frequency of their engagement with identified behaviours, ranging from: never; once or twice; two or three times per month; once a week; to several times per week. The scale for duration included: once; a few days; about a month; six months; the whole year; several years. The survey also included checklist questions about the victims' feelings and coping strategies, as well as some questions about the perceived responsibility of the university and the ways the university could prevent or reduce cyberviolence.

Measures and sample: second study (interviews)

For the second study, we interviewed 20 students (12 female and 8 male), aged 18–26. They were approached to participate because they had declared on the survey (described previously) that they were either victims or witnesses to cyberviolence, and had indicated that they were willing to take part in face-to-face interviews. A semi-directed interview protocol was designed to investigate the following aspects: (a) involvement as victim, aggressor, and witness; (b) the online context of the adverse situation; (c) the reasons why it happened; (d) their reporting and coping strategies; and (e) their suggestions on how to handle and manage the situation (both individually and at the university level). Data collection occurred outside the university in cafés in order to be in a neutral space. Information about the study was provided before starting the interview, and active consent for recording was sought. The results presented here focus on the students' experiences and suggestions for intervention.

Analyses

The way we define and measure violence and online aggression does influence the quality of response and analyses (Corcoran, McGuckin, & Prentice, 2015). For both studies, therefore, we did not propose a set definition of cyberbullying to the students. Instead, we drew a distinction between students who were victimized several times and those who reported only one negative experience. We labelled behaviour as cyberviolence when it involved occasional victimization and as cyberbullying for repeated victimization. We did not use "cyberbullying" as the umbrella term to avoid confusion as to what was being measured and to reduce opportunities for intra-national and cross-national comparisons. We completed logistic regression analyses to check the predictive power of the independent variables (socio-demographics, digital practices, etc.) with the following profiles: victims, authors, and victims/authors.

The 20 interviews were then transcribed and analysed using content analysis and inductive open coding to identify emerging themes, the prevalence of these themes, and to check for potential patterns.

Prevalence and reasons for victimization

Prevalence

Cyberviolence is not an issue that is restricted to secondary education students, as previously demonstrated in other countries (Molluzzo & Lawler, 2012; Walker et al., 2011; Zacchilli & Valerio, 2011). As shown in Table 1.1, over 50% of the survey respondents were victims of cyberviolence at least once during the academic year, 41% were victims only, 14% were authors only, and 12% (or just over 1 out of 10) were both victims and authors.

In contrast, repeated victimization, labelled here as cyberbullying, involved 10% of the students as victims only, 0.5% as authors only, while 1% of the respondents declared they were both victims and authors.

These results show that university students in France are affected by cyberviolence and cyberbullying, and that occasional online violence is more frequent than cyberbullying. As in other research (Molluzzo & Lawler, 2012), the most common forms of aggression are nasty or intimidating messages via SMS (26%), the sharing of personal information without previous consent (15%), unpleasant or nasty emails (16%), and sexting (10%).

The findings from the logistic regression analyses to check the predictive power of the independent variables (socio-demographics, digital practices, etc.) in relation to the following profiles – victims, authors, and victims/authors – show that gender is strongly associated with being a victim/author (OR = 1.83, $p < .001$), as well as a perpetrator of cyberviolence (OR = 2.28, $p < .001$). These results echo studies conducted by Chapell and colleagues (2006) and Faucher et al. (2014), which showed that male students at university were more likely to be involved as perpetrators. However, according to our results, being a female is not significantly associated with victimization. This contradicts previous research by Francisco, Veiga Simão, Ferreira, and Martins (2015) in Portugal; they found that females were more involved as victims and as perpetrators. MacDonald and Roberts-Pittman (2010) in the United States, on the other hand, did not find any difference between genders. As a result of these conflicting findings, the issue of gender needs further investigation.

TABLE 1.1 Involvement of Students in Cyberviolence and Cyberbullying

	Victims only (%)	*Authors only (%)*	*Victims/Authors (%)*
Cyberviolence (one aggression)	41	14	11
Cyberbullying (repeated victimization)	10	0.5	1
Total	51	14.5	12

Regardless of gender, victims are 3.6 times more likely to become authors (OR = 3.60, $p < .001$), and authors are equally more at risk to become victims (3.62, $p < .001$), thus confirming other research findings (Zacchilli & Valerio, 2011). These findings support the lifestyle theory, where certain behaviours such as delinquent lifestyles elevate one's odds of being victimized: the more one offends, the higher the risk of being victimized (Henson, Wilcox, Bradford, & Cullen, 2010). As in other research, our analyses show evidence that the amount of time spent online (5 hours and more, OR = 1.71, $p < .01$) and to a lesser extent, the involvement in online social networking (OR 1.52, $p < .05$), increases the odds of being a victim. The other variables most associated with perpetration are to be very active online, as the respondents who declared eight or more different activities are more likely to be authors of cyberviolence (OR = 2.19, $p < .05$), and to be both victim/authors (OR = 3.10, $p < .01$).

Reasons explaining victimization and perpetration

Among the main reasons for victimization from the victims' point of view, friendship disputes predominate (54%), followed by being different (4%), physical appearance, country of origin (2.1%), and religion (2.1%). The last two reasons confirm that there may be a higher risk of victimization for ethnic minority students, as previously shown by Näsi et al. (2014). As for perpetrators, 40% stated they cyber-aggressed their victims because they were annoyed with him/her, and 1 out of 10 said it was because they wished to get revenge on an ex-partner. Interviews show that friendship disputes were mostly based on rivalry between protagonists, with the individuals involved intent on finding their own place and status. This reasoning is explained by one of the interviewees:

> Disputes you can have when you are young, due to the difficulty to find your place, to get included into a group or not. I cannot remember something specifically; they were mainly unpleasant and nasty messages about her dress code and behaviour.
>
> *(female, undergraduate)*

Males reported being generally more excluded online compared to females, contrary to what happens offline. Some research has shown that being involved in online gaming increases aggressive behaviours (Anderson et al., 2010; Hasan, Bègue, Scharkow, & Bushman, 2013; Yang, 2012). Several male respondents confirmed these conclusions:

> I was on a game and someone ridiculed and excluded me from the game because I was not performing well enough.
>
> *(male, undergraduate)*

> I had problems with an online game. We disagreed, he insulted me. We sorted it out with a challenge and I won. The problem is over.
>
> *(male, undergraduate)*

> When I started playing online, they picked on me and called me names because I was not good and I was not scoring enough. They can be very violent and they insult you or throw you out if you are not competitive enough, but it is part of the game. If you are a gamer, you have got to be able to stand it.
>
> *(male, Master's student)*

These responses reinforce the centrality of competence and performance in deciding who is victimized, as well as the inability on the part of some of the aggressors to manage frustration, echoing the work of Przybylski, Deci, Rigby, and Ryan (2014). Research on social relations in online games shows that players are often excluded when not matching the established community's expectations. As indicated, males are predominantly involved in multi-player games (Anderson et al., 2010). As a consequence of this heavy involvement, they are more at risk to be excluded than they are in their offline life (Blaya, 2013). However, as one respondent noted: "Women are regularly subjected to discrimination in video games, which gives the feeling that all the males are morons". A female gamer stated that when playing online, she used a male pseudonym and avatar so that males do not discriminate against her. Therefore, while males are the most frequent participants in online gaming communities, and thus more frequently abused, females are still subjected to acts of exclusion.

Consequences and coping strategies

As is the case with traditional bullying, cybervictimization brings about negative consequences regarding the psychological well-being of young people: anxiety, low self-esteem, and depression are part of the negative effects that were identified among victims (Goebert, Else, Matsu, Chung-Do, & Chang, 2011; Kubiszewski, Fontaine, Hure, & Rusch, 2013). Cybervictimization also affects a student's social life and academic achievement, as expressed in the following sections. These negative impacts may be why over half of the participants (54%) chose not to answer the questions on the impacts of cybervictimization.

Impact on socio-emotional well-being and on social relationships

Survey responses showed that 7.9% of victims felt depressed ($Chi^2 = 1040.46$, $df = 1$, $p < .001$), and 7% indicated that it had altered their relationships with others ($Chi^2 = 169.00$, $df = 2$, $p < .001$). As explained by some of the interviewees, the experience can be very upsetting:

> It started with a photograph that was taken during a party and uploaded on Facebook. Boys started making unpleasant comments about my appearance. They were 5–6 and I found it particularly upsetting. I was living on my own, so I was quite lonely. I wanted to stop seeing what they wrote but at the same time, I wanted to know, I could not help it. I started feeling very low and depressed.
>
> *(female, undergraduate)*

The term "shame" or "ashamed" were terms commonly used by interviewees, particularly among female students (6 out of the 12 female respondents):

> I was not really depressed. It is just that I was so ashamed; I was more and more ashamed of myself. I felt ugly and useless because they were criticizing me permanently. I felt I had to change everything in me. I thought I was ugly. I started being obsessed with my physical appearance and every detail was of great importance so that they could not post any degrading comment anymore. I was in a state that made me reject what I was, I could not accept myself anymore so it was really difficult from a psychological point of view.
>
> *(female, undergraduate)*

This student was not only ashamed: her comments show how she became very anxious about her physical appearance – how the domination of the group of other girls overpowered her life. It affected her self-esteem, reflected her need to be accepted by the dominant group, and the impact and importance of having a positive reputation both online and offline (Coutant & Stenger, 2010).

Impact on academic achievement

Among the victims, 2.8% of the respondents to the survey ($Chi^2 = 208.83$, $df = 1$, $p < .001$) stated cybervictimization had negative effects on their exams and 2.6% ($Chi^2 = 211.32$, $df = 1$, $p < .001$) on the marks they received. Two of the victims stated they had to repeat their academic year. Nine of the students (1.9% – $Chi^2 = 226{,}23$, $df = 1$, $p < .001$) reported they debated leaving university. Four of the 20 students interviewed considered dropping out of university, as indicated by these quotations:

> I felt like crap. Everything I was saying was picked on, everything I was wearing was criticized by this group of girls. The only thing they were

> interested in was gossiping and boyfriends. I thought I could not cope anymore and that the only solution was to go for an online course.
>
> *(female, undergraduate)*

> I was new in the city and I knew no one, the other students had attended the same high schools and had known each other for a while. As I was not from the same region, they picked on me because of my accent. It carried on online and they started sending nasty comments on my accent and the way I dressed or talked. They picked on me continuously. I was not invited to parties and no one would sit next to me in the lecture theatre. I felt so lonely, I thought there was no way I could carry on like that and I wanted to leave.
>
> *(female, Master's student)*

In the examples described here, the victimization was both online and offline, impacting the victims' motivation to stay in school. A similar impact on victims' levels of concentration (abilities), motivation, and academic achievement was previously documented for secondary school students (Kowalski & Limber, 2013). However, we did not expect this to be a major factor among a more mature student population.

Coping strategies

The victims were asked about their coping strategies. Most respondents said that they ignored the problem, while just over 1 out of 10 tried to solve it (11.9%). Among the other strategies: 8.8% of the victims said they tried to ask the aggressor to stop the behaviour; one out of four shared it with someone else (a friend, their partner, parents); and only two students reported the problem to university staff – perhaps reflecting the lack of trust in the university staff to handle the situation, or a perception that it is not up to the university to manage cyberbullying. Just over 24% of the victims stated they had tried to seek support from friends. Moreover, 6 out of the 20 interviewees said they tried to find some distance from the situation:

> Relativize maybe. When you have done nothing wrong, there is no reason you should be belittled. Talk to friends so that they help you to put the situation into perspective and to find a solution if you do suffer because of it. It is very important not to keep it to yourself.
>
> *(male, undergraduate)*

> I tried to sort it out on my own and then I waited. I did not ask for any help to start with. Later, when my friends started putting me down on MSN also, I asked a friend to give me support and that did help me.
>
> *(female, undergraduate)*

Both the survey and the interview responses showed that students tended to avoid or ignore the problem, while only a minority tried to take an active approach to solving the situation. As a second step, victims tended to seek help from acquaintances or friends rather than family, which might be explained by the fact that they are young adults.

Intervention: what can be done at the university level?

In order to understand the students' expectations in terms of intervention at the university level, we performed a content analysis of the responses to the following open-ended question: "What do you think your university could/should do to prevent cyberviolence?" Only 39% of the students answered, and findings show (Table 1.2) that 1 out of 10 respondents think that it is not part of the responsibilities of the university to prevent cyberviolence.

Very few students stated that universities should punish cyberbullying behaviour or impose sanctions (2%), with the majority suggesting prevention and greater dialogue. Students wished to be actively involved in some form of peer mediation and support. This is confirmed by the fact that 38% of students think that young people are the ones who can find solutions to cyberviolence because they are the digital natives. In terms of direct intervention from the university, 7% of students would like the institution to set up prevention activities such as information campaigns and conferences. Raising awareness could contribute to developing a collective anti-violence ethos. Moreover, 7.6% of the respondents suggested that the university should strengthen and facilitate offline communication between students, but also between staff and students. The feeling of a lack of communication reflects a need for a stronger social bond – social bonding being one of the most protective factors against violence in schools (Catalano, Haggerty, Oesterie, Fleming, & Hawkins, 2004) – but also against preventing drop-outs (Wang & Fredricks, 2014). Similar processes may be considered within the college environment. Most of

TABLE 1.2 The Role of University to Prevent Cyberviolence According to the Students' Perceptions

What university could/should do to prevent cyberviolence	*Number of citations*	*Frequency*
It is not the university's responsibility	117	10.4%
Nothing	94	8.4%
Improve relations between individuals offline	85	7.6%
Prevention and awareness-raising activities	79	7%
Organize peer mediation and support groups	53	4.7%
Sanctions	23	2.0%
I do not know	40	3.6%

the students who asked for an improvement in communication were freshmen (43%), and all were undergraduates (100%). Once enrolled in a Master's degree program, students are more likely to have developed friendship networks, and therefore less likely to require support. Many students expressed loneliness during their beginning years at university, and thought the university should provide more support.

> Preventing cyberviolence should be one of the priorities of the university because college is often a place where you feel lonely, mainly for undergraduates.
>
> *(male, Master's student)*

> To create forums for students to help each other and not only on the internet, but also face-to-face.
>
> *(female, undergraduate)*

> To set up discussion groups where students could get to know each other better, including with university staff.
>
> *(female, undergraduate)*

One of the challenges in bullying and cyberbullying is to get victims and witnesses to speak up, as they tend to keep quiet for fear of retaliation or because of the lack of spaces where they can share their concerns and negative experiences. The majority of the participants in the study (60.8%) stated that they would report problems if there was a means of doing so anonymously and if they knew how and to whom they could report:

> It would be useful to spread information and to have identified potential referees in case a problem emerges. This should be free and available to the whole community.
>
> *(male, undergraduate)*

Quite a few students advocated for the creation of spaces for dialogue in the form of forums, conversation groups, and support groups. The porosity between offline and online spaces is a common response among those who recommend increasing communication offline to reinforce positive values (Doane et al., 2014). There is a growing trend towards counter-speech or rather "positive speech", as a way to prevent assaultive discourse, mainly in relation to increasingly hateful discourse targeting some specific communities. Even as early as the beginning of the 20th century, Brandeis (1927) was arguing for education over censorship, noting that the best remedy for harmful speech "is more speech, not enforced silence" (as cited in Richards & Calvert, 2000, p. 1). Learning to handle and contest hate speech through education is perceived by many as being a powerful and useful part of one's education.

> Try and develop models of counter-speech so that the students know that the internet can also be a place where you care for the others; show students how to write positive messages.
>
> *(female, Master's student)*

This last point supports the idea that colleges and universities have a prevention role to play in providing their students with the social and communicative skills required to build a better community, as well as to foster more positive social relationships.

Our findings highlight that students think they can play an active part in the prevention and intervention against cyberbullying and that a greater culture of caring and dialogue would contribute to a healthier learning environment. Students stress the need for greater information and raising awareness. As noted by the students themselves, universities should offer curriculum content (awareness raising, information on how to cope with the issue, consequences of online aggression, how to behave in an ethical way when online, writing and managing counter-speech), as well as organizational aspects (more space and time for dialogue, specific referees and adapted means for reporting incidents, a more caring attitude as a collective value).

Conclusion

This study sought to assess the extent of cyberviolence or cyberbullying in French universities. Findings show that cyberviolence is indeed of concern, since more than 50% of the respondents had been victimized, 14% were authors, while 12% declared a double status as both authors and victims. The more students are active on the internet (time spent online, multiple activities, social network activities), the higher the odds of becoming a victim, thus replicating conclusions from previous studies (Kubiszewski et al., 2013). Victims are more at risk to be offenders, and offenders are equally as likely to become victims. Gender is also strongly associated with cyberviolence, as males declared a greater involvement as both perpetrators and victim/authors. More specifically, online gamers seem to be at risk of victimization. As the interviews demonstrated, underperforming in the gaming community is linked to insults, humiliations, and exclusion – echoing findings by Przybylski and colleagues (2014).

Cyberviolence can have deleterious effects on some victims' academic careers (Cassidy, Faucher, & Jackson, this volume; Crosslin & Crosslin, 2014; Kowalski & Limber, 2013). It is, therefore, of paramount importance that university leaders take the issue seriously and that guidelines be included in students' portfolios when entering university – since, at present, nothing is being done to counter this issue at the university level in France. Students indicated the need for greater awareness and information, support services, and clear policy. Moreover, students expressed their wish to be actively included in the prevention process, which should be a first step towards success (Cross, Lester, Barnes, Cardoso, & Hadwen, 2015). As stressed by some of the participants, the two predominant aspects in terms of prevention are increased communication between individuals and a stronger culture of care and bonding. These demands clearly point out that beyond electronic communication and its ethical use, the social climate of the university is at the heart of deterrence of cyberviolence.

Note

1 We refer to cyberviolence as any type of violence perpetrated through electronic media of communication. Cyberviolence is different from cyberbullying in the sense that cyberviolence is not repeated violence and can be an occasional incident.

References

Adams, F. D., Lawrence, G. J., & Schenck, S. (2008). A survey on bullying: Some reflections on the findings. *NASCD News & Notes, 8*, 1–7.

Anderson, C. A., Shibuya, A., Ihori, N., Swing, E. L., Bushman, B. J., Sakamoto, A., . . . & Saleem, M. (2010). Violent video game effects on aggression, empathy, and prosocial behavior in Eastern and Western countries. *Psychological Bulletin, 136*, 151–173.

Bauman, S., & Newman, M. L. (2013). Testing assumptions about cyberbullying: Perceived distress associated with acts of conventional and cyber bullying. *Psychology of Violence, 3*(1), 27–38.

Berthaud, J., & Blaya, C. (2014). *Premiers résultats de l'enquête française Cyberviolence à l'université. Adjectif, Analyses et Recherches sur les TICE.* Retrieved from www.adjectif.net/spip/spip.php?article279

Berthaud, J., & Blaya, C. (2015). Pratiques numériques, perception de la violence en ligne et victimation chez les étudiants. *Recherches en éducation, Hors série* 7, 146–161.

Blaya, C. (2013). *Les ados dans le cyberspace, prises de risque et cyberviolence.* Bruxelles: De Boeck.

Blaya, C., & Fartoukh, M. (2015). Digital uses, victimization and online aggression: A comparative study between primary school and lower secondary school students in France. *European Journal on Criminal Policy and Research, 22*(2), 285–300.

Cassidy, W., Faucher, C., & Jackson, M. (this volume). "You need a think skin . . .": Impacts of cyberbullying in Canadian universities. In W. Cassidy, C. Faucher, & M. Jackson (Eds.), *Cyberbullying at university in international contexts* (pp. 112–125). Oxford, UK: Routledge.

Catalano, R. F., Haggerty, K. P., Oesterie, S., Fleming, C. B., Hawkins, J. D. (2004). The importance of bonding to schools for healthy development: Findings from the social development research group. *Journal of School Health, 74*, 252–262.

Chapell, M., Casey, D., De la Cruz, C., Ferrel, J., Forman, J., Lipkin, R., . . . & Whitaker, S. (2004). Bullying in university by students and teachers [Electronic Version]. *Adolescence, 39*, 53–64.

Chapell, M. S., Hasselman, S. L., Kitchin, T., Lomon, S. N., MacIver, K. W., & Sarullo, P. L. (2006). Bullying in elementary school, high school, and college. *Adolescence, 41*, 633–648.

Corcoran, L., McGuckin, C., & Prentice, G. (2015). Cyberbullying or cyber aggression? A review of existing definitions of cyber-based peer-to-peer aggression. *Societies, 5*, 245–255.

Cross, D., Lester, L., Barnes, A., Cardoso, P., & Hadwen, K. (2015). If it's about me, why do it without me? Genuine student engagement in school cyberbullying education. *International Journal of Emotional Education*, 7(1), 35–51.

Crosslin, K. L., & Crosslin, M. B. (2014). Cyberbullying at a Texas university: A mixed methods approach to examining online aggression. *Texas Public Health Journal, 66*, 26–31.

Coutant, A., & Stenger, T. (2010). Pratiques et temporalités des réseaux socionumériques: logique de flux et logique d'archive. *Mémoires et Internet – Médiation et Information, 32*, 125–136.

Doane, A. N., Pearson, M. R., & Kelley, M. (2014). Predictors of cyberbullying perpetration among college students: An application of the theory of reasoned action. *Computers in Human Behavior, 36*, 154–162.

Faucher, C., Jackson, M., & Cassidy, W. (2014). Cyberbullying among university students: Gendered experiences, impacts, and perspectives. *Education Research International, 2014*, 1–10.

Francisco, S. M., Veiga Simão, A. M., Ferreira, P. C., & Martins, M. J. D. D. (2015). Cyberbullying: The hidden side of college students. *Computers in Human Behaviour, 43*(0), 167–182.

Gibb, Z., & Devereux, P. G. (2016). Missing link: Exploring repetition and intentionality of distress in cyberbullying behaviors within a college population. *Translational Issues in Psychological Science, 2*(3), 313–322.

Goebert, D., Else, I., Matsu, C., Chung-Do, J., & Chang, J. Y. (2011). The impact of cyberbullying on substance use and mental health in a multiethnic sample. *Maternal Child Health Journal, 15*, 1282–1286.

Hasan, Y., Bègue, L., Scharkow, M., & Bushman, B. J. (2013). The more you play, the more aggressive you become: A long-term experimental study of cumulative violent video game effects on hostile expectations and aggressive behavior. *Journal of Experimental Social Psychology, 49*(2), 224–227.

Henson, B., Wilcox, P., Reyns, B. W, & Cullen, F. T. (2010). Gender, adolescent lifestyles, and violent victimization: Implications for Routine Activity Theory. *Victims & Offenders, 5*(4), 303–328.

Kennedy, M. A., & Taylor, M. A. (2010). Online harassment and victimization of college students. *Justice Policy Journal*, 7(1), 1–21.

Kowalski, R. M., Giumetti, G. W., Schroeder, A. N., & Reese, H. (2012). Cyberbullying among college students: Evidence from multiple domains of college life. In C. Wankel & L. Wankel (Eds.), *Misbehavior online in higher education* (pp. 293–321). Bingley, UK: Emerald.

Kowalski, R. M., & Limber, S. P. (2013). Psychological, physical, and academic correlates of cyberbullying and traditional bullying. *Journal of Adolescent Health, 53*(Suppl.), S13–S20.

Kraft, E., & Wang, J. (2010). An exploratory study of the cyberbullying and cyberstalking experiences and factors related to victimization of students at a public liberal arts college. *International Journal of Technologies, 1*(4), 74–91.

Kubiszewski, V., Fontaine, R., Hure, K., & Rusch, E. (2013). Le cyber-bullying à l'adolescence: problèmes psycho-sociaux associés et spécificités par rapport au bullying scolaire. *L'Encéphale. 39*(2), 77–84.

MacDonald, C. D., & Roberts-Pittman, B. (2010). Cyberbullying among college students: Prevalence and demographic differences. *Procedia – Social and Behavioral Sciences, 9*, 2003–2009.

Molluzzo, J. C., & Lawler, J. (2012). A study of the perceptions of college students on cyberbullying. *Information Systems Education Journal, 10*(4), 84–109.

Nagelkerke, N. (1991). A note on a general definition of the coefficient of determination. *Biometrika, 78*, 691–692.

Näsi, M., Räsänen, P., Oksanen, A., Hawdon, J., Keipi, T., & Holkeri, E. (2014). Association between online harassment and exposure to harmful online content: A cross-national comparison between the United States and Finland. *Computers in Human Behavior, 41*, 137–145.

Przybylski, A. K., Deci, E. L., Rigby, C. S., & Ryan, R. M. (2014). Competence-impeding electronic games and players' aggressive feelings, thoughts, and behavior. *Journal of Personality and Social Psychology, 106*(3), 441–457.

Richards, R. D., & Calvert, C. (2000). Counterspeech 2000: A new look at the old remedy for "bad" speech. *BYU Law Review, 2000*(2), 553–586.

Smith, P. K., Mahdavi, J., Carvalho, M., Fisher, S., Russell, N., & Tippett, N. (2008). Cyberbullying: Its nature and impact in secondary school pupils. *Journal of Child Psychology & Psychiatry, 49*, 376–385.

Smith, J. A., & Yoon, J. (2013). Cyberbullying presence, extent, & forms in a Midwestern post-secondary institution. *Information Systems Education Journal, 11*, 52–78.

Vance, J. W. (2010). *Cyber-harassment in higher education: Online learning environments.* Ed.D. dissertation. Retrieved from University of Southern California Digital Library (usctheses-m2954).

Wang, M.-T., & Fredricks, J. (2014). The reciprocal links between school engagement, youth problem behaviors, and school dropout during adolescence. *Child Development, 85*(2), 722–737.

Yang, S. (2012). Paths to bullying in online gaming: The effects of gender, preference for playing violent games, hostility, and aggressive behavior on bullying. *Journal of Educational Computing Research, 47*(3), 235–249.

Zacchilli, T., & Valerio, C. (2011). The knowledge and prevalence of cyberbullying in a college sample. *Journal of Scientific Psychology, 3*, 11–23.

2

RELATIONSHIPS AMONG UNIVERSITY STUDENTS/FACULTY AND CYBERBULLYING IN JAPAN

Tomoyuki Kanetsuna, Ikuko Aoyama, and Yuichi Toda

Current issues and brief history of research on bullying, cyberbullying, and other online problems in Japan

Brief history of research on bullying and cyberbullying, and current situation among school children

The history of *ijime*, the Japanese term most similar to the Western concept of bullying, can be traced back to the 1980s. The first research studies followed a tragic chain of suicides of children, who claimed in their suicide notes that being victims of *ijime* had led them to take their own lives. These suicides shocked Japanese society and called attention to the ferocious nature of *ijime*, which came to be seen as one of the biggest social problems in Japan. In the three decades since then, the government, local boards of education, schools, and academics have conducted numerous studies aimed at uncovering the nature, prevention, and intervention of *ijime* (Toda, 2016).

Actions against cyberbullying or *net-ijime* in Japan roughly started around 2006, following the rapid increase in mobile phone use and internet access among children and adolescents. According to the latest survey on internet use among youth in 2015, more than 27% of primary school students, 45% of junior high students, and 93% of high school students reported using smart phones. Among those, approximately 19% of primary school, 42% of junior high, and 92% of high school students reported having access to the internet from their mobile devices (Cabinet Office, 2016). As for the prevalence of cyberbullying, 1.4% of primary students, 7.8% of junior high students, and 18.7% of high school students reported being victimized online in some way (MEXT, 2016).

Internet-related problems among university students

Until recently there has not been much concern about cyberbullying at the post-secondary level, although other internet-related problems have been in the spotlight. Early studies focused on the negative effects of the rapid popularization of mobile phones on interpersonal relationships and living environments. From a study of 259 university students, Kohara (2004) argued that because many students possessed their own mobile phones, they could easily locate each other on large university campuses, which enabled them to actively decide with whom to spend time. As a result, students became less likely to pursue new friendships, while existing friendships tended to become increasingly limited and fixed. In contrast, Watanabe, Kubota, Ishizaki, and Oyanagi (2008) studied 271 university students and found that about 25% of them felt that their stress levels had increased by using mobile phones, while about half of them felt that having mobile phones improved their general enjoyment of life. Watanabe et al. (2008) argued that such stress was the result of mutual surveillance among friends exchanging excessive emails and short messages, which led to high levels of anxiety and concern about the lack of instant responses from friends.

These early studies clearly indicated both positive and negative consequences of the popularization of mobile phones and the internet. Around 2010, the spread of mobile phones and smart phones had increased further, with these mobile devices becoming one of the essential lifelines for university students. This led to a study of the repercussions of students' excessive use and their tendency to depend on mobile devices for their daily lives and mental health. Kamihama, Shimizu, Sawamura, and Shimizu (2013) studied 278 university students and found that female students used their mobile phones, emails, and the internet significantly more than males, and were more likely to become dependent on their mobile phones. They further found that such tendencies negatively impacted their daily lives, causing issues such as lack of sleep, decreased learning efficiency, and diminished academic achievements. Okamoto et al. (2014) examined the general usage of the internet among university students (N = 343) and found that about 3% of them reported that their time spent on the internet increased by more than eight hours per day since they entered university, and about 4% of them claimed that they used the internet more than 10 hours per day. These students clearly showed the strong tendency to depend on, or even to become addicted to the internet, claiming that "they cannot stop thinking about the internet" and "they cannot imagine life without it" (p. 9). Okamoto et al. (2014) further reported that those with high levels of dependency on the internet showed significantly higher levels of various mental health problems including depression, anxiety, loneliness, and poor interpersonal relationships.

Another internet-related problem among university students was the unofficial syllabus known as "*Ura-Syllabus*" in Japanese. Similar to rating sites such as "Rate my professors.com" (www.ratemyprofessors.com), students post information about the ease of obtaining credits in specific subjects, as well as complaints and rumours concerning faculty members and lecturers. The problem with this unofficial syllabus is that not all posted information is written fairly or impartially, and some posts are simply slanderous. Many universities have now started official evaluations of lectures and of students' daily lives at university, which gives students an opportunity to comment on lectures and university life in general, including services and facilities, club activities, and relationships with lecturers and staff. Such formalization of the evaluation process can be a good countermeasure to control and prevent students from inappropriately posting online about their university experiences, which may prevent the escalation of cyberbullying cases.

Flaming posts on the internet are another recent problem among university students. Since 2013, there has been a significant upsurge in the posting of pictures and videos of students exhibiting deviant and inappropriate behaviour via Twitter and other Social Networking Service (SNS) sites. Many of these pictures and videos seem to be posted in an attempt to attract attention and/or to be enjoyed by a limited group of friends. However, due to lack of proper knowledge about the internet and an absence of insight into how such a posting might affect others, these are often posted without restrictions and, therefore, can be circulated quickly and widely. As a consequence, in many cases, the person who posted the information is not only accused of deviant behaviour but also suffers verbal abuse from unspecified internet users. Furthermore, such accusations of deviant postings often do not remain on the internet, but they also impact the person who posted, revealing their offline identity. Many of those who post end up facing severe sanctions, including arrest and/or expulsion from their universities. Although many Japanese consider such an end to be the reasonable outcome of the person's own deed, sometimes the individual identified as the perpetrator and accused of the offences is innocent. Such unjust victimization is another serious online problem that can occur, unless due diligence is undertaken to fully investigate the situation.

Recently, tragic news about the suicide of a university student due to revelations of secrets on the internet shocked Japanese society (Sasagawa, 2016). A male student plunged to his death after one of his friends disclosed his homosexuality through SNS. The student's parents filed a complaint for compensation against the university for insufficiently protecting him, and against the person who exposed the secret online without his consent. The legal counsel of the parents claimed that because there is much discrimination and prejudice against LGBT individuals in society, their son must have felt great fear and anxiety, and the university did not take any measures to protect him from the classmate's exposure, but only to deal with the perceived problem that the student himself was homosexual (Sasagawa, 2016). Although the verdict of this trial is still pending, this news, along with other internet-related incidents covered by the media, is prompting Japanese society to rethink what it considers responsible online behaviour.

Tashiro (2012) raised an alert over these series of problematic online behaviours by university students, claiming that inadvertent dissemination of information on the internet caused serious problems including suspension, expulsion from university, and withdrawal of job offers.

Anonymity and issues related to cyberbullying and other online problems

Perceived online anonymity

Many of these internet-related problems were said to occur due to students' lack of foresight into what other people may think about their behaviour, insufficient consideration for how others may feel if they are attacked online, or limited awareness regarding having their secrets disclosed to many unknown people. One example is the tendency of students to wrongly assume their online audience. Many of the students who posted inappropriate content later stated that they merely intended to play a silly prank and to have fun among peers; they did not intend to offend a broader unknown online community (Tashiro, 2012). Unfortunately, they did not foresee how many people would view their online posts and what those people might think of their behaviour.

One reason for such thoughtless acts of university students is the commonly held belief about anonymity on the internet. Use of social media such as the online Bulletin Board System (BBS), weblogs, and various kinds of SNS has rapidly increased during the last decade, especially among adolescents and university students. Among those using such online social media in Japan, about 70% said they prefer anonymous communication (Internet White Paper, 2008). The MEXT (2008) claimed that anonymous communication on the internet makes it easy for youngsters to become both victims and perpetrators of cyberbullying. Aoyama, Saxon, and Fearon (2010) pointed out the difficulty for cyberbullying victims to seek social help, due to anonymity. They argued that because perpetrators can remain anonymous, the victims cannot identify who the bullies are in the first place. Furthermore, when hurtful gossip and rumours are spread on SNS, it is highly possible that the entire class or school are witnesses to the harassment, making it hard for the victims to seek help from peers (Aoyama et al., 2010). Ono and Saito (2008) also note in their study that due to anonymity on the internet, victims of cyberbullying often become highly suspicious, even with their close friends.

Orita (2009) argues, however, that the idea of being anonymous on the internet may be based on false beliefs. In other words, it is not too technologically difficult for a site administrator of a particular BBS or SNS, or for an internet service provider to identify by whom, when, and where a particular comment was posted (Orita, 2009). Furthermore, the latest survey of 3,000 primary, junior high, and high school students, and their parents using the Internet Literacy Assessment indicator for Students (ILAS) revealed that the majority of participants were aware that the internet is not fully anonymous (JISPA, 2016). If primary school students have been informed of knowledge about the anonymity of the internet, then it may be assumed that university-level students have the same knowledge. Yaguchi (2013) studied 315 university students and found that for those who had previously learned about the risks of the internet, 70% knew that anonymity on the internet is limited, while less than 60% of those who had not learned about the risks had appropriate knowledge about anonymity on the internet. Takeuchi, Toda, and Takahashi (2015) argue that even if it is merely a belief, strong beliefs about anonymity on the internet could lead to "Moral Disengagement" (Bandura, 1999) of people online, and this in turn may trigger the possibility of them easily becoming perpetrators.

Effects of the belief of anonymity on deviant online behaviour

The effects of anonymity on deviant online behaviour have been studied in the field of Computer-Mediated Communication (CMC) for the last two decades. Sproull and Kiesler (1986), for example, claimed that lack of nonverbal cues and attribute information, including the person's age, gender, and occupation, make it difficult for people to infer the other person's intention or their response to their own behaviour. As a result, people are more prone to act aggressively and exhibit disinhibition online. Sato, Hibino, and Yoshida (2010) also pointed out the negative effects of perceived online anonymity, arguing that the belief in anonymity reduces the fear and anxiety of being identified, and this, in turn, leads to more aggressive comments and behaviour.

Besides the influence of perceived anonymity on online behaviour, Chiba (2011) claimed that, in order to understand the cause of online flaming and aggressive behaviour, we must see it as a group phenomenon. The concept of "deindividuation" is defined as "the absence of self-awareness and self-evaluation following from certain situational conditions, and a resultant increase in the probability of uninhibited behaviour" (Diener, 1977, p. 144). While Zimbardo exposed the powerful effect of deindividuation with his famous Stanford Prison Experiment (www.prisonexp.org), CMC can also be said to deindividuate through its (albeit false) anonymity and the difficulty to distinguish between users. If we regard CMC as communication in a context of deindividuation, various problematic online behaviours can be traced back to a dilution of group norms caused by a belief in online anonymity (Chiba, 2011; Coyne & Farley, this volume).

In contrast, Reicher (1984) pointed out that the high level of anonymity on the internet does not lead to an unregulated state due to the dilution of group norms, but rather that it makes the transition from personal to social identity. This idea was later theorized by Postmes, Spears, and Lea (1998) as the Social Identity Model of Deindividuation Effects (SIDE model). According to this model, deindividuation led by online anonymity enhances the social identity of individuals, and this in turn strengthens the conformity to group norms. Taking this perspective, Chiba (2011) argued that the internet tends to create bonds between people with similar values and thoughts, who then tend to exclude those who think or act differently. This process often escalates arguments and enables people to reach biased consensus (Chiba, 2011). This perspective could explain why a person who publicly posts an inappropriate piece of information tends to believe that people who share the post will also share their amusement. It also explains why people with common values join forces to accuse an outsider's post as inappropriate and unacceptable. Regarding such group behaviour, Toda, Strohmeier, and Spiel (2008) argued that perpetrators of bullying often embrace the illusion that they are the majority force and think the victims are deserving of being bullied. Toda et al. further argued that such illusions of being a majority force could increase their motivation to bully and escalate the attack on the victims.

Anonymity and moral disengagement

Bandura (1999) theorized moral disengagement as the process of convincing oneself of being exempt from moral standards in a particular context by separating moral reactions from inhumane conduct and by disabling the mechanism of self-sanction. Such disengagement of moral self-sanction from inhumane conduct can manifest at both individual and collective levels. The dilution of individual and group norms due to deindividuation led by a belief in online anonymity discussed previously can be seen as a form of moral disengagement. Studies that examine the relationship between Bandura's collective moral disengagement and bullying have found that classroom-collective moral disengagement is positively correlated with perpetration and negatively with defending behaviours (see, for example, Gini, Pozzoli, & Bussey, 2015; Kollerová, Soukup, & Gini, 2017).

The study done by Gini and colleagues (2015), cited earlier, focused on the relationship between classroom-collective moral disengagement and involvement in traditional bullying at school. At the university level, however, this concept of "classroom collectivity" is weakened as classrooms are not configured in the same way as at school. While perpetrators and victims may not share the same social group in the case of cyberbullying at university, there is similarity with traditional bullying in the way a group of perpetrators collectively attack a targeted victim. In this case, we should consider the characteristics and possible effects of "Cyber-Collective Moral Disengagement" in regards to cyberbullying and other online problematic behaviours, which may correspond to the effects of "Classroom-Collective Moral Disengagement" of traditional bullying at school, as proposed by Gini and colleagues (2015).

Recent research on cyberbullying and online problems among university students

Relationships between traditional bullying and cyberbullying

It is important to identify the similarities and differences between cyberbullying and traditional bullying, as well as to discern the distinguishing features of cyberbullying. Olweus (2012), for example, suggested several overlaps between cyberbullying and traditional bullying, arguing that cyberbullying is a low-prevalence phenomenon, and most of those who experience cyberbullying, either being a victim or a perpetrator, are often also involved in traditional bullying. While Smith (2012) concurs with Olweus about the lower prevalence of cyberbullying compared to bullying, he stresses the distinctive features of cyberbullying: for example, the invisibility or anonymity of the perpetrators. He also points out that the concept of repetition, one of the major conditions of traditional bullying, can be more difficult to operationalize, as only a single act by a perpetrator can be seen, commented on, and forwarded by many others, and this constitutes a repetition.

Taking into account these arguments, Kanetsuna (2014a) examined the perceptions and general understanding of the nature of cyberbullying with 601 university students (288 males and 313 females) and 536 high school students (278 males and 258 females). He used hypothetical scenarios of four different forms of online victimization: (1) attacks on an online BBS and SNS (making repeated abusive comments, spreading rumours, and outing personal information), (2) by email (sending repeated abusive comments and pictures), (3) by online spoofing (unknown homepage was insidiously opened in victim's name, and personal information, both true and untrue, is disclosed), and (4) by using pictures and videos taken by mobile devices (taking embarrassing pictures and videos, and disclosing and sharing them online). Using these scenarios, he first asked about the experience of witnessing others being victimized and of being victimized themselves in each of the four categories. He then asked about the likely perpetrators and likely relationships between victims and perpetrators. Lastly, he inquired about likely motives for perpetration and probable reasons for victimization.

He found that the majority of university students (about 50% to 60% depending on the forms of aggression) had some awareness of all four types of online victimization, but only about 20% to 35% reported having actually witnessed others being cyber-victimized, and very few (1.3% to 3.4%) reported being victimized themselves. High school students showed very similar patterns, though they were found to be less aware (about 42% to 55%) and less experienced (16% to 33% had witnessed and 0.7% to 3.8% were victimized) than university students.

Regarding the differences between types, being attacked on BBS and SNS, and through pictures and videos taken by mobile devices were found to be more frequent than bullying by email and spoofing. This may be, in part, because online communication has shifted rapidly from email to instant-messenger services, especially among adolescents, and the forms of cyberbullying shifted accordingly. As for spoofing, instigating this type of cyberbullying may need more specialized technical knowledge about the internet, and therefore may not be an option for everyone.

Regarding the likely perpetrators and their relationships with victims, again both university and high school students showed very similar patterns, and the findings were fairly consistent with those for traditional bullying. For all types of cyberbullying, the perpetrators were most likely to be someone or a group of people that the victim knows very well in real life, such as "classmates" or "someone in a different class or year group (but the same school)", or even "one of the friends of the victim", rather than someone unknown to the victim either in person or online (Kanetsuna, 2014a).

As for the motives for the perpetration, "antipathy for the victim" was the most likely motive followed by "for fun" and "for stress release". In terms of the reason to target the victim, "because the victim is cheeky", was the most common answer, followed by because the victim is "somewhat different from others" and "cannot read the situation" (Kanetsuna, 2014a). These responses were consistent between university and high school students. This tendency to attribute the responsibility of victimization to the victims rather than the perpetrators was also found in traditional bullying and is prevalent among Japanese adolescents (Kanetsuna, 2016a).

All of these perceptions appear to be consistent with the findings of traditional bullying or *ijime* in Japan (e.g., Kanetsuna, 2016a). Because of the similarities in their perceptions and understanding of the nature of traditional bullying and cyberbullying, university students in Japan perceived cyberbullying as an extension of traditional bullying, which most often occurs within close relationships.

Risk perception, anxiety, and coping potential

Kanetsuna (2014b) also examined the subjective risk perception, anxiety about victimization, and coping potential concerning cyberbullying, using the same four hypothetical scenarios described earlier. He found that pictures and videos taken by mobile devices and online communication using BBS and SNS were perceived to have the greatest potential for cyberbullying and caused the most anxiety. This may be because taking pictures and videos with mobile devices is becoming increasingly popular among the young, and those pictures and videos are often easily shared with others through SNS, regardless of whether they are socially appropriate. What can be more fearsome is that it is almost impossible to recover those pictures and videos once posted, spread, and shared online with many unknown others. Being targeted by emails, on the other hand, was perceived to have the lowest risk of occurrence, cause the least fear, and be the easiest to cope with if it occurred. This may be because email is more personal, is less likely to be made public, and it is easier to track the perpetrator.

Kanetsuna (2014b) further reported that those who had experienced being cyberbullied or had witnessed others being targeted online had a higher risk perception, a higher level of anxiety about victimization, and a lower coping potential compared to those who had never experienced it themselves or had never seen someone else being victimized. This suggests that even if students have awareness of online perpetration and victimization, it may be difficult for them to consider their own vulnerability unless they had experiences as victims or at least witnessed someone else being victimized. This is important to consider when planning for effective prevention methods.

The effects of the belief in anonymity on risk perception and preventive attitudes

Taking into account the arguments by Smith (2012) and Kanetsuna (2014a, 2014b), Kanetsuna (2016b) examined the effects of beliefs about online anonymity on the levels of risk perception and anxiety about the internet use, the caution concerning different online risk behaviours including accessing, signing up, and posting comments on online BBS, SNS, and adult and dating sites, and uploading pictures of themselves as well as those of friends to those sites. With 1,185 students from two high schools and three universities, he found that those with a stronger belief in online anonymity showed lower levels of risk perception and lower levels of caution for various online risk behaviours. This finding suggests that those who believe they are anonymous on the internet are less likely to think they could be victimized online and therefore less likely to be careful about their online actions. In contrast, those who think they are at risk of victimization in some way were more likely to feel anxious about using the internet in general and being victimized, and as a result, more likely to be careful about various online behaviours.

This series of studies suggests that in order to prevent and protect youth in school and at university from various online risks including cyber-victimization, it is important to inform them that cyberbullying often occurs in relationships in the real world, and that the internet is not totally anonymous. Even without actual exposure to these risks, they should be aware of the various online risks and become familiar with the actions they can take to avoid such risks.

A propensity for acute social withdrawal, problematic internet use, and cyberbullying

Regarding cyberbullying and problematic internet use among Japanese university students, Aoyama (2014) focused on the association between having a propensity for acute social withdrawal. For the past decade, acute social withdrawal (*hikikomori*) has been a serious social and educational problem in Japan, and it has been pointed out that problematic use of the internet and mobile phones, in particular the excessive or addictive use of the internet, can be related to *hikikomori*. *Hikikomori* is also related to cyber-victimization. MEXT (2012) demonstrated how experiencing peer victimization can lead to school avoidance and social withdrawal. According to a study by the Office for Youth Affairs and Public Safety of Tokyo Metropolitan Government (2008), 44% of *hikikomori* youth have experienced traditional peer victimization. Although the relationship between online victimization and *hikikomori* had not been previously determined, the experience of cyberbullying was found to cause various psychological symptoms including depression, anxiety, high levels of stress, and low self-esteem, all of which could lead to social withdrawal.

With 581 high school and university students (248 and 333, respectively), Aoyama (2014) found that there was a moderate negative correlation between propensity for acute social withdrawal and problematic use of the internet and mobile phones, and a moderate positive correlation with the experience of online victimization. Although the Cabinet Office (2010) claimed that those who are socially withdrawn are more likely to use the internet excessively, Aoyama (2014) revealed that those who are not exactly socially withdrawn but merely have a propensity for it are less likely to show symptoms of excessive or addictive internet use. However, consistent with the findings of MEXT (2012), the experience of cyberbullying does seem to affect social withdrawal.

Prevention and intervention

There have been various approaches to tackling cyberbullying in Japan. These have included teaching internet literacy and morality to children and adolescents (MEXT, 2010), making it obligatory for mobile service providers to offer internet filtering service to youth under 18 and, at the same time, encouraging efficient use of such internet filtering services for computers and mobile phones (Ministry of Internal Affairs and Communications, 2016). Strict monitoring of compliance with such internet regulatory laws for telecommunication companies and of the usage of internet among youth are conducted by the police (National Police Agency, 2013). However, all of these approaches target school-aged children, and there have not been many approaches and activities for university students.

One example of approaches targeting university students was introduced by Takeuchi and Abe (2014). In this inter-school peer-support workshop, they trained university students as facilitators for high school students' discussions on internet violence and to provide information as to what is and is not illegal and/or dangerous. To lead these workshops, university students had to gather accurate information about the internet and mobile phones and had to acquire appropriate skills for proper use of the internet. This process not only benefited high school students, but it also encouraged university students to learn how to wisely use the internet and mobile phones. Takeuchi and Abe emphasized that doing such student-led activities requires that the teachers trust the students and collaborate with them. As there have not yet been many student-led approaches aimed at preventing *ijime* and *net-ijime* in Japan, it is worth further investigating such initiatives.

Conclusion and future perspectives

Cyberbullying among university students in Japan can be understood as a phenomenon that shares several essential features with traditional bullying at school: it is a group phenomenon and it most often manifests as collective relational aggression against a targeted victim. However, it also has a number of distinctive features. While traditional bullying, and possibly cyberbullying, among school-aged children most often occurs between close relationships based mostly on class and year groups at the school, university students lack similar grouping by class. Beliefs about online anonymity seem to play a key role in the aggressive and deviant online behaviours of university students because this perception has been shown to either weaken personal and collective norms to morally disengage, or to strengthen students' conformity to a particular group norm. Strong beliefs about anonymity on the internet not only affect online perpetration, but they also affect students' risk perception of online victimization and their attitude and behaviour toward prevention and self-protection. Therefore, it is important to disseminate appropriate knowledge about online anonymity and to be aware that one is always at risk of inadvertently becoming an online perpetrator or victim. At the same time, it is also important to cultivate a sense of belonging in the real world to avoid immersive and addictive use of the internet, which often leads to other problematic online behaviours. In order for youth and young adults to learn appropriate internet literacy and morality, including the limits of online anonymity, practices such as those discussed in Takeuchi and Abe (2014), though they have currently only been implemented in a limited way, need to be spread nationwide.

References

Aoyama, I. (2014). The association between an affinity for acute social withdrawal (hikikomori) and problematic use of Internet/cell phone and cyberbullying among Japanese high school and college students [in Japanese]. *Educational Studies: Bulletin of International Christian University, 56*, 43–49.

Aoyama, I., Saxon, T. F., & Fearon, D. D. (2010). Internalizing problems among cyberbullying victims and moderator effects of friendship quality. *Multicultural Education & Technology Journal, 5*(2), 92–105.

Bandura, A. (1999). Moral disengagement in the perpetration of inhumanities. *Personality and Social Psychology Review [Special Issue on Evil and Violence], 3*, 193–209.

Cabinet Office. (2010). *Fact-finding survey on social withdrawal of adolescents* [in Japanese]. Tokyo: Cabinet Office, Government of Japan.

Cabinet Office. (2016). *Environmental consideration for safe and secure Internet use for adolescents* [in Japanese]. Tokyo: Cabinet Office, Government of Japan.

Chiba, K. (2011). Sociological study of flaming in cyberspaces: Diffusion of discourse beyond the intention [in Japanese]. *Social Movement and New Types of Working, Report on Research Project, 231*, 24–37.

Coyne, I., & Farley, S. (this volume). Cyberbullying within working contexts. In W. Cassidy, C. Faucher, & M. Jackson (Eds.), *Cyberbullying at university in international contexts* (pp. 80–96). Oxford, UK: Routledge.

Diener, E. (1977). Deindividuation: Causes and consequences. *Social Behavior and Personality, 5*, 143–155.

Gini, G., Pozzoli, T., & Bussey, K. (2015). The role of individual and collective moral disengagement in peer aggression and bystanding: A multilevel analysis. *Journal of Abnormal Child Psychology, 43*, 441–452.

Internet White Paper. (2008). *General Incorporated Foundation of Internet Association Japan*. Tokyo: Impress R & D.

Japan Internet Safety Promotion Association (JISPA). (2016). *Internet Literacy Assessment indicator for Students (ILAS) Final Report 2015* [in Japanese]. Tokyo: Japan Internet Safety Promotion Association (JISPA).

Japanese Ministry of Education, Culture, Sports, Science and Technology (MEXT). (2008). *Study for unofficial school homepage (e.g. anonymous BBS) used by adolescents* [in Japanese]. Department of Juveniles. Tokyo: Japanese Ministry of Education, Culture, Sports, Science and Technology (MEXT).

Japanese Ministry of Education, Culture, Sports, Science and Technology (MEXT). (2010). *Guidelines for information, moral education at school, and cooperation with family and community* [in Japanese]. Tokyo: Japanese Ministry of Education, Culture, Sports, Science and Technology (MEXT).

Japanese Ministry of Education, Culture, Sports, Science and Technology (MEXT). (2012). *Annual fact-finding survey on problematic behaviour in school* [in Japanese]. Tokyo: Japanese Ministry of Education, Culture, Sports, Science and Technology (MEXT).

Japanese Ministry of Education, Culture, Sports, Science and Technology (MEXT). (2016). *Annual fact-finding survey on problematic behaviour in school* [in Japanese]. Tokyo: Japanese Ministry of Education, Culture, Sports, Science and Technology (MEXT).

Japanese Ministry of Internal Affairs and Communications. (2016). *Improvement of safe and secure computer-mediated environment for adolescents* [in Japanese]. Tokyo: Japanese Ministry of Internal Affairs and Communications.

Kamihama, T., Shimizu, S., Sawamura, S., & Shimizu, S. (2013). Utilization and the dependence tendency in mobile phone use among university students [in Japanese]. *Department of Education Research Bulletin of Iwate University, 72*, 1–10.

Kanetsuna, T. (2014a). *General perception and understanding for the nature of different forms of cyberbullying among adolescents*. Poster presented at International Society for Research on Aggression XXIst World Meeting, Atlanta, Georgia, US.

Kanetsuna, T. (2014b). *The relationships between risk perception, fear of victimization, and coping potential in Cyberbullying*. Paper presentation at 14th Biennial Conference of the European Association for Research on Adolescence, Izmir, Turkey.

Kanetsuna, T. (2016a). Comparisons between English bullying and Japanese ijime. In P. K. Smith, K. Kwak, & Y. Toda (Eds.), *School bullying in different cultures: Eastern and Western perspectives* (pp. 153–169). Cambridge, UK: Cambridge University Press.

Kanetsuna, T. (2016b). *Effects of anonymous beliefs of the Internet on the levels of caution for various online risk behaviour*. Paper presentation at 31st International Congress of Psychology, Pacifico Yokohama, Yokohama, Kanagawa, Japan.

Kohara, K. (2004). The Influence of the diffusion of mobile phones to the relationship of university students [in Japanese]. *Socio-Cultural Studies of Education, 10*, 1–17.

Kollerová, L., Soukup, P., & Gini, G. (2017). Classroom collective moral disengagement scale: Validation in Czech adolescents. *European Journal of Developmental Psychology, 15*(2), 1–8.

Morita, Y. (2001). *Cross-national comparative study of bullying* [in Japanese]. Japan: Kaneko Shobo.

Morita, Y., & Kiyonaga, K. (1994). *Bullying: The ailing classroom* [in Japanese]. Tokyo: Kaneko Syobo.

National Police Agency. (2013). *Propulsive movement of cyber-patrol* [in Japanese] (Report on National Police Agency, 130).

Okamoto, Y., Miyake, Y., Jinnin, R., Yashiki, H., Uchino, T., Isobe, N., . . . & Yoshihara, M. (2014). The Internet use situation in university students: Association between tendency of dependence and mental condition [in Japanese]. *Sogo Hoken Kagaku, 30*, 7–13.

Olweus, D. (2012). Cyberbullying: An overrated phenomenon? *European Journal of Developmental Psychology, 9*(5), 520–538.

Ono, A., & Saito, F. (2008). Educational psychological review about understanding and coping with cyber bullying [in Japanese]. *Bulletin of Senri Kinran University, 5*, 35–47.

Orita, A. (2009). A report on the username squatting problem of social-media [in Japanese]. *Information Processing Society of Japan Technical Report, 44*, 5–14.

Postmes, T., Spears, R., & Lea, M. (1998). Breaching or building social boundaries? SIDE-effects of computer-mediated communication. *Communication Research, 25*(6), 689–715.

Reicher, S. D. (1984). The St. Pauls' riot: An explanation of the limits of crowd action in terms of a social identity model. *European Journal of Social Psychology, 14*, 1–12.

Sasagawa, K. (2016, August 7). Plunge to his death after exposure of homosexuality [in Japanese]. *The Huffington Post.*

Sato, H., Hibino, K., & Yoshida, F. (2010). The effects of computer-mediated communication (CMC) on verbal aggression [in Japanese]. *Psychology Bulletin of Tsukuba University, 39*, 35–43.

Smith, P. K. (2012). Cyberbullying: Challenges and opportunities for a research program – A response to Olweus (2012). *European Journal of Developmental Psychology, 9*(5), 553–558.

Sproull, L., & Kiesler, S. (1986). Reducing social context cues: Electronic mail in organizational communication. *Journal of Management Science, 32*(11), 1492–1512.

Takeuchi, K., & Abe, K. (2014). "Smart" online violence in Japan and the United States: Discussing the similarity/difference of them and applicability of inter-school peer support system. *The Japanese Journal of Educational Practices on Moral Development, 8*(1), 28–31.

Takeuchi, K., Toda, Y., & Takahashi, T. (2015). How should we cope with smartphone and the Internet problems among adolescence? For further collaboration of society and educational psychologists [in Japanese]. *The Annual Report of Educational Psychology in Japan, 54*, 259–265.

Tashiro, M. (2012). Analysis of university students' Internet flaming, prevention, and proposal of correspondence [in Japanese]. *Bulletin of Otsuma Women's University School of Information, 21*, 233–240.

The Office for Youth Affairs and Public Safety of Tokyo Metropolitan Government. (2008). *Fact-finding survey of social withdrawal of adolescents.* Tokyo: The Office for Youth Affairs and Public Safety of Tokyo Metropolitan Government.

Toda, Y. (2016). Bullying (*Ijime*) and related problems in Japan: History and research. In P. K. Smith, K. Kwak, & Y. Toda (Eds.), *School bullying in different cultures: Eastern and western perspectives* (pp. 73–92). Cambridge, UK: Cambridge University Press.

Toda, Y., Strohmeier, D., & Spiel, C. (2008). Process model of bullying [in Japanese]. In T. Katoh & H. Taniguchi (Eds.), *Darkside of interpersonal relationships* (S.117–131). Kyoto: Kitaohji-Shobo.

Watanabe, N., Kubota, M., Ishizaki, T., & Oyanagi, K. (2008). The study of cellular phone, the state of use and the influence on the living environment of junior high school, high school, and university students [in Japanese]. *Bulletin of Niigata Seiryo University, 8*, 31–40.

Yaguchi, S. (2013). Internet usage among university students [in Japanese]. *Bulletin of Tokoha University Junior College, 44*, 125–132.

3

EXPERIENCES OF CYBERBULLYING AT A CHILEAN UNIVERSITY

The voices of students

Rayén Condeza, Gonzalo Gallardo, and Pablo Reyes Pérez

Introduction

This chapter presents the first exploratory study on cyberbullying from the perspective of undergraduate students at Pontificia Universidad Católica de Chile (UC). Located in Santiago, Chile's capital city, and with one campus in the southern region of the country, this is Chile's second oldest university. Each year, UC receives students with the best high school graduation rankings and the most outstanding scores on the national university selection exam. It is considered to be one of the best universities in Latin America (first in 2018 QS ranking for the region). Throughout the past years, this institution has made progress in terms of social and geographical inclusion through the implementation of scholarships and additional admission mechanisms. However, the majority of students still represent a higher socio-economic status.

As in other countries, in Chile, the research on cyberbullying has focused mainly on behaviours at middle and high school levels (Varela, Pérez, Schwaderer, Astudillo, & Lecannelier, 2014). The interest for this type of study in higher education is increasing, driven by the frequent use of information and communication technologies (ICT) by university students (Faucher, Jackson, & Cassidy, 2015), for whom ICT is not something "new", "but rather it is an accepted and normalized part of everyday life" (Myers & Cowie, 2017, p. 1172). In Chile, 91% of people between 18 and 29 years old use smartphones to connect to the web, making them the more intensive users compared to other age groups (Gobierno de Chile, 2016).

Among university students, digital environments are active contexts of everyday life that offer opportunities and pose risks, such as aggression, social exclusion, and suffering in many shapes and degrees (Bartlett et al., 2014; Faucher et al.,

2015; Walker, Sockman, & Koehn, 2011). In order to promote well-being for all, higher education managers are now responsible for gathering information about this phenomenon to generate actions, limit its scope, and support its victims (Myers & Cowie, 2017).

In Chile, as well as in the rest of South America, investigations into this topic at higher education are rare. Cyberbullying is a social phenomenon and public health issue that is "polymorphous, multi-causal, complex and that is also a cause of suicide in young people" (García Peña, Moncada Ortiz, & Quintero Gil, 2013, p. 299). Evidence such as this should promote the development of policies and proactive practices that reduce the effects and impacts of cyberbullying (Cassidy, Faucher, & Jackson, 2013; Myers & Cowie, 2017; Walker et al., 2011).

This study may help to address the issue of cyberbullying at the university level in Chile by shedding light on its extent and providing additional data to inform existing protocols and regulations within UC, which are oriented toward fostering well-being and respect among students and professors. The university currently has an Office of the Ombuds and a helpline (2013), a Directorate for Inclusion (2015), and a Protocol to prevent sexual assault and support sexual assault victims (2016). The effort to promote a respectful environment between students and professors is included as a particular dimension evaluated by students in the teaching survey. Furthermore, addressing cyberbullying as an institutional concern supported by evidence may promote the discussion of regulations aimed at developing specific lines of action within UC and in other institutions.

Inequality and transformations in Chilean higher education

The school system in Chile is highly unequal and segregated (Bellei, 2013; Programa de Naciones Unidas para el Desarrollo PNUD, 2017). There are three types of schools: (a) public (free and funded by the state); (b) private-voucher (private owners, tuition fee paid by the state); and (c) private fee-paying (tuition fee paid entirely by the families). The latter "serve the upper class, with 94% of enrolment coming from the two wealthiest deciles. Public schools mostly serve the lower and the lower-middle class. Private-voucher schools recruit broadly from the middle and upper-middle strata" (Mizala & Torche, 2012, p. 135).

Notwithstanding the above, in the last 20 years, Chile has experienced a massive increase in access to universities, with a subsequent diversification of students (OECD Report Chile, 2007). In the Latin American context, Chile has the highest participation rate in higher education of students from the poorest quintile (27.4%), followed by Bolivia (24.8%) and Argentina (21.6%) (Brunner & Miranda, 2016). This development poses an opportunity for progress in social mobility, considering the highly unequal and segregated school system (Koljatic & Silva, 2012). In recent years, UC has diversified gradually, through specific affirmative action policies. According to its Admissions Department, 60% of students accepted in 2017 had studied at private schools, 27% at a private-voucher school, and 12% at a public school.

Well-being and social relationships at universities

Universities have the potential to break down barriers and bring people together, contributing to the well-being of the university community and (ultimately) the creation of a fairer society. Well-being may be understood as the satisfaction of personal, relational and collective needs. Among relational needs, it is important to mention the need for care, compassion, affection, bonding, social support, solidarity, and a sense of belonging in a community (Prilleltensky, 2004).

Nobody feels *part* of a community just by enrolling in university; it is essential to *perceive yourself as a part* of it based on positive experiences (Strayhorn, 2016; Tinto, 2015). Generally, good relationships among classmates contribute to improved involvement in the learning processes. If students feel valued and accepted by their classmates, they also feel more motivated (Grau & Pino-Pasternak, 2012). Unfortunately, relationships among peers at universities are not always pleasant (Lehmann, 2014; Roberts & Rosenwald, 2013). Social integration becomes more complex when there are no networks available at the university, and, instead, contact is mediated through negative prejudices among peers (Gallardo, Lorca, Morrás, & Vergara, 2014; Sobrero, Lara-Quinteros, Méndez, & Suazo, 2014). If career administrators create safe environments and promote positive intergroup contact, initial prejudices can potentially be overcome (Gallardo, Espinosa, Vergara, Sanhueza, & Cruz, 2016; González, 2005).

What is cyberbullying?

Cyberbullying is a complex phenomenon of interaction among peers that carries serious social and personal consequences (Ortega-Ruíz & Zych, 2016). Studies concerning this issue are relatively new and mostly descriptive (Bartlett et al., 2014). Cyberbullying is a type of bullying between peers, where behaviours are carried out using virtual media (text messages, chats, emails, webpages, Twitter, blogs, Facebook, YouTube or videogame chats, among others) causing different types of damage (Cassidy et al., 2013; Condeza & Fontcuberta, 2015). Its distinctive features include (Cassidy et al., 2013):

- Receiving vulgar, aggressive, threatening, hurtful or unpleasant messages via ICT.
- Degrading, defamatory, sexist, racist or homophobic images or messages through different media.
- Virtual identity theft (for instance, on Facebook or Twitter).
- Deliberate exclusion from an online group or community.

Cyberbullying exhibits the main features of bullying, regarding aggressive behaviour set in a repeatedly abusive relationship, carried out with the intention of causing damage to someone who has relatively less ability to defend themselves (Potocnjak, Berger, & Tomicic, 2011). However, in the specific case of cyberbullying, these features have different nuances (Bartlett et al., 2014; Cassidy et al., 2013; Faucher et al., 2015; Mishna et al., 2012; Ortega-Ruíz & Zych, 2016):

- Sometimes the online context provides anonymity for the offenders;
- There are very few immediate consequences for the offenders;
- It is more difficult to empathize with the victims when it is not possible to verify their emotional reaction;
- The audience witnessing cyberbullying is wider than it is for bullying;
- Messages could remain online for a lengthy period of time (making them harder to forget and facilitating re-victimization);
- The imbalance of power is variable and it can shift: people with less power can use technology to defend themselves.

The following consequences of cyberbullying have been observed in higher education contexts (Aricak, 2009; Faucher et al., 2014, this volume; Myers & Cowie, 2017; Walker et al., 2011):

a *Emotional issues*, such as depression, anxiety, low self-esteem, a sensation of threat towards their emotional and body confidence, and even suicidal thoughts;
b *Behavioural and academic issues*, such as a decrease in class attendance, commitment to studies and academic performance, and difficulty to fulfil academic tasks due to reduced productivity, self-confidence, and concentration;
c *Relational issues*, at the university and beyond, including the end of friendships and romantic relationships.

Some researchers found gender differences in the experiences and consequences of cyberbullying. For example, Faucher and colleagues (2014) indicated that female university students acknowledge the negative effects of online harassment to a higher degree than do male students. They are more likely to talk about the situations with friends or family, and they also tend to make more attempts to put an end to these actions. Women may be especially vulnerable when experiencing hostility, humiliation, violation of privacy, or exclusion in the context of friendships and romantic relationships. Sexual orientation (in the case of homosexual and transsexual students) may represent a factor that increases the risk of victimization (Margolin, 2011; Rivers, 2016, as referenced in Myers and Cowie, 2017; Pescitelli, this volume).

Current study

This study aims to understand the scope of cyberbullying among undergraduate students at UC, identify risk factors and describe the specific influence of university life on this phenomenon.

We employed a survey based on the research of Cassidy, Jackson, and Faucher (2012), adapted to fit into the sociocultural Chilean reality, in order to understand the students' points of view regarding cyberbullying, as well as their experiences as victims, witnesses, or bullies.

The survey consisted of 36 items, using the following variables: major, year in major, gender, age, people with whom they live, region of origin, type of high school they attended, nationality, identification with ethnic groups, and presence of special needs. Frequency of daily media use was also considered. Those who declared being victims were asked about the media through which they experienced said violence, and whether they shared this experience with others. A space was provided for students to tell their stories, and open-ended questions covered possible solutions and concrete preventive actions.

The research was approved by the University Research Ethics Committee. The survey was made available to all UC undergraduate students (n = 22,605) through an online platform. We received 961 completed surveys, which represents 4% of the total number of undergraduate students. The main findings of the survey are described as follows, identifying four sections: (1) experiences from undergraduate cyberbullying victims, (2) witnesses of cyberbullying, (3) offenders, and (4) general perceptions of the undergraduate student community about cyberbullying.

TABLE 3.1 Description of the Sample

Variable	*Category*	*N*	*%*
Gender	Male	317	33.0
	Female	640	66.6
	Missing data	4	0.4
School	Public	115	12.0
	Private-voucher	277	28.8
	Private fee-paying	557	58.0
	Missing data	12	1.2
Generation	First year	285	29.7
	Second year	151	15.7
	Third year	157	16.3
	Fourth year	149	15.5
	Fifth year	118	12.3
	Sixth year/ older	100	10.4
	Missing data	1	0.1

The respondents to the survey are described in terms of gender, high-school origin and college year. Women represent 66.6% of respondents, twice as many as men (33.0%). In this sample, they are over-represented in relation to the gender breakdown of UC first-year students in 2017 (55.3% women and 44.7% men). According to the type of secondary school of origin, the distribution is similar to that of the 2017 enrolment process: 12% of first-year students came from public schools, 27% from private-voucher schools, and 60% from private fee-paying schools. Finally, response rates decreased progressively as the year of enrolment increased, ranging from 29.7% (first year) to 10.4% (sixth year), with the exception of a slight increase between the second and third year (15.7% to 16.3%).

Experiences of cyberbullying victims

Twelve point five percent of participants mentioned being a victim of cyberbullying during the past year, while 2.4% of the students claimed to be a victim of cyberbullying at the time they answered the survey.

Seventy-two point four percent of the participants who claimed to have experienced cyberbullying mentioned that their offenders were mainly people from outside the university context, followed by university peers, with 45.1% referring to friends or friend groups, and 36.8% to university acquaintances.

Students were asked to indicate the media and the frequency in which they experienced cyberbullying in the last year. Facebook is the main platform used for

TABLE 3.2 Cyberbullying Behaviour Prevalence

			Confidence interval (95%)	
Category	*n*	*%*	*inf*	*Sup*
CB victim during past year	120	12.5	10.4	14.7
CB victim at university	61	6.3	4.8	8.0
Current CB victim	23	2.4	1.5	3.5

TABLE 3.3 Offender Distribution Declared by CB Victims

Declared offender	*n*	*%*
External to university	84	72.4
Friend or friend group from university	51	45.1
Acquaintance from university	39	36.8
Scholar or assistant	6	5.7
Worker from university	2	1.9

TABLE 3.4 Platforms and Frequency of CB

	Never	*1 or 2 times a month*	*3 or more times a month*	*Once a week*	*Every week*
Facebook	41.5%	41.5%	8.5%	5.9%	2.5%
Pictures via mobile phone	48.7%	38.3%	7.0%	1.7%	4.3%
Texts via email	78.1%	15.8%	2.6%	1.8%	1.8%
Identity theft	85.8%	10.6%	1.8%	0.0%	1.8%
Text message	87.1%	6.9%	2.6%	0.9%	2.6%
Twitter	87.8%	8.7%	0.9%	0.9%	1.7%
Pictures via email	88.8%	9.5%	0.0%	0.9%	0.9%
Forums or academic platforms	98.3%	0.9%	0.9%	0.0%	0.0%
Skype	95.0%	0.0%	0.8%	0.8%	3.4%

cyberbullying with a frequency of once or twice a week to once a month, ranging from 41.5% to 5.9%, respectively. Students who suffered from cyberbullying at least every week in the last year (i.e., the highest frequency alternative presented in the survey) report pictures sent by mobile phone (4.3%) as the predominant platform. Perhaps surprisingly, Skype is the second most common platform for cyberbullying with the highest range of frequency (3.4%), followed by text messages (2.6%).

Regarding the reasons or causes behind cyberbullying, 50.8% of the victims claimed not to be aware of the motivations of their offenders or to know the reasons why they were targeted. In the cases where victims were able to identify possible motivations behind the offenders' actions, they mentioned their physical appearance (36.6%), interpersonal relationship issues (30%), socio-economic status (20.8%), gender (20%), academic success (18.3%), age (10%), academic difficulties (9.2%), physical disability (4.2%), and geographical origin (4.2%).

In addition, respondents had the opportunity to describe other causes that, in their view, may have motivated cyberbullying from their peers. These included sexual orientation, political ideas, ending romantic relationships, or differences in age with respect to peers. The following quotations illustrate some of these self-reported reasons victims gave for why they were targeted at UC:

> Last year we were on strike for an indefinite amount of time. I expressed my opinion on the Facebook page of my major. A classmate of mine made a comment on the same post, saying that I was "fucking selfish". Others made fun of me because I said I was going to miss a flight because of the strike.
>
> *(male student, sixth year)*

> When I broke up with my partner a couple of years ago, my group of friends at university started judging me because I got into another relationship too soon after that, and they started spreading lies among them. After that, some people sent me aggressive messages insulting me and my new partner. My ex posted things on Facebook and started a wave of WhatsApp messages insulting me or ignoring me whenever I spoke on a WhatsApp group we shared.
>
> *(female student, fifth year)*

> In the context of a discussion forum in the UC students' Facebook group, a group of students were posting homophobic and transphobic comments and memes. I wrote a comment defying them, and they turned it into a meme, reposting it in the same Facebook group and on their own profiles.
>
> *(male student, third year)*

In relation to the consequences experienced, 51.7% of cyberbullying victims declared having felt physically or emotionally threatened, 52.5% experienced mental health difficulties, 47.9% showed physical symptoms, and 46.6% felt it affected their academic performance. Cyberbullying also caused difficulties in terms of interpersonal relationships (43.7%), academic performance (26.1%), and class attendance (25.9%). Eighteen point six percent of the victims considered dropping out of university, as illustrated by the following quotation from one respondent who had been victimized: "I have anxiety episodes to this day, every time I see my classmate (cyberbully). I had to drop out of my classes the last month and I have been under psychological and psychiatric treatment for almost a year now" (female student, second year).

Out of the total number of students who reported being victimized during the past year, 54.1% made attempts to stop it. Only 36.6% were able to do so, reinforcing the low amount of control of the situation that cyberbullying victims perceive to have.

Regarding support networks, 80.3% of students who defined themselves as cyberbullying victims mentioned having talked about their experience with a friend or classmate, 67.2% did so with a friend from outside university, 55.9% decided to share their experience with family members, and 47% did so with their partner. Teachers and professionals at the university were not sought out for support (only 8.2% of victims went to student affairs, 6.6% to teachers, and 3.3% to teaching assistants). Very few went to the police (3.3%). Student Health services, the university helpline, or the university counsellor were not mentioned.

Experiencing cyberbullying as a witness

The cyberbullying experience extends beyond the victim-offender relationship, involving spectators or indirect participants. These individuals may hear about the negative consequences that befall the victims, the lack of punishment for offenders, or they may observe the cyberbullying directly. Thirty-eight point one percent of the participants mentioned having witnessed cyberbullying. Some of these students said that they were emotionally affected, expressing discomfort and concern about this type of relationship among classmates, with some reporting that they felt empathy and attempted to support the victims. The following examples are indicative of the comments received:

> I thought that it was not right to expose a classmate like that, it upset me, and I believed that it was a shame that we treated each other like that.
>
> *(female, fourth year)*

> I felt powerless about the offenders' anonymity, and I felt ignorant because I did not know what to do.
>
> *(female, second year)*

> I was very angry . . . I felt rage, and I just wanted to let my friend know that she could count on me any time.
>
> *(female, fifth year)*

Beyond expressions of concern, or some attempt to show support to the victim, in most cases, this discomfort did not translate into action:

> I thought it was horrible, but I did nothing to stop it.
>
> *(female, sixth year)*

> I did not do anything, but I'm angry.
>
> *(female, sixth year)*

> I worry that people will be attacked in this way. However, I admit that I did not take any action in this regard.
>
> *(male, sixth year)*

> It angered me, but since it was not my friend, I cannot intervene.
>
> *(male, first year)*

It is also relevant to note that among the participants who identified themselves as witnesses of cyberbullying, 44.5% mentioned that they were sometimes afraid of becoming cyberbullying victims themselves.

Cyberbullying from the perspective of the offenders

Only 3.3% of the total number of participants reported having been cyberbullying offenders, while 7.8% claimed not to know if they had participated. Regarding those who identified themselves as being involved in cyberbullying, the majority said they only participated once or twice (85.7%), describing these instances as specific experiences rather than recurring. Ten point seven percent of those who said they cyberbullied, however, declared having participated in cyberbullying many times per week.

According to statements by students self-identified as offenders, their actions were directed towards class acquaintances or strangers rather than partners or close friends.

No one mentioned having targeted teachers or other authorities. These results suggest that aggressive behaviour among peers in this sample is more likely to occur with distant relationships, with friendships perhaps offering some protection from cyberbullying. This observation is worth investigating in future studies.

General conceptions about cyberbullying

Overall, 45.9%, or almost half, of the participants in this study had been involved in a cyberbullying situation during the past year, if one combines those who reported being a victim, witness, or offender. Also, of concern is that more than half of the respondents consider cyberbullying to be a *normal* online phenomenon (54.9%), with 23.5% noting that cyberbullying is unavoidable, although 23.7% agreed that the university should play a major part in preventing and stopping it. Importantly, 81.5% of the students stated that they would like to help create a more respectful and caring online environment. Most are willing to report cyberbullying, provided that it is anonymous (79.3%). Just under one-quarter of respondents (21.2%) think that freedom of speech permits them to say whatever they like online.

In thinking about future interventions, students were asked to evaluate strategies that the university could implement to prevent or limit the effects of cyberbullying. The three strategies that obtained the highest rating from the proposed list were: (1) provide counselling and support services to victims; (2) develop a specific policy; and (3) offer support to people who engage in cyberbullying. Some students added written suggestions for possible actions that the university might develop to institutionally address cyberbullying. For example, "conduct a campaign for good treatment and dedicate days in all academic units" (male, sixth year). Other students demanded moral sanctions and public rejection of the perpetrators along the lines of "an eye for an eye": "Punishments without mercy for cyberbullying" (male, second year). Or, "Punish those who bully so they learn that it is not right" (female, third year). Other students considered the aggressor as a member of the community who needs help: "it would be good to target those who attack, as they have often suffered aggression" (female, first year). Some voices were without hope, stating that there was nothing the university could do about cyberbullying.

Discussion and conclusions

One of the main objectives of this study was to discover the scope of cyberbullying experienced by UC undergraduate students. Our findings indicate that 45.9% (or close to half) of the participants in this study had been exposed to cyberbullying in the last year, whether as a victim, witness, or perpetrator. Regardless of their role in cyberbullying, it impacts the well-being and learning experiences of all participants (Aricak, 2009; Cassidy, Faucher, & Jackson, this volume; Faucher et al., 2014, this volume; Myers & Cowie, 2017; Walker et al., 2011). Although this study leads us to infer that cyberbullying occurs in Chilean higher education, additional studies are needed to investigate the phenomenon in greater depth at UC, as well as at other universities in Chile.

While the percentage of reported victims of cyberbullying among university students is lower than in many other countries (Faucher et al., 2014), the presence of negative online relationships among students in Chile is worth acknowledging. Recognizing oneself as a victim is never easy, and it becomes even more difficult when cyberbullying behaviours are normalized in some circles, or when there are no public campaigns to identify cyberbullying as a problem, a relational or a public health issue. We are highly motivated to disseminate the findings from this first Chilean study as a way to encourage a prevention campaign. Making cyberbullying prevention a priority at the post-secondary level could encourage more students to feel comfortable revealing that they have been victims or even perpetrators, as well as empower by-standers to offer concrete support or to intervene when an incident is occurring.

The repercussions of cyberbullying identified by participants in this study are in line with other studies (e.g., Aricak, 2009; Faucher et al., 2014; Myers & Cowie, 2017; Walker et al., 2011). Victims of cyberbullying at UC experienced similar emotional, behavioural, academic and relational issues, discomfort and suffering which, in some cases, lasted for several months. The sum of these consequences makes cyberbullying a pressing issue for higher education institutions in Chile and for society as a whole.

Therefore, the questions remain: what should be done? And what actions should be promoted? A first step is to work towards de-naturalizing the acceptance of these actions among students. This is a key challenge in the UC context. More than half of the participants in this study described cyberbullying aggressions as "normal". Medium-term actions could be to identify cyberbullying as a common problem that affects the welfare of all, and for which everyone has a responsibility to act. The newspaper in charge of the Directorate of Student Affairs, "Vive la UC", could be a relevant and important tool because undergraduate students report that it is the medium with the greatest impact.

To make visible the invisible, to problematize the everyday, and to de-naturalize mistaken assumptions is a path towards awareness. It is a process. In order to make progress, it will not be enough to merely spread awareness of the subject. To problematize and de-naturalize cyberbullying requires the promotion of critical reflection and analysis in each academic unit, among teachers, between teachers and students, and also among students, ideally organized through student centres (democratic organizations chosen by students from each major). As Montero (2011) states:

> It is not possible to denature a stereotype, a commonplace, a traditional and firmly entrenched belief, a norm, a habit or, in general, a way of behaving whose presence in daily life is explained only because "that's the way things are", or "because that is the way people behave" or "because it has always been done", if there is not a process of criticism that submits the subject matter to review, discussion and analysis.
>
> *(p. 262)*

How to move forward? Myers and Cowie (2017) emphasize that prevention and intervention against cyberbullying must be the institution's responsibility. Faucher et al. (2015) mention that preventive actions should be implemented at the very beginning of university life, "such as during the initial orientation sessions and on the first day of a course" (p. 115), in order to promote immediate awareness of cyberbullying as an issue. Other possible lines of action would be to offer reporting options and direct support for witnesses, encouraging them to step forward and "break the silence" that permeates these practices (Myers & Cowie, 2017).

Doing so is not easy. As this study suggests, students do not look for support from institutional agents (university helpline, counsellor's office, teachers); rather, they resort to family and friends. Furthermore, some students do not believe that the university should be responsible for intervening in, or preventing, these issues. It will be a challenge to generate a change of attitude and perception. Defining cyberbullying in institutional policies, describing the harmful consequences, and creating clear action protocols are all initiatives worth considering (Faucher et al., 2015).

Actively promoting good peer relationships in educational contexts is also important. Creating affection and close bonds among classmates promotes self-esteem, well-being, and a sense of belonging (Strayhorn, 2016; Tinto, 2015). Neither bullying nor cyberbullying behaviours can be explained in terms of the bully's personality, the witnesses' indifference, or the victim's lack of strategies: this is a systemic issue (López de Lerida, Berger, & Pizarro, 2012). It is essential to encourage and model respect and good relationships within educational communities and in society as a whole.

Finally, it is necessary to activate and disseminate resources already available at UC, and also to create new approaches for effective intervention, to stop violence when detected, protect victims, and generate opportunities for learning and reparation for aggressors. Among the resources already available at UC are the Ombuds, the undergraduate and teacher regulations, the unit of psychological support (Bureau of Health students), and the helpline "Fono-Ayuda UC", which offers guidance, support, and information about procedures and channels for victims and witnesses of harassment and physical or psychological abuse or violence. In addition, just as UC created the "Protocol against sexual harassment and abuse", it could create a protocol of "Good treatment in cyber space". As with the "Protocol against sexual harassment", it would be important to source codes and norms through dialogue among the different members of the community. Mass diffusion of information regarding cyberbullying and disseminating the results of this study in a fact-sheet or easily readable infographic could contribute to increasing awareness of the problem. Promoting national and international meetings of higher education in this field will continue to foster the interdisciplinary international research networks such as the one that gave rise to this study.

Finally, this topic demands collective reflection throughout the campus context and in every career program. Furthermore, more research is needed to support policy development and the implementation of new practices at the university and state levels. For example, regarding the Chilean higher education system, the government could consider the implementation of specific policies and protocols in this area as a requisite for university accreditation, encouraging institutional attention to this area of student well-being across the country.

Limitations and future research

It is necessary to move forward with the investigation about this issue by providing stratified samples according to student population parameters. In our study, female participants, as well as certain academic fields, are over-represented (for instance, students from the Faculty of Engineering, College and Faculty of Medicine). This could have an effect on the cyberbullying prevalence rates. Additionally, it is necessary to have a better understanding of cyberbullying experiences at university, taking a qualitative approach in subsequent research studies.

Acknowledgements

We thank all the students who trusted us with their experiences.

References

Aricak, O. T. (2009). Psychiatric symptomatology as a predictor of cyberbullying among university students. *Egitim Arastirmalari-Eurasian Journal of Educational Research, 34*, 167–184.

Bartlett, C., Gentile, D., Anderson, C., Suzuki, K., Sakamoto, A., Yamaoka, A., & Katsura, R. (2014). Cross-cultural differences in cyberbullying behaviour: A short-term longitudinal study. *Journal of Cross-Cultural Psychology, 45*(2), 300–313.

Bellei, C. (2013). El estudio de la segregación socioeconómica y académica de la educación chilena [The study of the socioeconomic and academic segregation of Chilean education]. *Estudios Pedagógicos, 39*(1), 325–345.

Brunner, J. J., & Miranda, D. (2016). *Educación Superior en Iberoamérica Informe 2016 [Higher Education in Ibero-America Report 2016]*. Santiago de Chile: CINDA (Centro Interuniversitario de Desarrollo)/RIL Editores.

Cassidy, W., Faucher, C., & Jackson, M. (2013). Cyberbullying among youth: A comprehensive review of current international research and its implications and application to policy and practice. *School Psychology International: Special Issue on Cyberbullying, 34*(6), 575–612.

Cassidy, W., Faucher, C., & Jackson, M. (this volume). "You need a thick skin . . .": Impacts of cyberbullying in Canadian universities. In W. Cassidy, C. Faucher, & M. Jackson (Eds.), *Cyberbullying at university in international contexts* (pp. 112–125). Oxford, UK: Routledge.

Cassidy, W., Jackson, M., & Faucher, C. (2012). *Survey to investigate the extent, nature and impact of Cyber-Bullying among university students in select universities in Canada*. Canada: Simon Fraser University.

Condeza, R., & Fontcuberta, M. (2015). Redes sociales: luces y sombras en el ámbito de la Comunicación & Educación [Social networks: Lights and shadows in the field of Communication & Education]. In V. Tomé, E. Bévort, & V. Reia-Baptista (Eds.), *Research on social media: A glocal view [Investiugacao em media sociais: uma visiao glocal]* (pp. 51–78). Lisboa: RVJ.

Ezcurra, A. M. (2005). Diagnóstico preliminar de las dificultades de los alumnos de primer ingreso a la educación superior [Preliminary diagnosis of the difficulties of first-year students entering higher education]. *Perfiles Educativos, 27*(107), 118–133.

Faucher, C., Cassidy, W., & Jackson, M. (this volume). Power in the tower: The gendered nature of cyberbullying among students and faculty at Canadian universities. In W. Cassidy, C. Faucher, & M. Jackson (Eds.), *Cyberbullying at university in international contexts* (pp. 66–79). Oxford, UK: Routledge.

Faucher, C., Jackson, M., & Cassidy, W. (2014). Cyberbullying among university students: Gendered experiences, impacts, and perspectives. *Education Research International, 2014*, 1–10 [online]. Retrieved from https://www.hindawi.com/journals/edri/2014/698545/

Faucher, C., Jackson, M., & Cassidy, W. (2015). When online exchanges byte: An examination of the policy environment governing cyberbullying at the university level. *Canadian Journal of Higher Education/Revue canadienne d'enseignement supérieur, 45*(1), 102–121.

Gallardo, G., Espinosa, C., Vergara, M., Sanhueza, M., & Cruz, S. (2016). Apoyo institucional para la inclusión educativa universitaria: actividades deportivas de integración [Institutional support for inclusion at higher education: Sports integration activities]. In PAIEP (Comp.), *Primer Congreso de Inclusión en la Educación Superior: Acciones afirmativas para igualar oportunidades*. Santiago de Chile: PAIEP USACH.

Gallardo, G., Lorca, A., Morrás, D., & Vergara, M. (2014). High school to college transition experiences of students admitted in a Chilean traditional university (CRUCH) through Inclusive Special Admission. Pensamiento Educativo. *Revista de Investigación Educacional Latinoamericana, 51*(2), 135–151.

García Peña, J., Moncada Ortiz, R., & Quintero Gil, J. (2013). El bullying y el suicidio en el escenario universitario [Bullying and suicide in the university scenario]. *Revista colombiana de ciencias sociales, 4*(2), 298–310.

Gobierno de Chile. (2016). *Séptima encuesta de Acceso, Usos y Usuarios en Internet* [Seventh Survey on Access, Uses and Users on the Internet]. Santiago: Subtel/Ipsos.

González, R. (2005). Movilidad social: el rol del prejuicio y la discriminación [Social mobility: The role of prejudice and discrimination]. *En foco, Expansiva, 59*, 1–23.

Grau, V., & Pino-Pasternak, D. (2012). Colaborar para aprender en contextos de diversidad. El aprendizaje mediado por pares y la riqueza de las diferencias [Collaborate to learn in contexts of diversity. Peer-mediated learning and the richness of differences]. In I. Mena, M. R. Lissi, L. Alcalay, & N. Milicic (Eds.), *Educación y divesidad. Aportes desde la Psicología educacional* (pp. 71–94). Santiago de Chile: Ediciones UC.

Koljatic, M., & Silva, M. (2012). Opening a side-gate: Engaging the excluded in Chilean higher education through test-blind admission. *Studies in Higher Education, 38*(10), 1427–1441.

Lehmann, W. (2014). Habitus transformation and hidden injuries: Successful working-class university students. *Sociology of Education, 87*(1), 1–15.

López de Lerida, S., Berger, C., & Pizarro, B. (2012). Intimidación o Convivencia: Polos opuestos en la experiencia de la diversidad escolar [Intimidation or Coexistence: Opposite poles in the experience of school diversity]. In I. Mena, M. R. Lissi, L. Alcalay, & N. Milicic (Eds.), *Educación y Diversidad. Aportes desde la Psicología Educacional* (pp. 123–152). Santiago: Ediciones UC.

Mishna, F., Khoury-Kassabri, M., Gadalla, T., & Daciuk, J. (2012). Risk factors for involvement in cyber bullying: Victims, bullies and bully-victims. *Children and Youth Services Review, 34*, 63–70.

Mizala, A., & Torche, F. (2012). Bringing the schools back in: The stratification of educational achievement in the Chilean voucher system. *International Journal of Educational Development, 32*(1), 132–144.

Montero, M. (2011). *Introducción a la Psicología Comunitaria. Desarrollo, conceptos y procesos* [Introduction to community psychology. Development, concepts and processes]. Buenos Aires: PAIDÓS.

Myers, C., & Cowie, H. (2017). Bullying at university: The social and legal contexts of cyberbullying among university students. *Journal of Cross Cultural Psychology, 48*(8), 1172–1182.

OECD Report, Chile. (2007). *Recognition of non-formal and informal learning. Country Background report Chile*. Prepared by the Lifelong Learning System Chilecalifica in collaboration with the Higher Education Division of the Ministry of Education and National Service the Training and Employment. Retrieved from www.oecd.org/chile/41836939.pdf.

Ortega-Ruíz, R., & Zych, I. (2016). La ciberconducta y la psicología educativa: retos y riesgos [Cyber-conduct and educational psychology: Challenges and risks]. *Psicología Educativa, 22*, 1–4.

Pescitelli, A. (this volume). *MySpace* or yours? An exploratory study of homophobic and transphobic cyberbullying of post-secondary students. In W. Cassidy, C. Faucher, & M. Jackson (Eds.), *Cyberbullying at university in international contexts* (pp. 52–65). Oxford, UK: Routledge.

Programa de Naciones Unidas para el Desarrollo-PNUD. (2017). *Desiguales. Orígenes, cambios y desafíos de la brecha social en Chile* [Unequal. Origins, changes and challenges of the social gap in Chile]. Santiago: PNUD.

Potocnjak, M., Berger, C., & Tomicic, T. (2011). Una aproximación relacional a la violencia escolar entre pares en adolescentes Chilenos: Perspectiva adolescente de los factores intervinientes [A relational approach to school violence among peers in Chilean adolescents: Adolescent perspective of the intervening factors]. *Psykhe, 20*(2), 39–52.

Prilleltensky, I. (2004). Prólogo. Validez psicopolítica: el próximo reto para psicología comunitaria [Foreword. Psychopolitical validity: The next challenge for community psychology]. In M. Montero (Ed.), *Introducción a la Psicología Comunitaria. Desarrollo, conceptos y procesos* (pp. 5–14). Buenos Aires: PAIDÓS.

Roberts, J. S., & Rosenwald, G. C. (2013). Ever upward and no turning back: Social mobility and identity formation among first generation college students. In D. P. McAdams, R. Josselson, & A. Lieblich (Eds.), *Turns in the road: Narrative studies of lives in transition* (pp. 91–119). Washington, DC: American Psychological Association (APA).

Sobrero, V., Lara-Quinteros, R., Méndez, P., & Suazo, B. (2014). Equidad y diversidad en universidades selectivas: la experiencia de estudiantes con ingresos especiales en las carreras de la salud [Equity and diversity in selective universities: Experiences of students admitted to health majors via equity programs]. *Pensamiento educativo, Revista de Investigación educacional latinoamericana, 51*(2), 152–164.

Strayhorn, T. (2016). *Student development theory in higher education: A social psychological approach*. New York & London: Routledge.

Tinto, V. (2015). Through the eyes of students. *Journal of College Student Retention: Research, Theory and Practice, 19*(3), 254–269.

Varela, J., Pérez, J. C., Schwaderer, H., Astudillo, J., & Lecannelier, F. (2014). Caracterización del cyberbullying en el gran Santiago de Chile, en el año 2010 [Characterization of cyberbullying in the city of Santiago, Chile, in 2010]. *Revista Quadrimestral da Associação Brasileira de Psicologia Escolar e Educacional, 18*(2), 347–354.

Walker, C. M., Sockman, B. R., & Koehn, S. (2011). An exploratory study of cyberbullying with undergraduate university students. *TechTrends: Linking Research and Practice to Improve Learning, 55*(2), 31–38.

4

MYSPACE OR YOURS?

An exploratory study of homophobic and transphobic cyberbullying of post-secondary students

Aynsley Pescitelli

The vast majority of cyberbullying research to date focuses on elementary, middle, and high school students; yet, post-secondary students are not immune to this behaviour, nor are they immune to the resultant harms. In fact, "while traditional bullying decreases as adolescents move into university, cyberbullying may remain constant from the high school years" (Wensley & Campbell, 2012, p. 652). Although studies have just begun to examine cyberbullying among post-secondary students, there is even less research examining the LGBTQ (lesbian, gay, bisexual, transgender, queer, and/or questioning) experience. Of the studies that have been conducted, most address LGBTQ students as part of the wider student population (Bauman & Baldasare, 2015; Finn, 2004; Lindsay & Krysik, 2012; Wensley & Campbell, 2012), or comparing patterns of cyberbullying of LGBTQ individuals to their peers (Cooper & Blumenfeld, 2012; Finn, 2004), rather than studying this group in particular. This chapter addresses LGBTQ students' experiences with homophobia[1] and transphobia[2] in online environments.

Literature review

Homophobia and transphobia in post-secondary settings

Research on homophobia and transphobia in post-secondary institutions has most often been conducted in the United States and the United Kingdom. These studies have generally neglected to focus on the "T" in LGBT (Beemyn, 2012), often examining only discrimination encountered by gay, lesbian, and bisexual students. The bulk of this research has focused on the anti-homosexual attitudes of heterosexual post-secondary students. In their study of anti-gay attitudes of U.S. college students, Cotten-Huston and Waite (1999) found that one-time, in-class interventions were largely ineffective in influencing attitudes towards homosexuality. In a four-year longitudinal project with U.S. university students, however, Jayakumar (2009) found that most students (75%) had lower levels of sexual prejudice in their final year of university. Finally, in their examination of heterosexist language in American college settings, Woodford, Howell, Silverchanz, and Yu (2012) focused specifically on the popular phrase "that's so gay", as well as wider use of the term "gay" in a derogatory fashion. Almost all (90% of LGB participants) reported hearing the phrase at least once in the last year (with 47% hearing it more than 10 times). Woodford et al. (2012) argue that the common use of such terms, particularly in school settings, has likely led to a degree of desensitization among LGB students, and that findings indicate high levels of resiliency among their sample.

Although this area remains an under-researched one (Rivers, 2016), a small number of studies have also addressed transgender students specifically. In their undergraduate survey, Nagoshi et al. (2008) found that male students' scores on both homophobia and transphobia were significantly higher than those of their female counterparts. Homophobic and transphobic males were also significantly more likely to self-report high levels of aggression and masculinity. In a UK study (Ellis, 2009), LGBT students from 42 universities reported experiencing homophobia and transphobia most often in public places. Such harassment was overwhelmingly perpetrated by other students. Although homophobic and transphobic events were commonly experienced by participants, most believed that on-campus anti-LGBT attitudes were fairly uncommon.

Cyberbullying and LGBTQ students

The rates of, and consequences resulting from, the cyberbullying of LGBTQ youth are a cause for concern. In Varjas, Meyers, Kiperman, and Howard's (2013) study of American LGB adolescents, 94% of participants reported experiencing cyberbullying, with the majority believing that their sexual orientation was the reason for their cyber-victimization. In their comparison of American LGBT and allied youth, Cooper and Blumenfeld (2012) found similar rates of cyber-victimization in terms of bullying which was based on race/ethnicity and biological sex – LGBT individuals, however, were much more likely to be cyberbullied for reasons related to their sexual or gender identity. LGBT participants were also more likely to receive messages of a threatening or intimidating nature. Although both allied and LBGT groups reported experiencing negative emotional responses following cyberbullying victimization, rates of depression were higher among LGBT participants, as were rates of suicidal thoughts and attempts. GLSEN, CiPHR, and CCRC's[3] (2013) online study of LGBT and non-LGBT U.S. youth also showed much higher levels of online bullying and harassment among their LGBT participants. "Nearly three in four respondents (71%) in this study reported having been bullied specifically because of their sexual orientation, gender expression, or both in the past year" (GLSEN et al., 2013, p. 8). LGBT participants also reported much higher rates of sexual harassment than their non-LGBT peers, both online and through text messaging (GLSEN et al., 2013).

While there is still a dearth of research in this area, researchers are starting to explore the topic by comparing the experiences of LGBTQ and non-LGBTQ post-secondary students. Finn (2004) found higher rates of stranger-perpetrated email harassment among sexual minority-identified participants at the University of New Hampshire. In an Australian study, Wensley and Campbell (2012) found that, compared to their heterosexual peers, non-heterosexual male university students were significantly more likely to be victims of cyberbullying. Overall rates of cyberbullying in this study were comparable to those found in middle and high school settings, suggesting that cyberbullying continues to be a problem experienced by post-secondary students. Although, in a re-examination of Finn's (2004) study at Arizona State University, Lindsay and Krysik (2012) did not find LGBT students' stated sexual orientation to be linked to more frequent experiences of online harassment.

The continuing presence of subtle and overt homophobic and transphobic harassment in post-secondary settings is quite troubling, especially since the internet provides a wider context in which to perpetrate similar forms of bullying. If homophobia and transphobia are this prevalent in face-to-face contexts, there is a strong possibility that it is even more common on the internet, where anonymity and disinhibition may further encourage such behaviour. Although several of these studies discuss the overlap of online bullying and LGBTQ young adults, very few have focused on this topic exclusively. Furthermore, the studies conducted to date have been entirely or predominantly quantitative in nature. Thus, the research outlined in this chapter attempts to fill this gap and examine the topic through an exploratory, qualitative lens.

Research methods

Because very little research has been conducted to date on post-secondary students' experiences with homophobic and transphobic cyberbullying, this study is both exploratory and descriptive. The primary research question is: "What are post-secondary students' experiences with homophobia and transphobia in online environments?"

Participants were selected through purposive and snowball sampling methods. It was important that interviewees met several criteria for inclusion. These requirements included: current registration at a post-secondary institution in the Greater Vancouver area of British Columbia, being a minimum age of 19, and personal or witnessed experience of homophobic or transphobic cyberbullying.[4] Additional participants were recruited through a snowball sampling method, wherein early-stage interviewees spread the word about the study to contacts that also fit the sampling criteria. Snowball sampling is often used in research with hard-to-contact populations and studies that address sensitive topics (Dantzker & Hunter, 2012; Palys & Atchison, 2014). These considerations both apply in the current study, as information about an individual's sexual orientation and/or gender identity may not be readily apparent (Janoff, 2005); members of the LGBTQ community, however, may know others who meet study requirements who are unaware of the research being conducted.

Recruitment was carried out primarily through posters placed in general areas of multiple local university and college campuses, as well as in several inclusive spaces (both on campuses and in the community). Additional recruitment methods included: free and paid advertisements on online news and classified sites, as well as in local newspapers; Facebook recruitment through former participants and colleagues; email newsletters through LGBTQ organizations (on and off campus); and email recruitment through several departmental undergraduate mail lists.

The final sample consisted of six participants, including both undergraduate and graduate students from post-secondary institutions throughout the Greater Vancouver region. All information in Table 4.1, as well as further demographic information, was obtained through a follow-up questionnaire administered after each interview. Questionnaire results were submitted in the participants' own words and are reported as written. Interviewees were given additional space to expand on answers or to discuss anything not covered in the interview. Participants were provided the opportunity to select their own pseudonyms. They were also encouraged to define their own sexual orientation and/or gender identity, rather than having these personal features presumed or assigned. Finally, interviewees were asked how they would like to be referred to in the study (e.g., in masculine, feminine, or neutral terms) to allow them to have additional ownership over their representation.

In-depth, semi-structured interviews were conducted between January and June of 2013. Interview length ranged from 45 minutes to 1 hour and 50 minutes. Participants were given the opportunity to select a location for the interview

TABLE 4.1 Study Participants

*Pseudonym**	*Sexual Identity or Orientation***	*Gender Identity***
Clark Kent	Not identified	Not identified
Mercy	Straight, bi, or pansexual (situation dependent)	Female
Jeeves	Pansexual queer	Transmasculine
Fox	Lesbian	Not identified
Gia	Queer/lesbian/gay	Female/genderqueer
Damon	Pansexual/polyamorous	Transmasculine

* Selected by participants or assigned by researcher if self-selection declined.

** Self-identified by participants.

(as recommended by Legard, Keegan, & Ward, 2003). Interviews were recorded on a digital device (with permission), and field notes were taken to supplement recordings. Although this project was designated minimal risk by the institutional Office of Research Ethics, bullying, homophobia, and transphobia are difficult topics – interviews can involve the recounting of painful memories, experiences, and emotions. For this reason, interviewees were also provided with a list of local counselling contacts. Recorded interviews were transcribed and uploaded to *NVivo 10* qualitative analysis software for coding. Coding was conducted in several stages, beginning with an initial round of open coding, followed by axial coding, shifting the focus to more specific categories and key themes present throughout the entire sample (see Corbin & Strauss, 2008; Strauss, 1987; Scott & Garner, 2013).

Results

Venues in which cyberbullying most often occurs

Cyberbullying was encountered by participants in many different online settings, including chat rooms, through instant messaging, social networking sites (Facebook, MySpace, Twitter), video sharing sites (YouTube), news sites (*The Vancouver Sun*, *The Province*), gaming communities (*Call of Duty*, virtual worlds), and blogs (Tumblr). Although homophobia and transphobia were encountered in each of these venues, it was most commonly experienced through Facebook posts, online gaming, and YouTube comments and videos.

All participants reported regular use of Facebook. Reported forms of victimization on Facebook included threats, use of transphobic slurs (e.g., "tranny"), and insult wars between groups of people. There was an additional level of discomfort with Facebook victimization compared to the other listed media, since it is not an anonymous website and, in most cases, the cyberbullies were friends or acquaintances. There were a few instances where unknown individuals posted rude comments due to changes in Facebook privacy settings, but these were rare. Such knowledge of identity did play a role in one interviewee's, Jeeves', offline experiences, however. In this case, Facebook victimization extended into in-person victimization when cyberbullies spotted Jeeves at the mall and said hurtful things about him while he was nearby.

Fox and Mercy, meanwhile, had both been regularly exposed to victimization in online gaming environments. In Mercy's in-game experiences, homophobic comments were generally tied to players' religious beliefs. Such cases were typically attributed to "trolling", with players seeking to get a rise out of her and other LGBTQ gamers. In comparison, Fox's experiences with homophobic comments in *Call of Duty* were constant. Her online profile and uniform emblems identified her as both female and a lesbian, and she was regularly barraged by slurs (e.g., "dyke", "lesbo", "faggot"), as well as threats of rape.

Fox also experienced secondary cyber-victimization, as she was constantly being exposed to homophobic insults directed at male players, whether gay or straight. She states that "faggot" is by far the most common insult used in-game, and that she hears the term repeatedly in every game in which she participates.

> They jump on guys whether they're straight or not. When it comes to gaming like that, if you aren't good, then you're a fag. If you have to throw grenades, if that's the only way you can get kills instead of actually shooting somebody with a gun, which takes a little more precision, then you're a fag.
> *(Fox, personal communication, 2013)*

YouTube emerged as one of the most concerning online venues. Homophobic and transphobic views were sometimes expressed through videos, but were more commonly present in comments responding to videos. Some comments were directed at videos with LGBTQ contributors or in support of LGBTQ causes. Examples of this included music videos by gay or lesbian artists, or videos posted by activist groups. Others were posted in response to seemingly innocuous videos. Damon also described high levels of transphobic comments in response to trans-specific videos on YouTube, and talked about actively avoiding reading such comments.

MySpace *or yours?: do safe online spaces exist?*

There was clear consensus among participants that there is no such thing as a truly safe online space. Some sites or modes of communication were viewed as safer than others, but there was no sure-fire way to control what might be encountered – or what other people might say/post. Mercy felt that Facebook was the closest thing to this "safe space", since the user can control access to their personal information (i.e., who sees what). She also pointed to the ability to block people and record information. She did, however, acknowledge that Facebook makes controlling your own space challenging, by often having to monitor and change one's privacy settings. Damon seconded this, arguing that the boundaries on Facebook are ever-shifting, making it difficult to feel truly secure in that virtual environment.

An interviewee named Clark Kent argued that Tumblr is the closest thing to a safe online space, given the ability to control what appears on one's dashboard and who you follow. Fox also brought up the ability to use trigger warnings on Tumblr to avoid mentions of especially troubling content. Still, hurtful content sometimes slips through the cracks, and there is no guarantee that this content will not be encountered at some point.

> Even on Tumblr, the gayest site in the world, you will still find occasionally a bit of abuse. Especially toward gays, because there are some, you know,

> Republicans in America who will get online and make a whole bunch of posts about how evil gays are. There's a small conservative niche on Tumblr. And they're very adamantly and staunchly anti-gay.
>
> *(Fox, personal communication, 2013)*

There was agreement among participants that they have never personally experienced a safe space online. Clark Kent felt that, because online environments are shared, it is impossible to rely on other people for safety. Despite this belief, several interviewees thought that the creation of such spaces was possible. Fox argued that a safe space would have to be self-created and limited only to people you know and truly trust. Damon felt that boundaries would need to be clear and fixed, and that all members would have to agree to and abide by pre-set norms. These concerns are warranted but troubling, as participants have accepted the constant risk of harmful behaviours in an online setting. Given the frequent use of the internet by all participants, for both educational and social purposes, such a risk has the potential to seriously disrupt online activities and freedom.

Can't we all just get along?: cyberbullying within and outside of the LGBTQ community

Homophobic and transphobic cyberbullying were perpetrated in many ways, and participants reported experiencing both overt and subtle forms in online contexts. Overt forms of online homophobia and transphobia included threats, slurs, hate speech, insults, and harassment. More subtle forms included heteronormative or heterosexist comments and inadvertent forms of discrimination.

While much of the experienced homophobia and/or transphobia was perpetrated by individuals known or presumed to be heterosexual, one of the more unexpected findings was experiences with cyber-victimization perpetrated by other members of the LGBTQ community. Such harassment was often experienced by trans-participants, with Jeeves and Damon reporting the bulk of such occurrences. In these cases, cyberbullies were members of the LGB and/or trans communities. When discussing transphobic bullying by members of the LGB community, Damon pointed to recent debates surrounding the presence of trans-males on social networking applications traditionally used by gay men (e.g., Grindr, SCRUFF, GROWLr). Damon reported that this resulted in a considerable amount of transphobia on these sites. Damon also maintained that there is a certain lack of understanding of trans issues in the wider LGB community, arguing that a lot of the transphobia coming from them is unintentional: possibly the result of wanting to be supportive but not knowing how.

Jeeves referred to trans-on-trans cyberbullying as a form of "queer community self- policing". In such cases, transphobic comments related to individuals being perceived as "not trans enough to be trans". For example, Jeeves often experienced discrimination and confusion because his partner is genderqueer, and many members of the trans community presume that he, as a trans-male, should be dating a woman. Damon reported similar experiences. Damon also explained that trans people are not always on the same page about issues, definitions, or concerns, which can lead to disagreements. Ultimately, such in-community debate and discord was perceived by participants as being more harmful than helpful.

Perceived reasons for online homophobia and transphobia

When discussing their experiences with homophobic and transphobic cyberbullying, interviewees believe such actions occurred for several reasons. Some participants had fairly good ideas of why they were bullied, or were told outright by perpetrators. Others could only guess based on the content or context of posts and discussions. Perceived reasons included the perpetrators' religious beliefs, mean-spiritedness, impulsivity, ignorance, exhibitionism, lack of boundaries, and anonymity. The most prevalent reasons were disconnect or detachment in online contexts, strongly held opinions, and the wider societal acceptance of transphobia.

Disconnecting on the internet

In their discussions of cyberbullying, all participants pointed to the ease with which individuals can detach themselves and their behaviours when online. This disconnect generally tied into the anonymity afforded by the internet, as well as the fact that offline consequences are either not apparent or far removed. Several interviewees pointed to the lack of real-world cues missing in online discussions, such as body language, tone of voice, and facial cues. It is often difficult to gauge responses at all – let alone severity of response. Clark Kent pointed out that this is especially problematic if you do not have an offline relationship with the person.

> I mean, we call them by their username, and it's that identity on the internet that we're getting pissed off at. Not the actual person behind the screen. Unless we know that person. Then we can link it to another identity.
>
> *(Clark Kent, personal communication, 2013)*

The non-linear nature of the internet can also be problematic, as people are often receiving communications at later times, which may affect how far removed the perpetrator is from the situation and possible repercussions.

Several participants argued that the internet brings out the worst in people. They argued that specific aspects of the internet encourage people to say things they likely would not say offline. Gia had her own theory about this phenomenon, arguing that anonymity plus an audience encourages abusive behaviour that users would never be courageous (or foolish) enough to engage in offline. She also discusses the troubling tendency of people distinguishing their online activities from in-person ones by using the term IRL (in real life), delineating their offline experiences. She reached an epiphany while watching a documentary on the subject.

> I watched a documentary once on the *Pirate Bay* . . . called *The Pirate Bay AFK*, and I didn't know what that meant, but during the documentary, someone says IRL. And they're like, "well, actually, we don't say IRL (in real life) we say away from keyboard [AFK], because the internet is real life". It is real life! This is your actual life, and what you do on it is going to impact others and impact you. You have to behave accordingly. But yeah, saying IRL I feel sort of backs up these people who just say whatever they want on the internet.
>
> *(Gia, personal communication, 2013)*

This IRL versus online distinction may allow cyberbullies to separate themselves from their online actions, as well as minimize the perception of the harm experienced by victims.

Strongly held opinions: everyone has one and they're not afraid to share them online

Several participants were of the mindset that online homophobia and transphobia often stemmed from the personal opinions and deeply held beliefs of perpetrators. Some interviewees felt that people were entitled to their own opinions, providing they did not force them on others. Others felt that, while individuals were entitled to their own beliefs, they could control their personal associations and exposures to them. Jeeves reported ending online friendships over strong clashes in beliefs, particularly if they related to his trans status.

While several participants were pro-education and wanted to promote an understanding of LGBTQ issues, they realized that some opinions are difficult, if not impossible, to change. Gia related this to her own beliefs, understanding that her own strongly held convictions were unlikely to be easily changed. She did, however, acknowledge that it was always worth trying. While some people may be unwilling to listen to or accept other viewpoints, others may be more receptive. Gia believed it was worth attempting to clarify opinions or educate individuals, even if they only took a small part away from her larger argument.

What's the big deal?: wider societal acceptance of transphobia

Several participants thought that transphobia often occurs online due to a wider societal acceptance of transphobic behaviour. While overt homophobia has become much less acceptable, transphobia has not followed the same trend. Damon discussed how popular culture's emphasis on transphobia as a joke or humorous concept might lead the wider society to view such actions as acceptable.

Aynsley: Does transphobia tend to be anonymous in your experiences online?

Damon: No. Transphobia is very accepted as a form of, humour right now. . . . So many mainstream movies, like, at least one a year will come out with something really explicitly transphobic. And there won't be any narrative to act as though that was an absurd thing to see.

Aynsley: Not the same backlash you'd see for something very homophobic or racist.

Damon: Yeah, exactly. That wouldn't survive in this political climate right now. But we're in a time and a climate that is supportive of that. So people don't feel, like, it's not the sort of thing, if people harbour those feelings and thoughts, that they feel the need to hide them. It's not shameful right now.

(Damon, personal communication, 2013)

Transphobic slurs were also an all-too-common occurrence, directed at participants and others in online and offline settings. Both Jeeves and Damon encountered the slur "tranny" very often, generally being used by people outside of the trans community. Jeeves noted that he personally considers the term to be an acceptable one for trans-identified individuals to use, but that it becomes problematic and offensive when used by those outside of the community. Damon argued that is a difficult concept, as most people do not even define such terms as slurs. He linked the heavy use of such slurs to ignorance, stating that many people do not realize the offensiveness of transphobic comments. Jeeves agreed that sometimes the use of such terms is linked to not knowing any better, so he often assumes innocent intent and aims to educate people who use these terms incorrectly.

Discussion and conclusions

It is clear from the findings of this study that not only does cyberbullying extend beyond high school, but cyberbullying experienced by participants within the LGBTQ community was anything but rare. Interviewees encountered cyberbullying throughout their lives and continued to experience it as adult post-secondary students. This finding is consistent with many post-secondary studies indicating that cyberbullying does not simply stop at high school graduation (Faucher, Jackson, & Cassidy, 2014; Zalaquett & Chatters, 2014). Study participants recounted online experiences of both the positive and negative variety, and generally coped with online harassment in a mature fashion. Interviewees often gave perpetrators the benefit of the doubt, assuming positive or neutral, rather than negative intent. While these findings are promising and point to high levels of resiliency (as was similarly noted by Woodford et al., 2012), other findings are more troubling.

The perception of a strong societal acceptance of transphobic views is saddening, as is the common experience of cyberbullying within the LGBTQ community. Similar findings emerged in Dispenza, Watson, Chung, and Brack's (2012) study of in-person career-related discrimination experienced by female-to-male trans adults. In their study, transphobic discrimination was perpetrated by both LGB and trans individuals. Findings of transphobic actions perpetrated by the LGB community are not entirely surprising, as heterosexist beliefs are also sometimes held by LGB individuals (Weiss, 2003). As pointed out by Jackson, Faucher, and Cassidy (this volume), any policies developed in this area should take into account the vulnerability to potential homophobic and transphobic discrimination.

As this present study was conducted in 2013, however, it is possible that societal views and norms may have shifted since the research period (either positively or negatively), both within and outside of the LGBTQ community. Furthermore, students are now using different sites and applications, rendering some of the earlier sites nearly obsolete. This provides additional venues and options for cybervictimization that may have been neglected, as well as options for potentially safer online communities.

Ultimately, this study offers an important jumping-off point. This information is useful for raising awareness of problems that exist, persist, and may need more (or less) focus. Awareness is the first step in problem solving, and these data are certainly a step in the right direction in improving the internet experiences of LGBTQ individuals, and in creating truly safe online spaces.

Action points

- As recommended by Faucher, Jackson, and Cassidy (2015), administrators should consider both gender and sexuality when drafting policies and procedures related to online activities. Past research indicates that rates of cybervictimization may be higher among LGBTQ students (Finn, 2004; Wensley & Campbell, 2012) and consequences may be more severe (Cooper & Blumenfeld, 2012), so it is important to examine the particular needs of and risk factors associated with LGBTQ students online.
- Administrators should also consider the needs of LGBTQ students and community members when creating general university policies and procedures. If a university espouses a zero-tolerance response to homophobia and transphobia, it can be helpful in dealing with such behaviours in the online context as well (particularly with more subtle or unintentional forms of discrimination). Examples may include the creation of gender-neutral washrooms, or LGBTQ-supportive spaces and organizations on campus.

- To ensure that LGBTQ students feel they are a valued part of the community, universities and colleges should ensure that they are providing adequate orientation and identity options on official documents and institutional surveys (see Rivers, 2016). They should move away from dichotomous gender options (or the additional option that literally "others" those who do not identify as male or female). It is difficult to feel one's voice is heard when your identity is not properly acknowledged by your institution.
- When defining terms such as "cyberbullying" or "cyber-harassment", it is worthwhile to consider the role of harm and how harm may be experienced. While many commonly employed definitions consider only those behaviours where harm was deliberate (Hinduja & Patchin, 2009; Langos, 2012), it may be more useful to direct attention to the harm that is experienced by the victim, rather than the intent of the perpetrator (Walker, Sockman, & Koehn, 2011). It is apparent from the experiences of this study's participants that, while interviewees experienced harm from online actions and defined said behaviour as cyberbullying, they still often presumed neutral or even positive intent on behalf of their cyberbullies. We cannot discount such experiences when the impact is equally severe. Unintentional cruelty can lead to the same consequences as intentional cruelty.

Notes

1 Homophobia is often referred to as a "fear or hatred of homosexuality and gays and lesbians in general" (Pickett, 2009, p. 93). It is also often used to explain orientation-based discrimination experienced by bisexual and questioning individuals (Blackburn, 2012; Conoley, 2008; Weiss, 2003).

2 While homosexuality and bisexuality relate to sexual orientation, transgender relates to gender roles and identities (Nagoshi et al., 2008). Transgender is likely often subsumed under the wider LGB category because it has only been distinguished from homosexuality within the past century (Pickett, 2009; Weiss, 2003). Transphobia is described as "fear and/or emotional disgust towards individuals who do not conform to society's gender expectations" (Watjen & Mitchell, 2013, p. 135).

3 The Gay, Lesbian & Straight Education Network, the Center for Innovative Public Health Research, and the Crimes Against Children Research Center, respectively.

4 I did not explicitly define cyberbullying for potential participants, as I was interested in how they personally perceived and defined the issue.

References

Bauman, S., & Baldasare, A. (2015). Cyber aggression among college students: Demographic differences, predictors of distress, and the role of the university. *Journal of College Student Development, 56*(4), 317–330.

Beemyn, G. (2012). The experiences and needs of transgender community college students. *Community College Journal of Research & Practice, 36*(7), 504–510.

Blackburn, M.V. (2012). *Interrupting hate: Homophobia in schools and what literacy can do* about it. New York, NY: Teachers College Press.
Conoley, J. C. (2008). Sticks and stones can break my bones and words can really hurt me. *School Psychology Review, 37*(2), 217–220.
Cooper, R. M., & Blumenfeld, W. J. (2012). Responses to cyberbullying: A descriptive analysis of the frequency of and impact on LGBT and allied youth. *Journal of LGBT Youth, 9*(2), 153–177.
Corbin, J., & Strauss, A. (2008). *Basics of qualitative research techniques and procedures for developing grounded theory* (3rd ed.). Thousand Oaks, CA: Sage Publications.
Cotten-Huston, A. L., & Waite, B. M. (1999). Anti-homosexual attitudes in college students. *Journal of Homosexuality, 38*(3), 117–133.
Dantzker, M. L., & Hunter, R. D. (2012). *Research methods for criminology and criminal justice* (3rd ed.). Mississauga, ON: Jones & Bartlett Learning Canada.
Dispenza, F., Watson, L. B., Chung, W. B., & Brack, G. (2012). Experience of career-related discrimination for female-to-male transgender persons: A qualitative study. *The Career Development Quarterly, 60*, 65–81.
Ellis, S. J. (2009). Diversity and inclusivity at university: A survey of the experiences of lesbian, gay, bisexual and trans (LGBT) students in the UK. *Higher Education, 57*(6), 723–739.
Faucher, C., Jackson, M., & Cassidy, W. (2014). Cyberbullying among university students: Gendered experiences, impacts, and perspectives. *Education Research International, 2014*, 1–10.
Faucher, C., Jackson, M., & Cassidy, W. (2015). When online exchanges byte: An examination of the policy environment governing cyberbullying at the university level. *Canadian Journal of Higher Education, 45*(1), 102–121.
Finn, J. (2004). A survey of online harassment at a university campus. *Journal of Interpersonal Violence, 19*(4), 468–483.
GLSEN, CiPHR, & CCRC. (2013). *Out online: The experiences of lesbian, gay, bisexual, and transgender youth on the Internet*. New York, NY: GLSEN.
Hinduja, S., & Patchin, J. W. (2009). *Bullying beyond the schoolyard: Preventing and responding to cyberbullying*. Thousand Oaks, CA: Corwin Press.
Jackson, M., Faucher, C., & Cassidy, W. (this volume). What's policy got to do with it? The focus on cyberbullying policy at the university level. In W. Cassidy, C. Faucher, & M. Jackson (Eds.), *Cyberbullying at university in international contexts* (pp. 198–211). Oxford, UK: Routledge.
Janoff, D.V. (2005). *Pink blood: Homophobic violence in Canada*. Toronto, ON: University of Toronto Press.
Jayakumar, U. M. (2009). The invisible rainbow of diversity: Factors influencing sexual prejudice among college students. *Journal of Homosexuality, 56*, 675–700.
Langos, C. (2012). Cyberbullying: The challenge to define. *Cyberpsychology, Behavior, and Social Networking, 15*(6), 285–289.
Legard, R., Keegan, J., & Ward, K. (2003). In-depth interviews. In J. Ritchie & J. Lewis (Eds.), *Qualitative research practice: A guide for social scientists and researchers* (pp. 138–169). Thousand Oaks, CA: Sage Publications.
Lindsay, M., & Krysik, J. (2012). Online harassment among college students. *Information, Communication & Society, 15*(5), 703–719.
Nagoshi, J. L., Adams, K. A., Terrell, H. K., Hill, E. D., Brzuzy, S., & Nagoshi, C. T. (2008). Gender differences in correlates of homophobia and transphobia. *Sex Roles, 59*, 521–531.

Palys, T., & Atchison, C. (2014). *Research decisions: Quantitative, qualitative, and mixed methods approaches* (5th ed.). Toronto, ON: Nelson Education.

Pickett, B. L. (2009). *The A to Z of homosexuality*. Plymouth, UK: Scarecrow Press.

Rivers, I. (2016). Homophobic and transphobic bullying in universities. In H. Cowie & C. Myers (Eds.), *Bullying among university students: Cross-national perspectives* (pp. 48–60). New York, NY: Routledge.

Scott, G., & Garner, R. (2013). *Doing qualitative research: Designs, methods, and techniques* (1st ed.). Upper Saddle River, NJ: Pearson Education.

Strauss, A. (1987). *Qualitative analysis for social scientists*. New York, NY: Cambridge University Press.

Varjas, K., Meyers, J., Kiperman, S., & Howard, A. (2013). Technology hurts? Lesbian, gay, and bisexual youth perspectives of technology and cyberbullying. *Journal of School Violence, 12*(1), 27–44.

Walker, C. M., Sockman, B. J., & Koehn, S. (2011). An exploratory study of cyberbullying with undergraduate university students. *TechTrends, 55*(2), 31–38.

Watjen, J., & Mitchell, R. W. (2013). College men's concerns about sharing dormitory space with a male-to-female transsexual. *Sexuality & Culture, 17*, 132–166.

Weiss, J. T. (2003). GL vs. BT: The archaeology of biphobia and transphobia within the U.S. gay and lesbian community. In J. Alexander & K. Yescavage (Eds.), *Bisexuality and transgenderism: InterSEXions of the others* (pp. 25–56). Binghamton, NY: Harrington Park Press.

Wensley, K., & Campbell, M. (2012). Heterosexual and nonheterosexual young university students' involvement in traditional and cyber forms of bullying. *Cyberpsychology, Behavior, & Social Networking, 15*(2), 649–654.

Woodford, M. R., Howell, M. L., Silverchanz, P., & Yu, L. (2012). "That's so gay!": Examining the covariates of hearing this expression among gay, lesbian, and bisexual college students. *Journal of American College Health, 60*(6), 429–434.

Zalaquett, C. P., & Chatters, S. J. (2014). Cyberbullying in college: Frequency, characteristics, and practical implications. *SAGE Open, 4*(1), 1–8.

5

POWER IN THE TOWER

The gendered nature of cyberbullying among students and faculty at Canadian universities

Chantal Faucher, Wanda Cassidy, and Margaret Jackson

It is not surprising that cyberbullying has appeared as an issue in the context of post-secondary education for several reasons. First, information and communication technologies (ICT) increasingly permeate our daily lives; their presence is both pervasive and permanent. Second, cyberbullying exists in elementary and secondary schools, as well as in the workplace; therefore, it could easily be predicted to occur in the post-secondary sector as well. Third, the role of power in bullying behaviour has long been recognized, and the hierarchical and competitive nature of universities lends itself to the emergence of problems related to the exercise of power. Furthermore, the slowly emerging literature on cyberbullying in the post-secondary realm provides indications that the problem is gendered. This chapter offers a gendered analysis of experiences with cyberbullying reported by university students and faculty based on the power dynamics that characterize the post-secondary context. The gender differences that emerge help to carve out a clearer understanding about cyberbullying behaviour at the university level. The findings advance a gendered interpretation of vulnerability to cyberbullying, which is closely tied to power imbalances among members of the university community. Such findings have the potential to inform the development of more appropriate policies and intervention programs/solutions to address the gendered nature of this behaviour.

Background

Cyberbullying in higher education can be situated on a continuum between cyberbullying in kindergarten to grade 12 (K–12) education and cyberbullying in the workplace (Adams & Lawrence, 2011; Faucher, Cassidy, & Jackson, 2015; Langos & Giancaspro, this volume; McKay, Arnold, Fratzl, & Thomas, 2008;

Zalaquett & Chatters, 2014). Time spent online is a significant variable as far as experiences with cyberbullying are concerned (Cassidy, Jackson, & Faucher, 2016; Donner, 2016; Turan, Polat, Karapirli, Uysal, & Turan, 2011; Wright, 2016; Yubero, Navarro, Elche, Larrañaga, & Ovejero, 2017; Zhang, Land, & Dick, 2010). Those who spend more time online are more likely to experience cyberbullying. As time spent online, for both personal and academic purposes, becomes more strongly anchored in the daily life of university students and faculty members, cyberbullying experiences are expected to follow.

In findings reported elsewhere, we noted that 24% of 1,925 students surveyed at four Canadian universities had experienced cyberbullying in the past 12 months (Faucher, Jackson, & Cassidy, 2014) and 25% of 331 faculty members surveyed had reported the same (Cassidy et al., 2016). Other studies on cyberbullying in the post-secondary context in different countries have similarly reported the existence of such experiences among students to varying degrees (e.g., Beran, Rinaldi, Bickham, & Rich, 2012; Blaya, this volume; Dilmaç, 2009; Francisco, Simão, Ferreira, & Martins, 2015; Langos & Giancaspro, this volume; Molluzzo & Lawler, 2012; Schenk & Fremouw, 2012; Turan et al., 2011; Walker, Sockman, & Koehn, 2011; Wensley & Campbell, 2012) as well as among faculty members (e.g., Blizard, 2016; McKay et al., 2008; Minor, Smith, & Brashen, 2013; Vance, 2010).

Although some youth (Fiske, 2016) and university students (Crosslin & Golman, 2014) may find the term outdated or childish, cyberbullying is perceived by a majority of post-secondary students and faculty as a problem that requires greater attention (Cassidy et al., 2016; Crosslin & Golman, 2014; Langos & Giancaspro, this volume). The perception of cyberbullying as childish behaviour, or at least behaviour which one is expected to handle independently, likely inhibits students' (and faculty members') willingness to report incidents of cyberbullying (Francisco et al., 2015) and relates to their preference for autonomous coping strategies (Orel, Campbell, Wozencraft, Leong, & Kimpton, 2017; Wozencroft, Campbell, Orel, Kimpton, & Leong, 2015).

What has become apparent in the gradually mounting body of work on cyberbullying in post-secondary is that the role of gender warrants closer consideration. Multiple studies employing convenience sampling methods have had a large over-representation of female participants (see Table 5.1). Although the disproportional representation of female participants in these studies is not significant in and of itself (and in some studies, the gender disparity is accounted for by representation in the student body), it does serve to alert us to a gender disparity in attention to the issue of cyberbullying in universities. It also invites us to consider the ways in which the experiences of cyberbullying may differ by gender.

This emerging literature on cyberbullying in post-secondary institutions has begun to reveal certain key gender differences, but more information is needed. Francisco et al. (2015) found that female students in Portugal were more prone to be aggressors and victims in cyberbullying. Such findings are paralleled in the work of Zalaquett and Chatters (2014), Snell and Englander (2010), and Turan

TABLE 5.1 Disparities in Gender Participation Among Studies of Cyberbullying in Post-Secondary Institutions

Authors (year)	*Country*	*Participants*	*n*	*% female*
Adams and Lawrence (2011)	USA	Students	269	65.4
Akbulut and Eristi (2011)	Turkey	Students	254	68.1
Beran, Rinaldi, Bickham, and Rich (2012)	Canada & USA	Students	1,368	49.4
Blaya (this volume)	France	Students	Surveys: 1,125 Interviews: 20	70 60
Blizard (2016)	Canada	Faculty	36	75
Cassidy, Jackson, and Faucher (2016)	Canada	Faculty	331	68
Condeza, Gallardo, and Reyes (this volume)	Chile	Students	961	66.6
Crosslin and Golman (2014)[1]	USA	Students	54	85
Dilmaç (2009)	Turkey	Students	666	65.3
Donner (2016)	USA	Students	522	66.1
Faucher et al. (2014)	Canada	Students	1,925	74
Finn (2004)	USA	Students	339	64.9
Francisco et al. (2015)	Portugal	Students	519	77.6
Langos and Giancaspro (this volume)	Australia	Students	213	43.7
Minor et al. (2013)	USA	Faculty	68	41.2
Molluzzo and Lawler (2012)	USA	Students	121	58
Orel et al. (2017); Wozencroft et al. (2015)	Australia	Students	282	72.3
Schenk and Fremouw (2012)	USA	Students	799	71.6
Snell and Englander (2010)	USA	Students	213	73
Turan et al. (2011)	Turkey	Students	579	56.8
Vance (2010)	USA	Students & faculty	225 students 56 faculty	63
Walker et al. (2011)	USA	Students	120	58.3
Wensley and Campbell (2012)	Australia	Students	528	80.7
Wright (2016)	USA	Students	1,483	60
Yubero et al. (2017)	Spain	Students	243	67.9

[1] Note: all studies cited used survey methodology, except Crosslin and Golman (2014), which used focus groups.

et al. (2011). Francisco et al. (2015) also reported that male cyberbullies tended to act alone, whereas female cyberbullies tended to act in groups.

On the other hand, studies by Akbulut and Eristi (2011) in Turkey, Blaya (this volume) in France, and Englander (2008) in the U.S. found cyberbullying to be more common among male than female college students. Donner (2016) examined the gender gap in college students' involvement in three forms of online crime, including cyber-harassment, and found male involvement to be persistently higher than that of female students. Dilmaç (2009) also found male students more likely to report they had engaged in cyberbullying others, whereas female students were more likely to report being victims of cyberbullying. Still others have found no gender differences in prevalence of cyberbullying (Schenk & Fremouw, 2012; Vance, 2010; Walker et al., 2011; Yubero et al., 2017).

One of the earliest studies in this field found LGBT students were twice as likely to experience online harassment as heterosexual students (Finn, 2004). Wensley and Campbell (2012) found higher cyberbullying perpetration rates among non-heterosexual female students, and higher victimization rates among non-heterosexual male students. Molluzzo and Lawler (2012) questioned students regarding their awareness of cyberbullying against particular groups at their institution and the main target groups identified were: gay, lesbian, and female.

Preferred coping strategies may also vary by gender – female students were more likely than males to use help-seeking coping strategies, whereas male students were more likely to retaliate against the cyberbullying (Orel et al., 2017). Schenk and Fremouw (2012) found that the most frequent types of coping strategies were similar for male and female students (i.e., telling someone, avoiding friends or peers, getting revenge), but some differences emerged with female students also frequently responding that they would avoid the internet or their cell phone, and male students reporting the use of substances such as alcohol or drugs to cope.

Theoretical framework

A number of theoretical frameworks have attempted to account for gender differences with respect to cyberbullying. Work on gender and cyberbullying in elementary and secondary schools has adopted the frames of relational aggression for girls (Jackson, Cassidy, & Brown, 2009) and cognitive and affective deficits for boys (Topcu & Erdur-Baker, 2012). Relational aggression is used to exert a negative impact on friendships, group belonging, or standing by spreading rumours, gossip, and slander (Crick et al., 1999). Cognitive and affective deficits may be more likely to contribute to boys' involvement in cyberbullying. Such deficits may limit empathy as well as the ability to identify emotions and paralinguistic cues. Both of these frames have some applicability to what is reportedly occurring in universities as well (Faucher et al., 2014), but they are certainly lacking in some respects.

Donner (2016) has used social learning theory to account for the gender gap in cyber-harassment and other cyber crimes among college students. He examines socialization variables, such as self-control and immersion into cyber-environments, in order to explain the gap. However, such variables cannot fully account for the gender differences in male and female students' level of involvement in cyber crimes.

To orient our analysis of the gender differences, we borrow from the field of intimate partner violence in situating our gendered analysis of cyberbullying against the backdrop of the Duluth model (Pence & Paymar, 1993). This model is a cognitive-behavioural approach used in counselling for males found guilty of domestic violence. The model is premised on the Power and Control Wheel, which specifies a range of ways in which power and control may manifest in an abusive relationship. Of particular interest in our analysis of cyberbullying relationships are the elements relating to the use of intimidation, coercion, threats, harmful language, emotional abuse, social standing, male privilege, exclusion, harassment, and using technology to send unwanted messages.

Much as in the field of intimate partner violence, the cyberbullying of women and girls should not be divorced from the gendered hierarchies of power that exist both online and offline and which contribute to the violence in the lives of women and girls in numerous forms (Crooks, 2016; Halder & Jaishankar, 2009; Navarro & Jasinski, 2013; Shariff & Gouin, 2005). While the internet may be a source of empowerment for women and girls (Crooks, 2016), it can also contribute to maintaining their disadvantaged position in society (Navarro & Jasinski, 2013). The internet has furthered the ways in which gender exploitation may occur, including pornography, sex trafficking, gender and sexual harassment, and cyber-stalking (Halder & Jaishankar, 2009; Navarro & Jasinski, 2013; Shariff & Gouin, 2005).

Power dynamics are integral to the hierarchical structure of post-secondary institutions. Not only is power manifested through rank and status, but gender, gender identity, sexuality, age, race, and ethnicity also are impactful features. Furthermore, the manifestation of contrapower harassment (where the person with ostensibly less power in the relationship harasses the individual with more power) in student-faculty relations has been noted (DeSouza, 2010). De Souza (2010) suggests that students, who may appear to be less powerful than faculty members, may use the anonymity of the internet to engage in uncivil behaviour in retaliation for actual or perceived slights.

A number of possible explanations have been offered for the use of contrapower harassment by post-secondary students in particular. The stress and pressure experienced by students may cause a range of undesirable behaviours including incivility, harassment, and bullying (Knepp, 2012). Furthermore, in a context where faculty members hold control over students' grades in particular, students may experience some degree of frustration and powerlessness (Blizard, 2016). Some students adopt consumerist views of education and feel some degree of entitlement with respect to their grades, such that they may react negatively when faculty members do not meet their expectations (Blizard, 2016; DeSouza, 2010; Knepp, 2012; McKay et al., 2008). These situations may be further compounded by universities overlooking student incivility in order to retain students (Knepp, 2012) and collective agreements that account for top-down harassment, but not for harassment of faculty by students (McKay et al., 2008). "The system is also weighted heavily in favour of the student, through the process of linking tenure and promotion to student evaluations" (McKay et al., 2008, p. 89).

Furthermore, a range of studies relating to contrapower harassment has clearly pointed to the fact that those faculty members who are most likely to be treated in this way by students are those who are perceived to have the least power in the university based mostly on gender, age, sexuality, gender identity, race/ethnicity, and rank (DeSouza, 2010; Knepp, 2012; Lampman, 2012; Sallee & Diaz, 2012). Lampman (2012) points out that women are at greatest risk of being bullied or disrespected by students in universities because they are underrepresented in the highest ranks and in leadership roles within universities, less likely to work full-time, and less likely to have tenured positions. Women's authority tends to be resisted by subordinates (as is the case for others with less power, such as minorities and those in low-ranking positions). Thus, when women do not accommodate student requests for extensions, make-up exams, etc., they may be perceived as breaking the prescriptive gender stereotype according to which women are sensitive, nurturing, caring, etc. (Lampman, 2012). Lampman's study of 524 professors from 100 colleges and universities in the U.S. also found that women faculty were more likely than male faculty to report experiences of severe contrapower harassment.

Contrapower harassment, however, is not the only manifestation of bullying behaviour found in universities. Bullying between colleagues or peers has also been reported. Lester's (2009) study of workplace harassment among community college faculty found the use of power to be significant. "Unlike other forms of bullying that use direct threats and obvious harassment, using formal power occurs by using institutionally or positionally relevant powers to silence and/or control faculty colleagues" (p. 452). Racism and sexism were prevalent throughout the forms of bullying noted in the study.

In Hollis's (2012) survey of 401 individuals employed at one of 175 higher education institutions in the U.S., higher rates of experience with workplace bullying were found among respondents who were African Americans, women, and members of the LGBT community. Witnesses of academic workplace bullying noted that those with less power within the higher education administration were more likely to be targeted. Taylor (2012) found that tenure status impacts faculty members' experiences with bullying in the academic workplace, both as targets and as bullies. Non-tenure-track faculty reported the highest levels of exposure and felt powerless to address the situation. Tenured faculty were more likely to be targeted if they were perceived as 'untouchable' (i.e., the intent of the bullying was to create conditions that would lead to their resignation, or it was due to envy). Tenure-track faculty members reported the lowest level of exposure. They are not as powerless as non-tenure track, but easier to terminate than tenured faculty.

Yamada, Cappadocia, and Pepler's (2014) Canadian study of psychology graduate students and their supervisors provides additional evidence on the use of power in universities. The academic context is particularly vulnerable to workplace bullying "due to the competitive and individualistic nature of obtaining promotions and progress through faculties and graduate programs" (p. 59). Graduate students are particularly vulnerable due to the power imbalance with their supervisors, who may control their grades, recommendations, references, financial support, and career opportunities.

In order to better understand bullying between peers, Walker et al. (2011) applied social dominance theory, which suggests that power differentials may exist based on age, gender, and other socially valued attributes and that 'legitimizing myths' may operate to allow for any discrimination that exists along these lines. In their comparison of the proportion of student respondents who reported experiencing at least one of 13 specific scenarios (which constituted cyberbullying according to the operational definition used by the authors) with the proportion of respondents who reported that they had been cyberbullied, a significant discrepancy arose (over 30% said yes to the former, 11% to the latter). The authors suggest that students may consider some of these behaviours to be accepted parts of online social life, which could suggest that legitimizing myths are operating.

In the following section, we briefly outline the methods employed in our examination of cyberbullying among post-secondary students and faculty, followed by a summary of the findings, and their analysis in relation to the lens of power.

Methods

In order to examine the nature, extent, impacts, and solutions to cyberbullying in the post-secondary context, the authors developed two online surveys disseminated at four Canadian universities. The universities are situated in different parts of the country and vary in size and profile. The surveys each contained over 100 items asking respondents about basic demographic information, background on ICT usage patterns, experiences with cyberbullying in the past 12 months, and solutions and opinions about the problem. Both closed and open-ended questions were included. The research ethics office of the researchers' university as well as of the participating universities reviewed and approved the study. The data were collected over short periods between late 2012 and early 2014 at the different universities.

Cyberbullying was defined in the surveys as using language that can defame, threaten, harass, bully, exclude, discriminate, demean, humiliate, stalk, disclose personal information, or contain offensive, vulgar, or derogatory comments. The intent to harm was emphasized. Respondents were also provided with a list of examples such as receiving nasty, mean, rude, vulgar, hurtful, or harassing email or text messages; having terrible, derogatory, sexist, racist, or homophobic things written about you online; someone posting an embarrassing photo or video of you online; someone pretending to be you online; and being deliberately excluded from an online group or chat.

Descriptive statistics were examined for the closed-ended questions and thematic content analysis was conducted on the open-ended questions.

Findings

More detailed findings from these surveys have been reported separately elsewhere (Cassidy et al., 2016; Faucher et al., 2014). We focus here on the analysis of similarities and differences between the results of the two surveys as they relate to gender, which has emerged as a key consideration.

As noted previously, participation in both of these surveys was consistent with what appears to be a trend in the literature to date on cyberbullying in the post-secondary sector in that voluntary female participation far outnumbered male participation. On the student survey, the female-to-male ratio was 3:1, and for the faculty survey it was 2:1. A very small number of respondents provided an alternate gender identity, and it was not possible to include these respondents in the gender analysis. What is clear in terms of the female-to-male ratios is that they are not consistent with the reported gender ratios for Canadian university students or faculty (Council of Canadian Academies, 2012; websites of participating universities).

The student sample consisted of 1,925 students, 74% of whom were women and 51% of whom were Caucasian. The students were primarily undergraduates and were fairly evenly drawn from first, second, third, and fourth years. The faculty sample was composed of 331 faculty members, 68% women, 84% Caucasian and included professors, teaching assistants, instructors, lecturers, advisors, and other teaching-related university personnel. There was a fairly even distribution between those with less than five years of experience and those with more than five years and/or permanent or tenured positions.

Respondents to both surveys reported similar rates of cyberbullying victimization overall (24.1% of students and 25% of faculty had been cyberbullied in the last 12 months). However, although rates for male and female students were fairly similar (25.4% and 23.8%, respectively), female faculty members (27%) were much more likely than male faculty members (18%) to have been cyberbullied. The rates for cyberbullying of faculty members by students were more similar for men and women (13% and 16%, respectively), but there was a wider gap between those who reported being cyberbullied by a faculty colleague (8% of male respondents and 14% of female respondents). For students, male respondents were more likely than female students to have been cyberbullied by someone they did not know, whereas female students were more likely to report having been cyberbullied by a friend or acquaintance at the university. For faculty, the vast majority of cyberbullying victims knew the perpetrators (students and/or faculty).

Students experienced cyberbullying in a wide range of formats: social networks, email, text messages, non-course-related blogs, forums, or chat rooms. Social networks and text messages were more frequently cited by female respondents, whereas the non-course-related blogs, forums, or chat rooms were more often mentioned by male respondents. Male respondents were overrepresented among those who reported experiencing extensive cyberbullying via email, email photo, text message, course-related sites, other blogs, forums, or chat rooms, impersonation, and "other" which predominantly consisted of cyberbullying in online gaming. On the other hand, faculty overwhelmingly experienced cyberbullying over email, with professor-rating sites and course-related sites, blogs, forums, and chat rooms a distant second and third.

When asked for the reasons for which they had been cyberbullied, students who knew the reasons generally provided answers such as interpersonal problems, their physical appearance, or other reasons such as differences of opinions/beliefs, it was part of an online game, or it was a joke. Males also cited their ethnicity as a reason for which they were cyberbullied, while female students mentioned their gender as a primary reason for the cyberbullying they experienced. Female faculty respondents also cited their gender as a primary reason for which they became targets of cyberbullying. Other reasons cited by faculty tended to be related to their work. When they were targeted by students, they felt it was often due to teaching-related reasons (such as students being unhappy with a grade they received or some aspect of the course they were taking), or their position or role at the university. When they were targeted by colleagues, faculty members primarily cited work-related reasons, such as a professional difference of opinion, competition between colleagues, professional jealousy, their professional status, or attempts to establish power and control. Their position or role at the university was also cited, as was age in some cases.

Approximately 5% of respondents to the student survey admitted to having cyberbullied someone at the university in the past 12 months. When asked about their intent, male and female respondents identified insulting as a primary intent, as well as defaming when the cyberbullying targeted faculty members. Furthermore, some male respondents also identified intents such as humiliating, harassing, and threatening. Faculty respondents were not asked about whether they had engaged in cyberbullying, but they were asked about the perceived intent of the cyberbullying that was directed at them. They reported similar intents to those cited by students: insulting, demanding, demeaning, belittling, being derogatory, spreading rumours, harassing, and being rude or vulgar.

In both surveys, female victims were much more likely than male victims to talk to someone about what they were experiencing, though few students or faculty reported the cyberbullying to someone at the university. They tended to prefer telling close friends, family, or partners. Faculty members also told colleagues, but they did not tell superiors or others who might help them in an official capacity.

Also in both surveys, female respondents reported a far wider range and extent of impacts stemming from their cyberbullying experiences. In all categories of effects about which they were surveyed, female students and faculty members were more likely than their male counterparts to acknowledge the effects, including mental and physical health issues, impacts on ability to work/study, impacts on relationships inside and outside the university, desire to remain at the university, feeling their emotional security and/or physical safety were threatened, and thoughts of suicide and self-harm.

Discussion

In line with most studies to date on the cyberbullying of post-secondary students and/or faculty, the vast majority of those who voluntarily participated in this study were women. We also note some differences between the experiences with cyberbullying for male and female study participants, suggesting that an analysis that takes gender into account is relevant.

Among students, the prevalence of cyberbullying victimization appears to be generally gender neutral, and no clear gender pattern has emerged in the existing literature, which contains contradictory findings as to whether female students are more or less likely to be victims and/or perpetrators (Akbulut & Eristi, 2011; Blaya, this volume; Dilmaç, 2009; Donner, 2016; Francisco et al., 2015; Schenk & Fremouw, 2012; Snell & Englander, 2010; Turan et al., 2011; Vance, 2010; Walker et al., 2011; Yubero et al., 2017; Zalaquett & Chatters, 2014). The different types of cyberbullying behaviours examined and different cyber-environments frequented by male and female students may account for some of the variations observed. For instance, in our study, students had experienced cyberbullying in a wide range of online settings, and there were significant variations between the online spaces where female and male respondents had experienced cyberbullying.

For faculty, however, the gender pattern noted in this study more clearly points to a greater likelihood for female faculty members to be targeted. Such a finding is in line with existing studies on cyberbullying and other forms of incivility and harassment in universities (Blizard, 2016; DeSouza, 2010; Hollis, 2012; Knepp, 2012; Lampman, 2012; Sallee & Diaz, 2012). The clearer pattern may also be partially accounted for by the vast consensus that email was the primary means through which the cyberbullying targeting faculty members was carried out, with professor-rating sites and course-related sites also being identified. These forms of technology may not have as much gender variability in usage as those noted in relation to the cyberbullying targeting students.

Although victimization is spread between men and women, the reasons for the targeting of women also point to other disadvantaged groups who may experience similar vulnerabilities, such as individuals from the LGBTQ communities or racial and ethnic minorities.

The examination of intents (actual or perceived) of the cyberbullying against both students and faculty members highlights a number of elements from the Power and Control Wheel. The elements of using technology to send unwanted messages, as well as threats and harassment, were directly cited by the respondents. Furthermore, intents such as belittling, demeaning, insulting, and humiliating the target all refer to the element of emotional abuse. Attacks on the targets' social standing were highlighted through intents such as defaming and spreading rumours. Lastly, messages that were perceived by the targets as demanding bring to mind the element of coercion.

Conclusion and action points

Universities reproduce power hierarchies in society. Although the numbers of women in post-secondary education are growing, even to the point of surpassing the number of men in some areas, these numbers do not appear to be sufficient to de-stabilize the long-standing hierarchical structures grounded in gender, race, and class discrimination and privilege that have shaped these institutions.

Cyberbullying is inscribed within this context and may merely be the newest manifestation of power relations and gender inequality in the post-secondary context. As with the field of intimate partner violence from which the Power and Control model is borrowed, men and women both experience such violence. However, women are more likely to be victims of family violence in Canada, as well as around the world, and they experience more frequent and more prolonged effects of the violence they endure (Statistics Canada, 2017; World Health Organization, 2013), as is also the case with the cyberbullying they experience.

Universities, as places of learning, must attend to the factors that prevent the learning environment from fostering positive outcomes by ensuring the well-being of all involved. Some suggestions stemming from the findings of this research that would help universities to address cyberbullying more effectively and to prevent it in the first place include:

- Develop, implement, communicate, enforce, and review university policies that speak to the issue of cyberbullying. Hold the campus community responsible for upholding standards of conduct (including online conduct) that support the well-being of all community members and promote an engaging learning environment.
- Generate awareness of the issue of cyberbullying, its nature, extent, and impacts on the university community.
- Create and promote services to assist those who have been victims of cyberbullying. Recognize the difficulties for victims coming forward to seek help

and remove those barriers. Understand the victims' needs and follow up to ensure they are met appropriately.

References

Adams, F. D., & Lawrence, G. L. (2011). Bullying victims: The effects last into college. *American Secondary Education, 40*(1), 4–13.

Akbulut, Y., & Eristi, B. (2011). Cyberbullying and victimisation among Turkish university students. *Australasian Journal of Educational Technology, 27*(7), 1155–1170.

Beran, T. N., Rinaldi, C., Bickham, D. S., & Rich, M. (2012). Evidence for the need to support adolescents dealing with harassment and cyber-harassment: Prevalence, progression, and impact. *School Psychology International, 33*(5), 562–576.

Blaya, C. (this volume). Cyberbullying among university students in France: Prevalence, consequences, coping and intervention strategies. In W. Cassidy, C. Faucher, & M. Jackson (Eds.), *Cyberbullying at university in international contexts* (pp. 9–22). Oxford, UK: Routledge.

Blizard, L. M. (2016). Faculty members' perceived experiences of cyberbullying by students at one Canadian university: Impact and recommendations. *International Research in Higher Education, 1*(1), 107–124.

Cassidy, W., Jackson, M., & Faucher, C. (2016). Gender differences and cyberbullying towards faculty members in higher education. In R. Navarro, S. Yubero, & E. Larrañaga (Eds.), *Cyberbullying across the globe: Gender, family, and mental health* (pp. 79–98). Basel, Switzerland: Springer.

Condeza, R., Gallardo, G., & Reyes, P. (this volume). In W. Cassidy, C. Faucher, & M. Jackson (Eds.), *Cyberbullying at university in international contexts* (pp. 36–51). Oxford, UK: Routledge.

Council of Canadian Academies. (2012). *Strengthening Canada's research capacity: The gender dimension – The expert panel on women in university research*. Ottawa, ON: Council of Canadian Academies.

Crick, N., Werner, N., Casas, J., O'Brien, K., Nelson, D., Grotpeter, J., & Markon, K. (1999). Childhood aggression and gender: A new look at an old problem. In D. Bernstein (Ed.), *Proceedings of the Nebraska symposium on motivation* (pp. 75–141). Lincoln, NB: University of Nebraska Press.

Crooks, H. R. (2016). An intersectional feminist review of the literature on gendered cyberbullying: Digital girls. *Jeunesse: Young People, Texts, Cultures, 8*(2), 62–88.

Crosslin, K., & Golman, M. (2014). "Maybe you don't want to face it" – College students' perspectives on cyberbullying. *Computers in Human Behavior, 41*, 14–20.

DeSouza, E. R. (2010). Frequency rates and correlates of contrapower harassment in higher education. *Journal of Interpersonal Violence, 48*(11), 1–27.

Dilmaç, B. (2009). Psychological needs as predictor of cyber bullying: A preliminary report on college students. *Educational Sciences: Theory & Practice, 9*(3), 1307–1325.

Donner, C. M. (2016). The gender gap and cybercrime: An examination of college students' online offending. *Victims & Offenders, 11*(4), 556–577.

Englander, E. K. (2008). *Cyberbullying and information exposure: User-generated content in post-secondary education.* In Massachusetts Aggression Research Center (MARC) Publications, Paper 11.

Faucher, C., Cassidy, W., & Jackson, M. (2015). From the sandbox to the inbox: Comparing the acts, impacts, and solutions of bullying in K-12, higher education, and the workplace. *Journal of Education and Training Studies, 3*(6), 111–125.

Faucher, C., Jackson, M., & Cassidy, W. (2014). Cyberbullying among university students: Gendered experiences, impacts, and perspectives. *Education Research International, 2014*, 1–10.

Finn, J. (2004). A survey of online harassment at a university campus. *Journal of Interpersonal Violence, 19*, 468–483.

Fiske, N. W. (2016). *Framing Internet safety: The governance of youth online*. Cambridge, MA: The MIT Press.

Francisco, S. M., Simão, A. M.V., Ferreira, P. C., & Martins, M. J. D. D. (2015). Cyberbullying: The hidden side of college students. *Computers in Human Behavior, 43*, 167–182.

Halder, D., & Jaishankar, K. (2009). Cyber socializing and victimization of women. *Temida*, 5–26.

Hollis, L. P. (2012). *Bully in the ivory tower: How aggression and incivility erode American higher education*. Wilmington, DE: Patricia Berkly.

Jackson, M., Cassidy, W., & Brown, K. (2009). "you were born ugly and youl die ugly too": Cyber-bullying as relational aggression. *In Education, 15*(2), part. 1, 68–82.

Knepp, K. A. F. (2012). Understanding student and faculty incivility in higher education. *The Journal of Effective Teaching, 12*(1), 33–46.

Lampman, C. (2012). Women faculty at risk: U.S. professors report on their experiences with student incivility, bullying, aggression, and sexual attention. *NASPA Journal About Women in Higher Education, 5*(2), 184–208.

Langos, C., & Giancaspro, M. (this volume). Cyberbullying in the Australian context: The shades of harm and implications for law and policy. In W. Cassidy, C. Faucher, & M. Jackson (Eds.), *Cyberbullying at university in international contexts* (pp. 181–197). Oxford, UK: Routledge.

Lester, J. (2009). Not your child's playground: Workplace bullying among community college faculty. *Community College Journal of Research and Practice, 33*(5), 444–462.

McKay, R., Arnold, D. H., Fratzl, J., & Thomas, R. (2008). Workplace bullying in academia: A Canadian study. *Employee Responsibility and Rights Journal, 20*, 77–100.

Minor, M., Smith, G. S., & Brashen, H. (2013). Cyberbullying in higher education. *Journal of Educational Research and Practice, 3*(1), 15–29.

Molluzzo, J. C., & Lawler, J. P. (2012). A study of the perceptions of college students on cyberbullying. *Information Systems Education Journal, 10*(4), 84–109.

Navarro, J. N., & Jasinski, J. L. (2013). Why girls? Using Routine Activities Theory to predict cyberbullying experiences between girls and boys. *Women & Criminal Justice, 23*(4), 286–303.

Orel, A., Campbell, M., Wozencraft, K., Leong, E., & Kimpton, M. (2017). Exploring university students' coping strategy intentions for cyberbullying. *Journal of Interpersonal Violence, 32*(3), 446–462.

Pence, E., & Paymar, M. (1993). *Education groups for men who batter: The Duluth Model*. New York: Springer.

Sallee, M., & Diaz, C. (2012). Sexual harassment, racist jokes, and homophobic slurs: When bullies target identity groups. In J. Lester (Ed.), *Workplace bullying in higher education* (pp. 41–59). New York: Routledge.

Schenk, A. M., & Fremouw, W. J. (2012). Prevalence, psychological impact, and coping of cyberbully victims among college students. *Journal of School Violence, 11*(1), 21–37.

Shariff, S., & Gouin, R. (2005). *Cyber-dilemmas: Gendered hierarchies, free expression and cyber-safety in schools*. Paper presented at Oxford Internet Institute International conference Safety and Security in a Networked World. Oxford, UK. Retrieved from www.oii.ox.ac.uk/cyber-safety.

Snell, P. A., & Englander, E. K. (2010). Cyberbullying victimization and behaviors among girls: Applying research findings in the field. *Journal of Social Sciences*, *6*(4), 510–514.

Statistics Canada. (2017). Family violence in Canada: A statistical profile, 2015. *Juristat*, *85*, 1–77.

Straus, M. A. (2008). Dominance and symmetry in partner violence by male and female university students in 32 nations. *Children and Youth Services Review*, *30*(3), 252–275.

Taylor, S. (2012). Workplace bullying: Does tenure change anything? The example of a Midwestern research university. In J. Lester (Ed.), *Workplace bullying in higher education* (pp. 23–40). New York: Routledge.

Topcu, Ç., & Erdur-Baker, Ö. (2012). Affective and cognitive empathy as mediators of gender differences in cyber and traditional bullying. *School Psychology International*, *33*(5), 550–561.

Turan, N., Polat, O., Karapirli, M., Uysal, C., & Turan, S. G. (2011). The new violence type of the era: Cyber bullying among university students –Violence among university students. *Neurology, Psychiatry and Brain Research*, *17*, 21–26.

Vance, J. W. (2010). *Cyber-harassment in higher education: Online learning environments*. Ed.D. dissertation. Retrieved from University of Southern California Digital Library (usctheses-m2954).

Walker, C. M., Sockman, B. R., & Koehn, S. (2011). An exploratory study of cyberbullying with undergraduate university students. *TechTrends*, *55*(2), 31–38.

Wensley, K., & Campbell, M. (2012). Heterosexual and nonheterosexual young university students' involvement in traditional and cyber forms of bullying. *Cyberpsychology, Behavior, and Social Networking*, *15*(12), 649–654.

World Health Organization. (2013). *Global and regional estimates of violence against women: Prevalence and health effects of intimate partner violence and non-partner sexual violence*. Geneva, Switzerland: World Health Organization.

Wozencroft, K., Campbell, M., Orel, A., Kimpton, M., & Leong, E. (2015). University students' intention to report cyberbullying. *Australian Journal of Educational and Developmental Psychology*, *15*, 1–12.

Wright, M. (2016). Cyber victimization on college campuses: Longitudinal associations with suicidal ideation, depression, and anxiety. *Criminal Justice Review*, *41*(2), 190–203.

Yamada, S., Cappadocia, M. C., & Pepler, D. (2014). Workplace bullying in graduate psychology programs: Students perspectives of student-supervisor relationships. *Training and Education in Professional Psychology*, *8*, 58–67.

Yubero, S., Navarro, R., Elche, M., Larrañaga, E., & Ovejero, A. (2017). Cyberbullying victimization in higher education: An exploratory analysis of its association with social and emotional factors among Spanish students. *Computers in Human Behavior*, *75*, 439–449.

Zalaquett, C. P., & Chatters, S. J. (2014). Cyberbullying in college: Frequency, characteristics, and practical implications. *Sage Open*, *4*(1), 1–8.

Zhang, A. T., Land, L. P. W., & Dick, G. (2010). Key influences of cyberbullying for university students. *PACIS 2010 Proceedings*, Paper 83.

6

CYBERBULLYING WITHIN WORKING CONTEXTS

Iain Coyne and Samuel Farley

Comparative to the literature on traditional workplace bullying and school-based cyberbullying, systematic empirical research exploring cyberbullying within working contexts is at an embryonic stage. Scholars are directing increasing attention to this research topic, and there is no doubt that our knowledge of cyberbullying at work will expand rapidly in the near future; yet, only a limited number of studies have focused specifically on cyberbullying within university employee samples (Cassidy, Faucher, & Jackson, 2014; Coyne et al., 2017). This chapter adopts a broader work-based perspective outlining and debating the extant literature and the implications this may have for a university workplace. The chapter commences with a brief review of workplace bullying research before focusing its attention on cyberbullying within working contexts. We follow with a discussion conceptualizing cyberbullying at work, debating its similarities with and differences from traditional workplace bullying. Next, we address evidence of cyberbullying rates and critically evaluate the measurement of this behaviour, as well as debate the impact of cyberbullying on individual and organizational well-being. We then turn our attention to understanding some of the antecedents of cyberbullying and theoretical notions of why this behaviour may occur within work settings. We conclude by outlining future areas of action.

Over the last 30 years, the proliferation of research evidence published on traditional workplace bullying has resulted in an enhanced understanding of what the behaviour is, measurements in establishing prevalence rates, the impact on individuals and organizations, situational and individual antecedents of bullying, theoretical models explaining bullying, and, more recently, strategies to reduce workplace bullying.

Evidence is consistent in highlighting a wide variety of psychological, psychosomatic, and physiological effects in victims (see Coyne, 2011) and witnesses of workplace bullying (Hoel, Cooper, & Faragher, 2004). Within university employee samples, investigations demonstrate consequences for victims including depression and anxiety (Björkqvist, Österman, & Hjelt-Bäck, 1994), a greater risk of alcohol abuse (Richman, Rospenda, Flaherty, & Freels, 2001), perceptions of shame (Lewis, 2004), and higher mental strain (Coyne et al., 2017). At an organizational level, data exist indicating increased absenteeism (Kivimaki, Elovainio, & Vahtera, 2000), lower job satisfaction (Bowling & Beehr, 2006), and negative perceptions of team performance (Coyne, Craig, & Smith-Lee Chong, 2004). In UK university samples specifically, Coyne et al. (2017) found a negative relationship between the experience of traditional bullying and job satisfaction. Empirical data, which illuminates the severe negative outcomes faced by individuals and organizations resulting from workplace bullying, augment the interest in this topic area and stresses the need to find solutions to reduce this behaviour.

Conceptualizing traditional workplace bullying

Perhaps one of the first confusing features individuals face when trying to understand the concept of workplace bullying is the use of different, yet seemingly similar, terms within the literature. Scholars are furnished with an assortment of such mixed terms, including mobbing (Zapf & Einarsen, 2001), abusive supervision (Tepper, 2000), workplace incivility (Pearson, Andersson, & Porath, 2005), and social undermining (Crossley, 2009). These terms appear to represent similar behaviours, yet are defended stoutly by proponents of each concept as possessing uniquely defined characteristics. Critically, Hershcovis (2010) advocates against differentiating concepts on the basis of "unique features": wherein measurement of these concepts tends not to reflect adequately the uniqueness espoused by scholars, and empirical evidence indicates minimal differences between concepts in their relationship to outcomes.

Albeit, some disagreement exists on what bullying is; Einarsen, Hoel, Zapf, and Cooper (2003) attempted to draw the body of research together to define workplace bullying. They suggest it is:

> harassing, offending, socially excluding someone or negatively affecting someone's work tasks. In order for the label bullying (or mobbing) to be applied to a particular activity, interaction or process it has to occur repeatedly and regularly (e.g. weekly) and over a period of time (e.g. about six months). Bullying is an escalating process in the course of which the person confronted ends up in an inferior position and becomes the target of systematic negative social acts. A conflict cannot be called bullying if the incident is an isolated event or if two parties of approximately equal "strength" are in conflict.
>
> *(p. 15)*

Inherent within this definition are criteria of frequency, duration, and power imbalance – all three of which differentiate workplace bullying from other related aggressive acts. Notably, unlike school bullying and general aggression research, workplace bullying definitions tend not to include intent. Arguments for this approach include the difficulty in measuring intent (Einarsen, Hoel, Zapf, & Cooper, 2011) and the possibility that perpetrators may disguise their true intentions to rationalize their behaviour to others (Samnani, 2013). Support exists on including frequency, duration, and power imbalance within workplace bullying definitions (Zapf & Einarsen, 2001); however, Rayner and Cooper (2006) argue how persistency allows a perpetrator to rationalize a one-off negative act as something that is not bullying. Furthermore, Saunders, Huynh, and Goodman-Delahunty (2007) illustrate differences between academic definitions of bullying and how the concept is conceptualized by its practitioners.

The extent of traditional bullying

Organizational and national surveys have provided stakeholders with an indication of the extent of workplace bullying. Chronologically, rates of those experiencing bullying that were reported include 8.8% in Finland (Salin, 2001), 10.6% in the UK (Hoel, Cooper, & Faragher, 2001), and 28% in the U.S. (Lutgen-Sandvik, Tracy, & Alberts, 2007). More recently, a meta-analysis across 86 studies by Nielsen, Matthiesen, and Einarsen (2010) illustrates a mean prevalence rate of 14.6%. In relation to university employees specifically, data show prevalence rates of 30–45% (depending on gender) (Björkqvist et al., 1994), 23% (Spratlen, 1995), and 6.2% (Einarsen & Skogstad, 1996).

We could argue that the plethora of survey data provides a clear indication that bullying pervades the workplace worldwide. The difficulty is in answering the question "to what extent"? As shown, bullying rates vary widely across studies and countries. While the meta-analysis offers a synopsis of existing data, it is not evident what the actual level of bullying *is*. Critics have pointed to problems in methodology within survey research (Cowie, Naylor, Rivers, Smith, & Pereira, 2002), including variability in the timeframe adopted for bullying (e.g., at least 6 months, over the year, or ever in career) and the lack of verification for self-reported bullying exposure. Additionally, the method used to establish victim status moderates the bullying rates recorded (Coyne, Smith-Lee Chong, Seigne, & Randall, 2003; Nielsen et al., 2010). Coyne et al. identify different victim rates (ranging from 3.9% to 39.6%) that depend on whether a definition of self-report, peer-report, or a combination of self-report and peer-report was used to classify one's victim status. Nielsen et al. emphasize variability of prevalence rates for a self-labelling approach using a definition (11.3%), self-labelling without a definition (18.1%), and a behaviour-based scale (14.8%).

Currently, no definitive guidance exists that advocates a specific way to assess bullying rates. Researchers have started to adopt a combination of self-reporting to a definition with behaviour-based scales as the default method for assessing prevalence rates. Additionally, support for the latent class cluster analysis methodology, which is more complex, has also been provided (Nielsen et al., 2009).

Antecedents of workplace bullying

Research on workplace bullying antecedents has focused principally on organizational factors that promote workplace bullying. Evidence has emerged indicating that organizations characterized as stressful (Hauge, Skogstad, & Einarsen, 2007), politicized (Salin, 2003), going through change (Harvey, Heames, Richey, & Leonard, 2006), and with poor leadership (Hoel, Glasø, Hetland, Cooper, & Einarsen, 2010) are likely to experience heightened levels of bullying. Modelling these factors, Salin (2003) suggests that for bullying to occur in an organization there needs to be an initial trigger event: something which allows the bullying to evolve (e.g., organizational change), a motivating process allowing a rationale for the behaviour (e.g., competition), and conditions that facilitate bullying (e.g., poor management). In commenting on research discussing bullying among university students, Coyne (2016) suggests Salin's model may explain university bullying as:

> the transition (change) to university . . . provides the trigger for bullying to evolve and the competitive environment . . . which normalizes abusive behaviour . . . provides the motivation to engage in bullying. When these are coupled with a lack of clear policies on bullying and power differentials . . ., you have the right environment for bullying to occur.
>
> *(p. 204)*

By comparison, individual-level explanations have received less attention, with some dismissing their usefulness for understanding workplace bullying. However, other researchers posit that disposition may help us understand the likely targets of bullying – based on the extent of their vulnerability or provocative nature (Coyne, Seigne, & Randall, 2000). Additionally, perpetrators of bullying have been hypothesized as possessing inflated self-esteem, low empathy, and a heightened need for power (Zapf & Einarsen, 2003).

Theoretically, bullying specific models have attempted to capture both individual and organizational characteristics as antecedents of bullying (e.g., Bowling & Beehr, 2006; Einarsen et al., 2003). Other scholars have focused on bullying from a conflict perspective (Strandmark & Hallberg, 2007) or drawn on existing psychological models on job characteristics (Notelaers, Witte, & Einarsen, 2010), fairness perceptions (Parzefall & Salin, 2010), and job demands/resources (Baillien, De Cuyper, & De Witte, 2011). Although, there is still some way to go in testing the robustness of theoretical models explaining workplace bullying, these relatively recent advances are providing fruitful areas of future research.

Conceptualizing cyberbullying within working contexts

Empirical research on cyberbullying at work may be viewed as the younger sibling of traditional workplace bullying research – albeit one which is at the beginning of its growth spurt. We know comparatively little about this phenomenon in working contexts and, as a result, researchers have tended to cogitate about it: using ideas gleaned from traditional workplace bullying and/or cyberbullying among children/adolescents. Not surprisingly, current thinking is dominated by existing ideas in these other domains; yet, more surprisingly, similar issues and concerns raised in traditional bullying research afflict this area (e.g., differing definitions and debates about essential defining criteria).

Table 6.1 highlights a number of definitions of workplace cyberbullying and related concepts. Mirroring the traditional bullying literature, we see a variety of concepts promoted with some similarities and some "unique differences". The majority of the definitions (e.g., Farley, Coyne, Axtell, & Sprigg, 2016; Lim & Teo, 2009; Weatherbee & Kelloway, 2006) closely reflect their offline equivalent counterparts, with the addition of a technological component; others (e.g., Whitty & Carr, 2006; Willard, 2007) promote technologically specific concepts; while Vranjes, Baillien, Vandebosch, Erreygers, and De Witte (2017) suggest both a similar and technologically specific feature to the behaviour.

Firstly, these differences add another level of complexity to what Hershcovis (2010) would refer to as an "abundance of overlapping constructs" (p. 499). Now, not only do we have to contend with whether incivility, aggression, and bullying are similar or different, but we also need to take the online/offline component into consideration. Coyne et al. (2017) argue that as workplace cyberbullying involves frequency, is focused on high-intensity behaviours, and tends not to consider organizational outsiders, it differs conceptually from cyber-aggression and cyber-incivility. However, this position is exactly the criticism Hershcovis levels at offline "aggression" research.

Secondly, the different definitions echo the current debate on whether workplace cyberbullying is simply bullying using technology (Coyne et al., 2017) or whether it is conceptually distinct from offline bullying. In this latter respect, Vranjes et al. (2017) posit specific characteristics of cyberbullying which support the conceptually distinct hypothesis:

- Communication online is less rich as a result of a lack of non-verbal cues. Consequently, perpetrators are less aware of their impact on others.
- Online communication allows for anonymity and reduces the victim's control over the behaviour.
- Cyberbullying blurs the public/private boundary, becoming intrusive and restricting a victim's ability to escape.
- The power imbalance derives more from technical power.
- The volume and speed of the abuse (viral reach) is increased when the behaviour is online.

TABLE 6.1 Definitions of Cyberbullying at Work and Related Concepts

Authors	*Concept*	*Definition*
Whitty and Carr (2006, pp. 237–238)	Cyber-harassment	*"obscene or hate email that threatens or frightens, or emails that contain offensive content, such as sexist or racist material . . . this material can be sent by people . . . (either known or unknown to the person)"*
Weatherbee and Kelloway (2006, p. 461)	Cyberaggression	*"aggression expressed in a communication between two or more people using ICTs, wherein at least one person in the communication aggresses against another in order to effect harm"*
Willard (2007, p. 5)	Flaming	*"heated, short lived argument that occurs between two or more protagonists".*
Lim and Teo (2009, p. 419)	Cyber incivility	*"communicative behavior exhibited in computer-mediated interactions that violate workplace norms of mutual respect"*
Zhang and Leidner (2014, p. 2)	Workplace cyberbullying	*"instances where an employee is systematically exposed to repeated negative treatment from supervisors, colleagues or subordinates by electronic forms of contact over a long period of time, in a situation in which the perpetrator has more power than the target"*
Farley et al. (2016, p. 295)	Workplace cyberbullying	*"a situation where over time, an individual is repeatedly subjected to perceived negative acts conducted through technology (e.g. phone, email, web sites, social media) which are related to their work context. In this situation the target of workplace cyberbullying has difficulty defending him or herself against these actions"*
Forssell (2016, p. 457)	Workplace cyberbullying	*"Negative acts carried out by a group or an individual using digital media. The acts are carried out repeatedly and over time against a victim who cannot easily defend him or herself. Online harassment can be expressed by offensive or rude text messages, email, or someone posting unpleasant and offensive information (picture, videos, or text) on the Internet"*
Vranjes et al. (2017, p. 326)	Workplace cyberbullying	*"all negative behavior stemming from the work context and occurring through the use of ICTs, which is either (a) carried out repeatedly and over a period of time or (b) conducted at least once but forms an intrusion into someone's private life (potentially) exposing it to a wide online audience. This behavior leaves the target feeling helpless and unable to defend"*

Our contention is that while we acknowledge and agree there are contextual features to workplace cyberbullying not seen in traditional bullying, these features do not change the conceptualization of the concept (bullying is still bullying); rather, they may help to explain why people engage in the behaviour and/or the extent of impact on the target. This is perhaps best illustrated by discussing the definitional criteria of frequency, duration, and power imbalance seen in offline bullying definitions.

Traditionally, the frequency and duration component of bullying refers to the same person regularly experiencing negative behaviour over a long period of time. What constitutes repetition in the virtual environment is more ambiguous, especially when considering a single online act, shared in the public domain that can be viewed repeatedly by a broad audience – which may or may not be shared by the initial perpetrator. Nevertheless, while not conforming strictly to original ideas around frequency and duration, the victim will still *regularly* experience the behaviour over a *prolonged* period of time: they could even encounter the cyberbullying for longer (due to their inability to escape) and more frequently (the viral reach of the act). A second issue relating to repetition is the co-occurrence of online and offline bullying behaviour. School-based (Sticca, Ruggieri, Alsaker, & Perren, 2013) and work-related research (Coyne et al., 2017) has identified relationships between experiencing offline bullying and cyberbullying. Co-occurrence of both behaviours raises the issue of whether a respondent is experiencing cyberbullying or whether they are actually facing regular bullying (which has started to manifest in technological form). In the latter case, one could claim that the movement across media is indicative of frequency and duration.

Elements of power imbalance may differ when comparing cyberbullying to traditional bullying. Cyberbullying victims are potentially in a stronger position, as they can terminate negative interactions more easily by not responding to messages (Wolak, Mitchell, & Finkelhor, 2007). However, Heatherington and Coyne (2014) argue that a victim's perceived lack of power, rather than the bully's possession of it, characterizes the power differential in the virtual environment. We suggest that Vranjes et al.'s (2017) position of cyberbullying being conceptually different from offline bullying still falls under the remit of power differential – albeit extending our perception of what power is:

- Due to the spread of technology and the lack of boundaries within online communication, employees can be subjected to cyberbullying in their own homes, which may heighten feelings of powerlessness.
- Technological ability by the perpetrator or limited technology ability by the target can result in victim perceptions of powerlessness, as they are unable to force a perpetrator to remove abusive material or cannot influence what others write about them.

- Anonymity can increase uncertainty, as victims do not know the perpetrators – or even whether there is more than one perpetrator – thereby creating a feeling of powerlessness.

At the beginning of this section, we expressed surprise that similar concerns levelled at traditional workplace bullying seem to permeate the research on workplace cyberbullying. The debate on what the concept is – and whether it is different from its online counterpart – perhaps illustrates these concerns clearly. Ideally, as the research evidence matures, researchers and practitioners will reach a level of consensus on how to conceptualize this form of interpersonal abusive behaviour.

Types, rates, and impact of workplace cyberbullying

Recent research has begun to unearth behaviours that may occur during workplace cyberbullying situations. Behaviours experienced by employees include anonymous abusive emails sent to everyone within an organization, negative public posts uploaded on social networking websites (D'Cruz & Noronha, 2013), not receiving responses to emails or text messages, and necessary work-related information being withheld (Forssell, 2016). Examples reported by Human Resource (HR) professionals include employees posting inappropriate comments about their colleagues on the internet, distributing jokes via work email, and cyberstalking after an office romance had broken down (West, Foster, Levin, Edmison, & Robibero, 2014).

The limited evidence in working populations to date for cyberbullying has shown rates in the UK of 9.2% (Baruch, 2005), in the U.S./Canada of 9% (Ford, 2013), 10.7% in Australia (Privitera & Campbell, 2009), 2.8% in New Zealand (Gardner et al., 2016), and 9.7% in Sweden (Forssell, 2016). Within a university context, Giumetti, McKibben, Hatfield, Schroeder, and Kowalski (2012) reported 26% of a sample of U.S. university employees had experienced cyber-incivility, and Cassidy et al. (2014) reported rates of 17% among Canadian university faculty. Across three different UK university employee samples, Coyne et al. (2017) detailed cyberbullying victim rates between 13.6% and 20.8%.

At this juncture, one almost experiences a sense of déjà vu observing the variety of prevalence rates for bullying at work. The variation apparent in the prevalence of cyberbullying may be due to existing cyberbullying measures being either too narrow in scope, focusing only on one medium such as email (Baruch); assessing constructs such as cyber-aggression (Ford) or cyber-incivility (Guimetti et al.); or using an adapted version of the Negative Acts Questionnaire (NAQ) for use in cyber-contexts (Coyne et al.; Forssell). Different methodologies and different categorization approaches create the pattern of victim rates seen above. It is only very recently that a specific workplace cyberbullying measure (WCM) has been developed and validated (Farley et al., 2016), which may provide a metric for assessing victim and target rates of cyberbullying at work – including universities. As with traditional bullying, we may see the norm being the use of the WCM, with an additional self-reported item added, to assess victim rates of cyberbullying at work.

Paralleling traditional bullying research, evidence to date reveals experiencing cyberbullying has negative implications for both individuals and organizations. Cross-sectional investigations have shown relationships between cyberbullying, anxiety, and an intention to leave one's workplace (Baruch, 2005); general well-being and fear of future harassment (Ford, 2013); perceived stress and low optimism (Snyman & Loh, 2015); and mental strain and job dissatisfaction (Farley, Coyne, Sprigg, Axtell, & Subramanian, 2015). University-specific studies on cyber-incivility have shown correlations with general job stress and burnout (Giumetti et al., 2012), as well as on cyberbullying with negative emotion, mental strain, perceived injustice, and job dissatisfaction (Cassidy, Faucher, & Jackson, this volume; Coyne et al., 2017). Indeed, in this latter study, the authors hypothesized that the "unique features" of cyberbullying (espoused earlier) may result in more severe outcomes when compared to traditional bullying; they also provide data to show that the strength of relationship between cyberbullying experience, mental strain, and job dissatisfaction was stronger than for offline bullying.

Antecedents of and theoretical approaches to cyberbullying within work

Expected within a developing research area, knowledge on the antecedents of workplace cyberbullying is sparse. Gardner et al. (2016) offer some initial results from a two-wave study: finding significant correlations between poor physical health, low organizational support, and low effective organizational strategies when first experiencing cyberbullying and then again at three months later. If we concur with the view that cyberbullying within working contexts is conceptually similar to offline bullying, then researchers have a ready-made compendium of possible antecedents (e.g., change, competition, poor leadership, etc.) from an organizational and individual level, which could be considered within cyberbullying research. Using Salin's (2003) model, researchers should identify the precipitating, motivating, and facilitating factors of workplace cyberbullying. Currently, however, there is limited research focused on directly mapping offline workplace bullying antecedents to cyberbullying contexts. The question is, then, "where do we look for possible explanations of cyberbullying within working contexts"? Theoretically, there are a number of avenues we can follow.

Theories of computer-mediated communication

There is a vast literature on computer-mediated communication (CMC), which may help identify why people engage in or experience cyberbullying behaviour.

Reduced social cues

Firstly, the reduced cues hypothesis (Daft, Lengel, & Trevino, 1987; Kock, 2004) suggests CMC methods possess fewer social, contextual, and verbal cues; are lower in media richness and media naturalness; and can result in individuals being less present and more anonymous – a state described as "deindividuation". In relation to cyberbullying, it may be more likely for people communicating virtually to misinterpret messages as cyberbullying acts. More misunderstandings occur during online communication than in person (Byron, 2008), which may lead individuals to mistakenly perceive themselves as victims of cyberbullying, even when the sender meant no ill intent.

Deindividuation

The deindividuation effect of CMC could also help explain cyberbullying. Computer-mediated communication is often characterized by feelings of anonymity, making people less sensitive to the thoughts and feelings of others, and causing a disinhibition effect (Siegel, Dubrovsky, Kiesler, & Mcguire, 1986). The outcome of this effect can be benign or toxic (Suler, 2004), in which case communication becomes harsher and more abusive. Therefore – because people become absorbed in immediate communication cues, rather than focusing on self and others (Siegel et al., 1986) – they become submerged into their technology, leading to a loss of identity and uninhibited behaviour – such as cyberbullying.

The Social Identity model of De-individuation Effects (SIDE) (Spears & Lea, 1994) argues that, in the absence of personal communication cues, individuals shift their attention away from interpersonal differences to focus on a common group identity, as characterized by group norms. According to SIDE, new group members accept these norms through deindividuation. Research has identified that norms of CMC are confined to the boundaries of a group – and that groups vary in the number of requests, reactions, humour, emotion, and personal revelations they deploy (Postmes, Spears, & Lea, 2000). Group norms have implications when a newcomer joins a group, as their communication may be perceived as rude or aggressive (and vice versa), which may spark conflict and lead to cyberbullying.

Taken together, these theories provide a lens for understanding communication in the virtual environment, and how this communication (or lack of communication) promotes cyberbullying. In particular, these theories outline how aspects of online communication differ from face-to-face communication, as well as how these differences – in terms of lack of cues, misinterpretation of communication, deindividuation, disinhibition, and social identity – may result in cyberbullying behaviour.

Psychological theories of cyberbullying

Currently, only a small number of researchers have used models encompassing features of existing bullying theories (e.g., stress, emotions, and fairness perceptions) to help explain workplace cyberbullying.

Dysempowerment theory

Focused on university employee samples in the UK, Coyne et al. (2017) apply dysempowerment theory (Kane & Montgomery, 1998) to explain how cyberbullying may lead to individual mental strain and job dissatisfaction. Dysempowerment theory posits an employee appraises a "polluting" work event as a violation of his/her dignity (fairness perception), which results in a perception of subjective stress, leading to negative affect (emotion) and, in turn, disrupts the employee's attitudes and behaviour at work. The greater the volume of polluting acts perceived by an employee, the stronger the potential for dysempowerment. Therefore, dysempowerment theory could explain cyberbullying as a situation in which a target of workplace cyberbullying may perceive a series of events as a violation of their dignity (or as something unfair), exhibiting a negative affective response that impacts on their mental well-being and job attitudes. These results indicate a mediating effect of negative emotion on the relationship between the experience of cyberbullying, mental strain, and job dissatisfaction. However, data suggests interpersonal justice and negative affect were two separate routes, through which cyberbullying may have its own effect: with negative emotion exhibiting a stronger effect on mental strain than job dissatisfaction, and justice only mediating the relationship between cyberbullying and job dissatisfaction.

Farley et al. (2015) go one stage further in their theories: combining dysempowerment theory with the attributional model of workplace harassment (Bowling & Beehr, 2006). They suggest that attribution of blame for the "polluting" event of cyberbullying impacts perceptions of violations to one's dignity and influence negative emotional responses. Findings indicate negative emotion mediated the relationship between self-blame for a cyberbullying act and mental strain, whereas interactional injustice mediated the association between blaming the perpetrator and job dissatisfaction. Attributions of blame potentially go some way in explaining the different paths seen in the Coyne et al. study.

Emotion reaction model

Offering a perspective on why people experience and/or engage in cyberbullying (rather than modelling the impact of cyberbullying), Vranjes et al. (2017)

posit the moderation-mediation Emotion Reaction Model. They theorize that work-related stressors at the job (e.g., role conflict), team (interpersonal conflict), and organization levels (e.g., change) relate to experience and engagement in cyberbullying behaviour at work. This stressor-strain relationship is mediated by discrete emotions of anger, fear, and sadness – with anger promoting the engagement in cyberbullying (via a retaliation process) and fear/sadness promoting the experience of cyberbullying (via a powerlessness process). Additionally, control appraisal is espoused to moderate the relationship between stressors and emotions. When stressors are seen to be under an individual's control, anger arises; comparatively, fear and sadness arise when work stressors are attributed to situational factors. Emotional regulation is also identified as a moderator, but with different impacts, depending on the type of strategy adopted. Reappraisal buffers the effect of stressors on emotions, whereas suppression increases the relationship of emotions to the experience or engagement of cyberbullying.

When considering the lifespan of its research, it is a strength that the development and testing of theoretical ideas related to cyberbullying within working contexts has arisen at such an early stage. Both the Coyne et al. and Vranjes et al. approaches have foundations within stress theories (similar to offline bullying models), and also provide insights as to the why and consequences of cyberbullying in workplace settings. There is no reason to believe that a university context will be any different from other working contexts in terms of job, team, and organizational stressors – or else perceptions of what is or is not unfair behaviour, perceptions of blame, and emotional reactions.

Conclusion

The evidence base for offline workplace bullying is extensive. Increasingly, it becomes more and more robust in terms of its theory-driven nature and methodological approaches. Cyberbullying research within working contexts is limited by comparison, but it is comforting to know that scholars are increasingly becoming aware of and interested in this concept – as well as notions of how cyberbullying emerges. Concerns to its impact have evolved much earlier on in the lifespan of a research agenda.

Going forward, a number of action points can be offered:

1 Consensus on whether cyberbullying is different from or the same as offline bullying should be reached. Meta-analytic approaches akin to Hershcovis (2010) will allow us to test if there are empirical differences between concepts in their relationship to antecedents and outcomes, and should establish support for one position or the other.
2 Use and validation of specific workplace cyberbullying measures – as well as approaches in classifying victim status – should exist, as they allow comparisons to be made across organizations, sectors, and countries. Perhaps

aligning to the approach adopted within offline bullying is the optimal solution.

3 Further testing and (where appropriate) the updating of models offered to explain cyberbullying at work should be implemented. It would be useful to consider including ideas from the CMC literature within current psychological models, as they may help to explain why people perceive messages as a violation of dignity – or why disinhibited actions result from stressors and emotions.
4 There should be a consideration of other roles within the cyberbullying situation. In parallel with offline workplace bullying research, the focus has tended to be at the level of the victim (although Vranjes's model does also consider the perpetrator). Witnesses/bystanders have, to date, been largely neglected in this process, with limited research suggesting that – unlike offline bullying – witnesses of cyberbullying do not exhibit negative outcomes (Coyne et al., 2017).
5 Lastly, identification and the development of evidence-based interventions could be put in place to reduce cyberbullying at work (see Farley and Coyne, this volume).

References

Baillien, E., De Cuyper, N., & De Witte, H. (2011). Job autonomy and workload as antecedents of workplace bullying: A two-wave test of Karasek's Job Demand Control Model for targets and perpetrators. *Journal of Occupational and Organizational Psychology, 84*(1), 191–208.

Baruch, Y. (2005). Bullying on the net: Adverse behavior on e-mail and its impact. *Information & Management, 42*(2), 361–371.

Björkqvist, K., Österman, K., & Hjelt-Bäck, M. (1994). Aggression among university employees. *Aggressive Behavior, 20*, 173–184.

Bowling, N. A., & Beehr, T. A. (2006). Workplace harassment from the victim's perspective: A theoretical model and meta-analysis. *Journal of Applied Psychology, 91*(5), 998–1012.

Byron, K. (2008). Carrying too heavy a load? The communication and miscommunication of emotion by email. *Academy of Management Review, 33*(2), 309–327.

Cassidy, W., Faucher, C., & Jackson, M. (2014). The dark side of the ivory tower: Cyberbullying of university faculty and teaching personnel. *Alberta Journal of Educational Research, 60*(2), 279–299.

Cassidy, W., Faucher, C., & Jackson, M. (this volume). "You need a thick skin . . .": Impacts of cyberbullying in Canadian universities. In W. Cassidy, C. Faucher, & M. Jackson (Eds.), *Cyberbullying at university in international contexts* (pp. 112–125). Oxford, UK: Routledge.

Cowie, H., Naylor, P., Rivers, I., Smith, P. K., & Pereira, B. (2002). Measuring workplace bullying. *Agggression and Violent Behavior, 7*, 33–51.

Coyne, I. (2011). Bullying in the workplace. In C. P. Monks & I. Coyne (Eds.), *Bullying in Different Contexts* (pp. 157–184). Cambridge, UK: Cambridge University Press.

Coyne, I. (2016). Commentary: What universities can learn from workplace bullying research. In H. Cowie & C. Myers (Eds.), *Bullying among university students: Cross-national perspectives* (pp. 203–206). Abingdon, Oxon: Routledge.

Coyne, I., Craig, J., & Chong, P. S.-L. (2004). Workplace bullying in a group context. *British Journal of Guidance & Counselling*, *32*(3), 301–317.

Coyne, I., Farley, S., Axtell, C., Sprigg, C., Best, L., & Kwok, O. (2017). Understanding the relationship between experiencing workplace cyberbullying, employee mental strain and job satisfaction: A dysempowerment approach. *The International Journal of Human Resource Management*, *28*(7), 945–972.

Coyne, I., Seigne, E., & Randall, P. (2000). Predicting workplace victim status from personality. *European Journal of Work and Organizational Psychology*, *9*(3), 335–349.

Coyne, I., Smith-Lee Chong, P., Seigne, E., & Randall, P. (2003). Self and peer nominations of bullying: An analysis of incident rates, individual differences, and perceptions of the working environment. *European Journal of Work and Organizational Psychology*, *12*(3), 209–228.

Crossley, C. (2009). Emotional and behavioral reactions to social undermining: A closer look at perceived offender motives. *Organizational Behavior and Human Decision Processes*, *108*(1), 14–24.

D'Cruz, P., & Noronha, E. (2013). Navigating the extended reach: Target experiences of cyberbullying at work. *Information and Organization*, *23*(4), 324–343.

Daft, R. L., Lengel, R. H., & Trevino, L. K. (1987). Message equivocality, media selection, and manager performance: Implications for information systems. *MIS Quarterly*, *11*(3), 355–366.

Einarsen, S., Hoel, H., Zapf, D., & Cooper, C. L. (2003). The concept of bullying at work: The European tradition. In S. Einarsen, H. Hoel, D. Zapf, & C. L. Cooper (Eds.), *Bullying and emotional abuse in the workplace: International perspectives in research and practice* (pp. 3–30). London: Taylor and Francis.

Einarsen, S., Hoel, H., Zapf, D., & Cooper, C. L. (2011). The concept of bullying and harassment at work: The European tradition. In S. Einarsen, H. Hoel, D. Zapf, & C. L. Cooper (Eds.), *Bullying and harassment in the workplace: Developments in theory, research and practice* (2nd ed., pp. 3–40). Boca Raton, FL: CRC Press.

Einarsen, S., & Skogstad, A. (1996). Bullying at work: Epidemiological findings in public and private organizations. *European Journal of Work and Organizational Psychology*, *5*(2), 185–201.

Farley, S., & Coyne, I. (this volume). Intervening against workplace cyberbullying. In W. Cassidy, C. Faucher, & M. Jackson (Eds.), *Cyberbullying at university in international contexts* (pp. 173–177). Oxford, UK: Routledge.

Farley, S., Coyne, I., Axtell, C., & Sprigg, C. (2016). Design, development and validation of a workplace cyberbullying measure, the WCM. *Work & Stress*, *30*(4), 293–317.

Farley, S., Coyne, I., Sprigg, C., Axtell, C., & Subramanian, G. (2015). Exploring the impact of workplace cyberbullying on trainee doctors. *Medical Education*, *49*(4), 436–443.

Ford, D. P. (2013). Virtual harassment: Media characteristics' role in psychological health. *Journal of Managerial Psychology*, *28*(4), 408–428.

Forssell, R. (2016). Exploring cyberbullying and face-to-face bullying in working life – Prevalence, targets and expressions. *Computers in Human Behavior*, *58*, 454–460.

Gardner, D., O'Driscoll, M., Cooper-Thomas, H. D., Roche, M., Bentley, T., Catley, B., . . . Trenberth, L. (2016). Predictors of workplace bullying and cyber-bullying in New Zealand. *International Journal of Environmental Research and Public Health*, *13*(5), 448–462.

Giumetti, G. W., McKibben, E. S., Hatfield, A. L., Schroeder, A. N., & Kowalski, R. M. (2012). Cyber incivility @ work: The new age of interpersonal deviance. *Cyberpsychology, Behavior, and Social Networking*, *15*(3), 148–154.

Harvey, M. G., Heames, J. T., Richey, R. G., & Leonard, N. (2006). Bullying: From the playground to the boardroom. *Journal of Leadership & Organizational Studies, 12*(4), 1–11.

Hauge, L. J., Skogstad, A., & Einarsen, S. (2007). Relationships between stressful work environments and bullying: Results of a large representative study. *Work & Stress, 21*(3), 220–242.

Heatherington, W., & Coyne, I. (2014). Understanding individual experiences of cyberbullying encoutered through work. *International Journal of Organizational Theory and Behavior, 17*(2), 163–192.

Hershcovis, M. S. (2010). "Incivility, social undermining, bullying . . . oh my !": A call to reconcile constructs within workplace aggression research. *Journal of Organizational Behavior, 32*, 499–519.

Hoel, H., Cooper, C. L., & Faragher, B. (2001). The experience of bullying in Great Britain: The impact of organizational status. *European Journal of Work and Organizational Psychology, 10*(4), 443–465.

Hoel, H., Cooper, C. L., & Faragher, B. (2004). Bullying is detrimental to health, but all bullying behaviours are not necessarily equally damaging. *British Journal of Guidance & Counselling, 32*, 367–387.

Hoel, H., Glasø, L., Hetland, J., Cooper, C. L., & Einarsen, S. (2010). Leadership styles as predictors of self-reported and observed workplace bullying. *British Journal of Management, 21*(2), 453–468.

Kane, K., & Montgomery, K. (1998). A framework for understanding dysempowerment in organizations. *Human Resource Management, 37*(34), 263–275.

Kivimaki, M., Elovainio, M., & Vahtera, J. (2000). Workplace bullying and sickness absence in hospital staff. *Occupational and Environmental Medicine, 57*(10), 656–660.

Kock, N. (2004). The psychobiological model: Towards a new theory of computer-mediated communication based on Darwinian evolution. *Organization Science, 15*(3), 327–348.

Lewis, D. (2004). Bullying at work: The impact of shame among university and college lecturers. *British Journal of Guidance and Counselling, 32*(3), 281–299.

Lim, V. K. G., & Teo, T. S. H. (2009). Mind your E-manners: Impact of cyber incivility on employees' work attitude and behavior. *Information & Management, 46*(8), 419–425.

Lutgen-Sandvik, P., Tracy, S. J., & Alberts, J. K. (2007). Burned by bullying in the American workplace: Prevalence, perception, degree and impact. *Journal of Management Studies, 44*(6), 837–862.

Nielsen, M. B., Matthiesen, S. B., & Einarsen, S. (2010). The impact of methodological moderators on prevalence rates of workplace bullying: A meta-analysis. *Journal of Occupational and Organizational Psychology, 83*(4), 955–979.

Nielsen, M. B., Skogstad, A., Matthiesen, S. B., Glasø, L., Aasland, M. S., Notelaers, G., & Einarsen, S. (2009). Prevalence of workplace bullying in Norway: Comparisons across time and estimation methods. *European Journal of Work and Organizational Psychology, 18*(1), 81–101.

Notelaers, G., Witte, H. De, & Einarsen, S. (2010). A job characteristics approach to explain workplace bullying. *European Journal of Work and Organizational Psychology, 19*(4), 487–504.

Parzefall, M.-R., & Salin, D. M. (2010). Perceptions of and reactions to workplace bullying: A social exchange perspective. *Human Relations, 63*(6), 761–780.

Pearson, C., Andersson, L., & Porath, C. (2005). Workplace incivility. In S. Fox & P. E. Spector (Eds.), *Counterproductive work behavior: Investigations of actors and targets* (pp. 177–200). Washington, DC: American Psychological Association.

Postmes, T., Spears, R., & Lea, M. (2000). The formation of group norms in computer-mediated communication. *Human Communication Research, 26*, 341–371.

Privitera, C., & Campbell, M. A. (2009). Cyberbullying: The new face of workplace bullying? *Cyberpsychology & Behavior: The Impact of the Internet, Multimedia and Virtual Reality on Behavior and Society, 12*(4), 395–400.

Rayner, C., & Cooper, C. L. (2006). Workplace bullying. In E. K. Kelloway, J. Barling, & J. J. Hurrell (Eds.), *Handbook of workplace violence* (pp. 121–145). Thousand Oaks, CA: Sage Publications.

Richman, J. A., Rospenda, K. M., Flaherty, J. A., & Freels, S. (2001). Workplace harassment, active coping, and alcohol-related outcomes. *Journal of Substance Abuse, 13*(3), 347–366.

Salin, D. (2001). Prevalence and forms of bullying among business professionals: A comparison of two different strategies for measuring bullying. *European Journal of Work and Organizational Psychology, 10*(4), 425–441.

Salin, D. (2003). Ways of explaining workplace bullying: A review of enabling, motivating and precipitating structures and processes in the work environment. *Human Relations, 56*(10), 1213–1232.

Samnani, A.-K. (2013). "Is this bullying?" Understanding target and witness reactions. *Journal of Managerial Psychology, 28*(3), 290–305.

Saunders, P., Huynh, A., & Goodman-Delahunty, J. (2007). Defining workplace bullying behaviour professional lay definitions of workplace bullying. *International Journal of Law and Psychiatry, 30*(4–5), 340–354.

Siegel, J., Dubrovsky, V., Kiesler, S., & Mcguire, T. (1986). Group processes in computer-mediated communication. *Organizational Behavior and Human Decision Processes, 37*, 157–187.

Snyman, R., & Loh, J. (2015). Cyberbullying at work: The mediating role of optimism between cyberbullying and job outcomes. *Computers in Human Behavior, 53*, 161–168.

Spears, R., & Lea, M. (1994). Panacea or panoptica? The hidden power in computer-mediated communication. *Communication Research, 21*(4), 427–459.

Spratlen, L. (1995). Interpersonal conflict which includes mistreatment in a university workplace. *Violence and Victims, 10*(4), 285–297.

Sticca, F., Ruggieri, S., Alsaker, F., & Perren, S. (2013). Longitudinal risk factors for cyberbullying in adolescence. *Journal of Community and Applied Social Psychology, 23*, 52–67.

Strandmark, M. K., & Hallberg, L. R. (2007). The origin of workplace bullying: Experiences from the perspective of bully victims in the public service sector. *Journal of Nursing Management, 15*(3), 332–341.

Suler, J. (2004). The online disinhibition effect. *Cyberpsychology & Behavior: The Impact of the Internet, Multimedia and Virtual Reality on Behavior and Society*, 7(3), 321–326.

Tepper, B. J. (2000). Consequences of abusive supervision. *The Academy of Management Journal, 43*(2), 178–190.

Vranjes, I., Baillien, E., Vandebosch, H., Erreygers, S., & De Witte, H. (2017). The dark side of working online: Towards a definition and an emotion reaction model of workplace cyberbullying. *Computers in Human Behavior, 69*, 324–334.

Weatherbee, T. G., & Kelloway, E. K. (2006). A case of cyberdeviancy: CyberAggression in the workplace. In E. K. Kelloway, J. Barling, & J. J. Hurrell (Eds.), *Handbook of workplace violence* (pp. 445–487). Thousand Oaks, CA: Sage Publications.

West, B., Foster, M., Levin, A., Edmison, J., & Robibero, D. (2014). Cyberbullying at work: In search of effective guidance. *Laws, 3*(3), 598–617.

Whitty, M., & Carr, A. (2006). New rules in the workplace: Applying object-relations theory to explain problem internet and email behaviour in the workplace. *Computers in Human Behavior, 22*(2), 235–250.

Willard, N. E. (2007). The authority and responsibility of school officials in responding to cyberbullying. *The Journal of Adolescent Health, 41*(6), S64–S65.

Wolak, J., Mitchell, K. J., & Finkelhor, D. (2007). Does online harassment constitute bullying? An exploration of online harassment by known peers and online-only contacts. *Journal of Adolescent Health, 41*, 851–858.

Zapf, D., & Einarsen, S. (2001). Bullying in the workplace: Recent trends in research and practice – An introduction. *European Journal of Work and Organizational Psychology, 10*(4), 369–373.

Zapf, D., & Einarsen, S. (2003). Individual antecedents of bullying. In S. Einarsen, H. Hoel, D. Zapf, & C. L. Cooper (Eds.), *Bullying and emotional abuse in the workplace: International perspectives in research and practice* (pp. 165–184). London: Taylor and Francis.

Zhang, S., & Leidner, D. (2014). *Workplace cyberbullying: The antecedents and consequences.* Paper presented at the 20th Americas Conference on Information Systems, Social-Technical Issues and Social Inclusion Track. Savannah.

PART II
Impacts

7

FROM TRADITIONAL BULLYING TO CYBERBULLYING

Cybervictimization among higher education students

Elisa Larrañaga, Santiago Yubero, Raúl Navarro, and Anastasio Ovejero

From traditional bullying to cyberbullying

Several studies have identified a correlation between participating in traditional bullying and cyberbullying (Hemphill et al., 2012; Jang, Song, & Kim, 2014). Students who are perpetrators of traditional bullying may also be perpetrators through use of ICT, and traditional bullying victims may also be cyberbullying victims (MacDonald & Roberts-Pittman, 2010; Smith et al., 2008; Sontag, Clemans, Graber, & Lyndon, 2011; Ybarra & Mitchell, 2004). Other studies have found that students who are victims of both traditional bullying and cyberbullying may also be cyberbullies (König, Gollwitzer, & Steffgen, 2010; Smith et al., 2008; Sontag et al., 2011; Ybarra & Mitchell, 2004). In those cases, cyberbullying may be a way of retaliating (Willard, 2006) or an act of revenge using the anonymity and distance offered by the internet (König et al., 2010).

Additional studies have shown that those participating in bullying in high school may continue to bully at university (Faucher, Jackson, & Cassidy, 2014; Paullet & Pinchot, 2014; Zalaquett & Chatters, 2014). Zacchilli and Valerio (2011) have also reported the link between cyberbullying at university and involvement in bullying in primary school.

As far as higher education students are concerned, MacDonald and Roberts-Pittman (2010) also found a link between cyberbullying and bullying behaviours, with correlations ranging from .22 to .65. Tomsa, Jenaro, Campbell, and Neacsu (2013) reported that 31.5% of the cybervictims were also victims of traditional bullying; with regard to perpetration, 10.9% of cyberbullies were also engaged in traditional bullying. More recently, in a sample of Spanish university students, Caravaca et al. (2016) found that 40.7% of traditional bullying victims were also victims of cyberbullying.

Nevertheless, even when research data show that cyberbullying is a prevalent behaviour in higher education students, a portion of the students participating in qualitative studies tend to view cyberbullying as childish behaviour more typical of previous educational levels, although these students admit that cyberbullying is present in higher education (Baldasare, Bauman, Goldman, & Robie, 2012; Crosslin & Golman, 2014). In these qualitative studies, higher education students point out that cyberbullying depends on the intention of the perpetrator (Baldasare et al., 2012; Kota, Schoohs, Benson, & Moreno, 2014), and they often believe that it is just a joke that went too far. They also downplay the scale of the repeated nature of cyberbullying (Kota et al., 2014). As a matter of fact, qualitative studies have shown that some of the students do not see cyberbullying as a serious problem because they believe they can cope with it, in comparison with students in previous educational levels (Baldasare et al., 2012; Crosslin & Golman, 2014; Kota et al., 2014). These contradictory findings warrant a more detailed analysis of cyberbullying behaviour in institutions of higher education.

Cyberbullying prevalence in higher education

Although there is a growing body of research on cyberbullying among primary and secondary school students, cyberbullying among higher education students has been less explored. The first study was conducted by Finn in 2004, whose results revealed that between 10% and 15% of the 339 participants from the University of New Hampshire had experienced cyberbullying through email and instant messaging platforms. Starting in 2009, there was an increase in studies regarding cyberbullying in different universities, mainly in the United States (e.g., Hoff & Mitchell, 2009; Kraft & Wang, 2010; Schenk & Fremouw, 2012; Smith & Yoon, 2013; Selkie, Kota, Chan, & Moreno, 2015) and Turkey (e.g., Aricak, 2009; Dilmac, 2009; Turan, Polat, Karapirli, Uysal, & Turan, 2011). The self-reported victimization rates in different studies range from 9% (Molluzzo & Lawler, 2011) to 27.4% (Mateus, Veiga, Costa, & das Dores, 2015), and amount to 60% when students were asked if they knew any victims of cyberbullying (Turan et al., 2011). With regard to time frames, prevalence rates also differ greatly, ranging from 53% (Dilmac, 2009) to 81% (Akbulut & Eristi, 2011) when asking students if they have experienced any behaviour at any time in their lives; from 8.7% (Tomsa et al., 2013) to 36.7% (Aricak, 2009) if they are asked about the previous year; and 9% at the current moment (Paullet & Pinchot, 2014; for more details, see Larrañaga, Yubero, & Ovejero, 2016).

Studies in Spain started to emerge in 2015. The first one was carried out by Elipe, Mora-Merchán, Ortega-Ruiz, and Casas (2015), with a wide sample of 638 undergraduate students from Andalusia. Over half of the participants (54%) reported having experienced some kind of cyberbullying victimization in the past two months. Twenty-five percent of students experienced "insults about me said to others via internet or SMS messages," and another 25% of students received "direct personal insults via email or SMS messages." Only 2.2% indicated that somebody had created a false Facebook or MSN account to steal their identity; in those cases, this happened with an overall frequency of once or twice.

Using a sample of 543 college students from Murcia, Caravaca et al. (2016) found that 62.2% of students reported having been the victim of traditional bullying, and 52.7% reported that they had experienced cyberbullying. Forty point seven percent of participants had been victims of traditional bullying and cyberbullying in the past 12 months. Separating these numbers by category showed that 21.3% experienced traditional bullying only, and 12% were victims of cyberbullying only.

Yubero, Navarro, Elche, Larrañaga, and Ovejero (2017), with a sample of 243 college students from Castilla-La Mancha, followed a more restrictive criterion to categorize cyberbullying (participants' scores above 1 standard deviation above the mean). Nine point eight percent of the surveyed higher education students reported having been victims of cyberbullying. The most frequently experienced form of cyberbullying victimization was the online dissemination of lies and rumours (36%); 9.1% had experienced such instances quite a few or many times in the past year. The results of this study indicated that cyberbullying victimization in higher education was associated with traditional bullying experienced in primary and secondary school.

Cyberbullying correlates in college students

Research has provided evidence that being the target of cyberbullying negatively impacts mental health and increases the risks of psychological and social problems. Indeed, the National Institute of Health (2010) reported that the impact of cyberbullying could be even more damaging than that of traditional bullying. Zalaquett and Chatters (2014) point out that the psychological consequences are more serious in the case of higher education students. Cyberbullying at university may trigger the development of mental health problems and may even lead to suicide (e.g., Cassidy, Faucher, & Jackson, this volume; Dilmac, 2009; Lindsay & Krysik, 2012; Zacchilli & Valerio, 2011).

Smith and Yoon (2013) found that 10% of the 276 college student participants experienced cyberbullying victimization. The students first reported lowered self-esteem (21%), declining academic performance (18.5%) (even dropping out of university), fewer social relations (15.5%), and depression (13.2%). Schenk and Fremouw (2012) also reported depression and anxiety among cyberbullying victims at university. Schenk, Fremouw, and Keelan (2013) analysed the consequences in university cyberbullies and cyberbullying victims. Their results show that cyberbullies and cyberbullying/victims scored significantly higher than other control participants on the clinical scales of interpersonal sensitivity, depression, hostility, phobic anxiety, psychoticism, and suicidal tendencies.

In the short term, victims of cyberbullying at university see their self-esteem reduced and suffer from stress and depression; they also feel frustrated when the university authorities do not take this problem seriously (Cassidy et al., this volume; Rivituso, 2014). Additionally, college students are concerned about how information on the internet can affect their professional careers in the long term (Kota et al., 2014).

Faucher et al. (2014) highlight the social consequences of cyberbullying, which lead to a reduction in the number of relations established both at university and beyond. Qualitative research (Baldasare et al., 2012; Crosslin & Golman, 2014) confirms the fact that cyberbullying affects students' social connections. Their social lives suffer more when cyberbullying is perpetrated by friends and acquaintances because it is generated inside their own social networks and, therefore, more difficult to ignore (Baldasare et al., 2012).

Tokunaga (2010) points out that higher education students perceive turning to their parents for help as immature behaviour, making them turn to their friends instead. Maybe that is why the social support provided by friends seems to be a protective factor against cyberbullying victimization among higher education students (Yubero et al., 2017).

Cyberbullying within the framework of dating relationships

Interest in violence within the framework of dating relationships has increased in the past few years. The reason is the link between violence in younger couples and subsequent violence in adult, long-standing couples (González-Ortega, Echeburúa, & De Corral, 2008; Wekerle, 1999). The Centers for Disease Control and Prevention (CDC, 2014) defines dating violence as that type of violence – whether physical, sexual, or psychological/emotional – inflicted in dating relationships, as well as other acts of persecution and abuse. It also specifies that this type of behaviour may originate from former or current partners, either in person or through different electronic means. New technologies expand the settings in which violence in couples' relationships may arise (Durán & Martínez-Pecino, 2015), and constitute a new control and surveillance device, making young people become more accessible and, therefore, more prone to interpersonal intrusiveness (Van Ouytsel, Van Gool, Walrave, Ponnet, & Peeters, 2016). Jealousy and fighting are the most common motivators for this kind of aggression (Borrajo & Gámez-Guadix, 2015; Kellerman et al., 2013).

Research in this area distinguishes two types of online abuse in dating: direct aggression and control (Bennett, Guran, Ramos, & Margolin, 2011; Burke, Wallen, Vail-Smith, & Knox, 2011). Direct abuse behaviours refer to those behaviours aimed at harming the partner, for example, by sending offensive messages or by disseminating negative information about the significant other (Zweig, Dank, Yahner, & Lachman, 2013). Control refers to those behaviours aimed at pursuing or controlling the significant other, for example, by visiting his/her profile on his/her social network quite frequently and controlling who he/she is with or what he/she is doing (Burke et al., 2011; Tokunaga, 2010).

Finn (2004) found that between 10% and 15% of higher education students had been abused by their partners. Other studies also highlighted the fact that an important proportion of young people who are victims of cyberbullying identify their partner as the perpetrator, and partners are the people against whom many perpetrators direct their cyberbullying actions (Alexy, Burgess, Baker, & Smoyak, 2005). At an empirical level, it has been found that those who admit committing cyber-dating abuse also tend to participate in cyberbullying (Hinduja & Patchin, 2011). For example, Hinduja and Patchin (2011) found that those young people who perpetrated cyberbullying were three times more likely to engage in abusive cyber-dating behaviour than those who did not perpetrate aggression against their peers.

Research on cyberbullying among higher education students has started to analyse the extent to which cyberbullying is perpetrated within the framework of dating relationships. In 2011, Bennett et al., with 437 college students, reported that 77% had experienced cyberbullying from their significant other in the last year. Likewise, the results obtained by Burke et al. (2011), with a sample of 804 undergraduates aged between 18 and 23, showed that half of both female and male respondents reported the use of communication technology to monitor partners, either as the perpetrator or victim. Women were significantly more likely than men to monitor the email accounts of their partners (25% vs. 6%), and to regard doing so as appropriate behaviour. Crosslin and Golman (2014) showed that according to 30% of participants, cyberbullying may be used to create disagreement or harm romantic relationships by friends, acquaintances, and ex-significant others.

In Spain, Durán and Martínez-Pecino (2015), with a sample of 336 college students aged between 18 and 30, analysed abusive behaviour and cyberbullying in dating relationships. Fifty-seven point two percent of participants stated that they had been victimized through their cell phones, and 27.4% via the internet, while 47.6% stated they had abused through cell phones, and 14% via the internet. Another study (Martínez-Pecino & Durán, 2016), with 219 college students aged between 18 and 28, 61.4% of whom were women, also reported greater incidence through cell phones (48.4%) than via the internet (37.5%). This study also shows the influence of participants' hostile sexism on cyberbullying against women in dating relationships. Borrajo, Gámez-Guadix, and Calvete (2015), with a sample of 656 Spanish young people aged between 18 and 30 years (79.7% of which were college students), showed that justifying online abuse is associated with direct online aggression in dating relationships. Myths about love were associated to a greater extent with online control behaviours (e.g., monitoring social status changes in social networks and cell phone messages). In their qualitative study on the basis of individual, in-depth interviews with seven college students (five women and two men), Borrajo and Gámez-Guadix (2015) reported that control behaviours and harassment are the most frequent forms of online abuse within the framework of dating relationships.

As a consequence of online abuse within romantic relationships, these types of behaviours can even become normal or cause an end to the relationship (Borrajo & Gámez-Guadix, 2015). Regardless of the outcome, cyberbullying in a relationship has a major impact on health because it generates anxiety and depression in its victims (Bennett et al., 2011; Borrajo & Gámez-Guadix, 2016; Reed, Tolman, & Safyer, 2015).

Cyberbullying behaviours in higher education students from teacher education programs

Within the program named "The protection of cyberbullying victims: a study of the gender and family variables" (PSI2015–70822-R), as part of the Spanish National Program of Research, Development and Innovation (I + D + i) from the Spanish Ministry of Economy and Competitiveness, a pilot study was conducted with teachers in training (Yubero, Larrañaga, & Navarro, 2017). The purpose of the study was to analyse cyberbullying victimization among university students in education degree programs and to explore the coping strategies they found more useful to confront cyberbullying behaviour. Participants included 154 university students at the Faculty of Education in the University of Castilla-La Mancha; 75.3% were women, all participants ranging from 18 to 36 years old (M(age) = 20.62; SD = 3.03).

Among the instruments used, students were asked to complete the BullyHARM (*Bullying, Harassment, and Aggression Receipt Measure*; Hall, 2016). It consists of 22 items and six subscales: physical bullying, verbal bullying, social/relational bullying, cyberbullying, property bullying, and sexual bullying. In the BullyHARM, a series of specific bullying behaviours are presented to respondents, who then indicate the frequency with which they have experienced each behaviour. A four-point rating scale was selected with the following response options: *not in the past month*, *1 or 2 times in the past month*, *about 1 time a week*, and *about 2 or more times a week*. For this study, the subscales of physical bullying, verbal bullying, social/relational bullying, and cyberbullying were used. In the present sample, the internal consistency coefficient, measured through Cronbach's Alpha, was .86 for the victimization scale and .86 for the perpetration scale.

Finally, students from teacher education programs completed the *Management strategies* questionnaire (Fenaughty & Harré, 2013). Students were asked to evaluate the suitability of different actions to cope with distressing harassment (1 = not at all suitable, 5 = very suitable). These items included support elicited from parents, teachers, and peers, and self-directed actions, including technological and confronting/fighting solutions, and/or ignoring as a strategy.

Thirteen point six percent of the students had suffered cyberbullying during the last month. Three point two percent of the participants reported they had been a cyberbullying perpetrator. The most common type of cyberbullying victimization was "made a mean comment about me on the internet" (8.4%), followed by "sent me a mean email, instant message, or text message" (6.5%), and "posted something bad about me on the internet" (3.9%). Regarding cyberbullying perpetration, 1.9% had "posted something bad about others on the internet," 1.3% had "sent a mean email, instant message, or text message to others," and another 1.3% "made a mean comment about others on the internet."

Regarding the suitability of the coping strategies, students reported that social support was the best strategy (M = 3.89; SD = 1.68), though they ranked in the first place, "talk to a parent about it" (79%), second, "report it to bullying phone" (68.5%), and third, "talk to teacher about it" (68.1%). Self-action strategies reached a mean of 2.68 (SD = 0.85), and 56.4% reported that the victim should tell the bullies to stop the bullying, while 11.2% of the students thought that the victims should use retaliation strategies. The ignoring strategies reached a mean of 2.68 (SD = 0.81), with almost 25% of the participants believing that ignoring was a good strategy to avoid bullying, 12% thinking that victims should stop going to class, and almost 10% believing that the victim should not do anything.

According to this data, it is necessary to improve the training of teachers and raise awareness of future educators in order for them to identify cyberbullying and take action against it in the exercise of their future duties.

Implications for practice

Universities have a responsibility to protect students by providing a safe physical and digital environment. Several studies have pointed out that cyberbullying behaviour that emerged in prior educational levels may continue at university. Additionally, cyberbullying may be a form of aggression between partners or students who are emotionally connected. Resolute action is necessary to prevent such aggression and, instead, promote appropriate interactions with others. Consequently, preventive actions and interventions should be implemented within the university context, involving students, professionals, and academic authorities (Souza, 2011).

Qualitative studies have highlighted students' assertion that the lack of accountability within the university context facilitates cyberbullying, and that university authorities do not respond adequately. Consequently, higher education institutions should develop policies with clear guidelines for students about when and where to report (Jackson, Faucher, & Cassidy, this volume; Langos & Giancaspro, this volume). University personnel who receive these reports should feel confident that the design of the policy allows them to manage incidents effectively (Wozencroft et al., 2015).

Additionally, it is essential that universities extend their abuse protocols to include cyberbullying. These protocols should include specific actions to be taken when cyberbullying is detected in order to prevent its escalation, as well as other procedures to address situations that have already escalated, and to minimize the impact on the victims. This requires a legislative framework that clarifies and facilitates procedures to deal with cyberbullying from the perspective of university regulators and/or inspection services (Yubero et al., 2017).

Protocols should also include therapeutic and social support actions to ensure victim protection. Research has shown that social support may prevent victimization and buffer the effects of victimization, especially support provided by friends, notably in the case of university students. Indeed, the prevention and intervention procedures should work towards strengthening social networks of support among peers. Specifically, in cyberspace, universities should emphasize not only prevention work with strategies to stop cyberbullying, but should also cultivate relationships with those responsible for providing advice and support to victims (Yubero et al., 2017).

In peer-support programs with adequate training, students can help to educate their classmates about responsible use of technology, cyberbullying, and other technology issues. Through dialogue with peers about online risks, they may discuss experiences with cyberbullying as well as strategies to prevent and address it (Kanayama & Kurihara, this volume; Sabella, Patchin, & Hinduja, 2013). Peer helper programs and strategies have been proven successful in traditional bullying (Ttofi & Farrington, 2011). Among the practices implemented in higher education, the *Brief Internet Cyberbullying Prevention Program*, developed with university students in the United States (Doane, 2011), has been effective in decreasing cyberbullying prevalence and dismissing positive attitudes toward such behaviour.

Cyberbullying prevention may be incorporated into the university curriculum as well. It is necessary to better educate students on which behaviours constitute cyberbullying and on the psychological and emotional repercussions. Actions should include lectures and activities that help students discern the psychological indicators of victimization and perpetration. Students are more likely to intervene with each other if they are able to detect when there is a problem and are familiar with the options for resolution (Souza, 2011).

Teachers-in-training need to equip themselves with the skills to manage cyberbullying confidently, competently, and effectively. With regard to their future occupation, the skills to be acquired by the teaching staff should be in line with the demands of society and the changes that have taken place within it. It is therefore important that future teachers know ways to prevent and intervene when cyberbullying emerges. Several studies, however, indicate that the university system is deficient in the preparation of teachers on this subject (Eden, Heiman, & Olenik-Shemesh, 2013; Li, 2008; Yilmaz, 2010). Adequate preparation is still lacking in Spain, as is students' satisfaction with the training received (Álvarez-García et al., 2010; Rodríguez, 2008). For example, Benitez, Berbén, and Fernández (2006) asked 373 Education students about their knowledge in relation to bullying, and more than 30% did not know how to define bullying. Future educators need the knowledge and skills required to implement suitable actions to prevent and curtail bullying and cyberbullying behaviours.

References

Akbulut, Y., & Eristi, B. (2011). Cyberbullying and victimization among Turkish university students. *Australasian Journal of Educational Technology, 27*, 1155–1170.

Alexy, E. M., Burgess, A. W., Baker, T., & Smoyak, S. A. (2005). Perceptions of cyberstalking among college students. *Brief Treatment and Crisis Intervention, 5*, 279–289. doi:10.1093/brief-treatment/mhi020

Álvarez-García, D., Rodríguez, C., González-Castro, P., Núñez, J. C., & Álvarez, L. (2010). The training of pre-service teachers to deal with school violence. *Revista de Psicodidáctica, 15*(1), 35–56.

Aricak, O. T. (2009). Psychiatric symptomatology as a predictor of cyberbullying among university students. *Eurasian Journal of Educational Research, 34*, 167–184.

Baldasare, A., Bauman, S., Goldman, L., & Robie, A. (2012). Cyberbullying? Voices of college students. *Technologies in Higher Education, 5*, 127–155. doi:10.1108/S2044–9968(2012)0000005010

Benítez, J. L., Berbén, A. G., & Fernández, M. (2006). El maltrato entre alumnos: conocimientos, percepciones y actitudes de los futuros docentes. *Revista de Investigación Educativa, 24*(2), 329–352.

Bennett, D. C., Guran, E. L., Ramos, M. C., & Margolin, G. (2011). College students' electronic victimization in friendships and dating relationships: Anticipated distress and associations with risky behaviors. *Violence and Victims, 26*, 410–429. doi:10.1891/0886–6708.26.4.410

Borrajo, E., & Gámez-Guadix, M. (2015). Comportamientos, motivos y reacciones asociadas a la victimización del abuso online en el noviazgo: un análisis cualitativo. *Revista de Victimología, 2*, 73–95.

Borrajo, E., & Gámez-Guadix, M. (2016). Abuso "online" en el noviazgo: relación con depresión, ansiedad y ajuste diádico. *Psicología Conductual, 24*(2), 221–235.

Borrajo, E., Gámez-Guadix, M., & Calvete, E. (2015). Justification beliefs of violence, myths about love and cyber dating abuse. *Psicothema, 27*, 327–333. doi:10.7334/psicothema2015.59

Burke, S. C., Wallen, M., Vail-Smith, K., & Knox, D. (2011). Using technology to control intimate partners: An exploratory study of college undergraduates. *Computers in Human Behavior, 27*, 1162–1167. doi:10.1016/j.chb.2010.12.010

Campbell, M. A. (2005). Cyberbullying: An old problem in a new guise? *Australian Journal of Guidance and Counselling, 15*(01), 68–76. doi:10.1375/ajgc.15.1.68

Caravaca, F., Falcón, M., Navarro-Zaragoza, J., Luna-Ruiz-Cabello, A. L., Rodriges, O., & Luna-Maldonado, A. (2016). Prevalence and patterns of traditional bullying victimization and cyber-teasing among college population in Spain. *BMC Public Health, 16*, 176–185. doi:10.1186/s12889-016-2857-8

Cassidy, W., Faucher, C., & Jackson, M. (this volume). "You need a think skin . . .": Impacts of cyberbullying in Canadian universities. In W. Cassidy, C. Faucher, & M. Jackson (Eds.), *Cyberbullying at university in international contexts* (pp. 112–125). Oxford, UK: Routledge.

Centers for Disease Control and Prevention (CDC). (2014). *Understanding teen dating violence*. Retrieved from www.cdc.gov/violenceprevention/pdf/teen-dating-violence-factsheet-a.pdf

Crosslin, K., & Golman, M. (2014). "Maybe you don't want to face it": College students' perspectives on cyberbullying. *Computers in Human Behavior, 41*, 14–20. doi:10.1016/j.chb.2014.09.007

Dilmac, B. (2009). Psychological needs as a predictor of cyber bullying: A preliminary report on college students. *Educational Sciences: Theory and Practice, 9*, 1307–1325.

Doane, A. N. (2011). *Testing of a brief internet cyberbullying prevention program in college students*. Doctoral Thesis, Old Dominion University.

Durán, M., & Martínez-Pecino, R. (2015). Ciberacoso mediante teléfono móvil e Internet en las relaciones de noviazgo entre jóvenes. *Comunicar, 22*(44), 159–167. doi:10.3916/C44-2015-17

Eden, S., Heimann, T., & Olenik-Shemesh, D. (2013). Teachers' perceptions, beliefs and concerns about cyberbullying. *British Journal of Educational Technology, 44*(6), 1036–1052. doi:10.1111/j.1467-8535.2012.01363.x

Elipe, P., Mora-Merchán, J. A., Ortega-Ruiz, R., & Casas, J. A. (2015). Perceived emotional intelligence as a moderator variable between cybervictimization and its emotional impact. *Frontiers in Psychology, 6*, 486. doi:10.3389/fpsyg.2015.00486

Faucher, C., Jackson, M., & Cassidy, W. (2014). Cyberbullying among university students: Gendered experiences, impacts, and perspectives. *Educational Research International, 2014*, 1–10. doi:10.1155/2014/698545

Fenaughty, J., & Harré, N. (2013). Factors associated with young people's successful resolution of distressing electronic harassment. *Computers & Education, 61*, 242–250. doi:10.1016/j.compedu.2012.08.004

Finn, J. (2004). A survey of online harassment at a university campus. *Journal of Interpersonal Violence, 19*, 468–483. doi:10.1177/0886260503262083

González-Ortega, I., Echeburúa, E., & De Corral, P. (2008). Variables significativas en las relaciones violentas en parejas jóvenes: Una revisión. *Psicologia Conductual, 16*(2), 207–225.

Hall, W. J. (2016). Initial development and validation of the Bullyharm: The bullying, harassment, and aggression receipt measure. *Psychology in the Schools, 53*(9), 984–1000. doi:10.1002/pits.21957

Hemphill, S. A., Kotevski, A., Tollit, M., Smith, R., Herrenkohl, T. I., Toumbourou, J. W., & Catalano, R. F. (2012). Longitudinal predictors of cyber and traditional bullying perpetration in Australian secondary school students. *Journal of Adolescent Health, 51*(1), 59–65. doi:10.1016/j.jadohealth.2011.11.019

Hinduja, S., & Patchin, J. W. (2011). *Electronic dating violence: A brief for educators and parents*. Cyberbullying Research Center. Retrieved from https://cyberbullying.org/electronic_dating_violence_fact_sheet.pdf

Hoff, D. L., & Mitchell, S. N. (2009). Cyberbullying: Causes, effects, and remedies. *Journal of Educational Administration, 47*, 652–665. doi:10.1108/09578230910981107

Jackson, M., Faucher, C., & Cassidy, W. (this volume). What's policy got to do with it? The focus on cyberbullying policy at the university level. In W. Cassidy, C. Faucher, & M. Jackson (Eds.), *Cyberbullying at university in international contexts* (pp. 198–211). Oxford, UK: Routledge.

Jang, H., Song, J., & Kim, R. (2014). Does the offline bully-victimization influence cyberbullying behavior among youths? Application of general strain theory. *Computers in Human Behavior, 31*, 85–93. doi:10.1016/j.chb.2013.10.007

Kanayama, K., & Kurihara, S. (this volume). Preventive measures against cyberbullying at a university in Japan. In W. Cassidy, C. Faucher, & M. Jackson (Eds.), *Cyberbullying at university in international contexts* (pp. 168–172). Oxford, UK: Routledge.

Kellerman, I., Margolin, G., Borofsky, L., Baucom, B., & Iturralde, E. (2013). Electronic aggression among emerging adults: Motivations and contextual factors. *Emerging Adulthood, 1*(4), 293–304. doi:1 0.1177/2167696813490159

König, A., Gollwitzer, M., & Steffgen, G. (2010). Cyberbullying as an act of revenge? *Australian Journal of Guidance & Counselling, 20*(2), 210–224. doi:10.1375/ajgc.20.2.210

Kota, R., Schoohs, S., Benson, M., & Moreno, M. A. (2014). Characterizing cyberbullying among college students: Hacking, dirty laundry, and mocking. *Societies, 4*(4), 549–560. doi:10.3390/soc4040549

Kraft, E., & Wang, J. (2010). An exploratory study of the cyberbullying and cyberstalking experiences and factors related to victimization of students at a public liberal arts college. *International Journal of Technologies, 1*, 74–91. doi:10.4018/jte.2010100106

Langos, C., & Giancaspro, M. (this volume). Cyberbullying in the Australian university context: The shades of harm and implications for law and policy. In W. Cassidy, C. Faucher, & M. Jackson (Eds.), *Cyberbullying at university in international contexts* (pp. 181–197). Oxford, UK: Routledge.

Larrañaga, E., Yubero, S., & Ovejero, A. (2016). Gender variables and cyberbullying in college students. In R. Navarro, S. Yubero, & E. Larrañaga (Eds.), *Cyberbullying across the globe: Gender, family, and mental health* (pp. 63–77). Netherlands: Springer. doi:10.1007/978-3-319-25552-1

Li, Q. (2008). Cyberbullying in schools: An examination of preservice teachers' perception. *Canadian Journal of Learning and Technology, 34*(2). doi:10.21432/T2DK5G

Lindsay, M., & Krysik, J. (2012). Online harassment among college students. *Information, Communication, & Society, 15*, 703–719. doi:10.2139/ssrn.1941065

MacDonald, C. D., & Roberts-Pittman, B. (2010). Cyberbullying among college students: Prevalence and demographic differences. *Procedia: Social and behavioral Sciences, 9*, 2003–2009. doi:10.1016/j.sbspro.2010.12.436

Martínez-Pecino, R., & Durán, M. (2016). I love you but I cyberbully you: The role of hostile sexism. *Journal of Interpersonal Violence*. doi:10.1177/0886260516645817

Mateus, S., Veiga, A. M., Costa, P., & das Dores, M. J. (2015). Cyberbullying: The hidden side of college students. *Computers in Human Behavior, 43*, 167–182. doi:10.1016/j.chb.2014.10.045

Melander, L. A. (2010). College students' perceptions of intimate partner cyber harassment. *Cyberpsychology, Behavior, and Social Networking, 13*, 263–268. doi:10.1089/cpb.2009.0221

Molluzzo, J. C., & Lawler, J. P. (2011). A study of the perceptions of college students on cyberbullying. *Information Systems Education Journal, 10*(4), 84–109.

National Institutes of Health. (2010). *Depression high among youth victims of school cyberbullying: NIH researchers report*. Maryland: National Institute of Child Health and Human Development.

Novick, R. M., & Isaacs, J. (2010). Telling is compelling: The impact of student reports of bullying on teacher intervention. *Educational Psychology, 30*(3), 283–296. doi:10.1080/01443410903573123

Paullet, K., & Pinchot, J. (2014). Behind the screen where today's bully plays: Perceptions of college students on cyberbullying. *Journal of Information Systems Education, 25*(1), 63–69.

Reed, L. A., Tolman, R. M., & Safyer, P. (2015). Too close for comfort: Attachment insecurity and electronic intrusion in college students' dating relationships. *Computers in Human Behavior, 50*, 431–438. doi:10.1016/j.chb.2015.03.050

Rivituso, J. (2014). Cyberbullying victimization among college students: An interpretive phenomenological analysis. *Journal of Information Systems Education, 25*, 71–75.

Rodríguez, J. M. (2008). Los docentes ante las situaciones de violencia escolar. *Revista Electrónica Interuniversitaria de Formación del Profesorado, 11*(3), 32–39.

Sabella, R.A., Patchin, J.W., & Hinduja, S. (2013). Cyberbullying myths and realities. *Computers in Human Behavior, 29*(6), 2703–2711. doi:10.1016/j.chb.2013.06.040

Schenk, A. M., & Fremouw, W. J. (2012). Prevalence, psychological impact, and coping of cyberbully victims among college students. *Journal of School Violence, 11*(1), 21–37. doi:10.1080/15388220.2011.630310

Schenk, A. M., Fremouw, W. J., & Keelan, C. M. (2013). Characteristics of college cyberbullies. *Computers in Human Behavior, 29*, 2320–2327. doi:10.1016/j.chb.2013.05.013

Selkie, E. M., Kota, R., Chan, Y., & Moreno, M. (2015). Cyberbullying, depression and problem alcohol use in female college students: A multisite study. *Cyberpsychology, Behavior, and Social Networking, 18*(2), 79–86. doi:10.1089/cyber.2014.0371

Smith, J. A., & Yoon, J. (2013). Cyberbullying presence, extent, & forms in a midwestern post-secondary institution. *Information Systems Educational Journal, 11*, 52–78.

Smith, P., Mahdavi, J., Carvalho, M., Fisher, S., Russell, S., & Tippett, N. (2008). Cyberbullying: Its nature and impact in secondary school pupils. *The Journal of Child Psychology and Psychiatry, 49*, 376–385. doi:10.1111/j.1469–7610.2007.01846.x

Sontag, L., Clemans, K., Graber, J., & Lyndon, S. (2011). Traditional and cyber aggressors and victims: A comparison of psychosocial characteristics. *Journal Youth Adolescence, 40*, 392–404. doi:10.1007/s10964-010-9575-9

Souza, S. B. (2011). *Exploratory study about the perspectives of young Portuguese university students regarding the phenomenon and coping strategies*. Master's Thesis, Faculty of Psychology. Lisbon: University of Lisbon.

Tokunaga, R. S. (2010). Following you home from school: A critical review and synthesis of research on cyberbullying victimization. *Computers in Human Behavior, 26*, 277–287. doi:10.1016/j.chb.2009.11.014

Tomsa, R., Jenaro, C., Campbell, M., & Neacsu, D. (2013). Student's experiences with traditional bullying and cyberbullying: Findings from a Romanian sample. *Procedia. Social and Behavioral Sciences, 78*, 586–590. doi:10.1016/j.sbspro.2013.04.356

Ttofi, M. M., & Farrington, D. P. (2011). Effectiveness of school-based programs to reduce bullying: A systematic and meta-analytic review. *Journal of Experimental Criminology*, 7(1), 27–56. doi:10.1007/s11292-010-9109-1

Turan, N., Polat, O., Karapirli, M., Uysal, C., & Turan, S. G. (2011). The new violence type of the era: Cyber bullying among university students: Violence among university students. *Neurology Psychiatry & Brain Research, 17*, 21–26. doi:10.1016/j.npbr.2011.02.005

Van Ouytsel, J., Van Gool, E., Walrave, M., Ponnet, K., & Peeters, E. (2016). Exploring the role of social networking sites within adolescent romantic relationships and dating experiences. *Computers in Human Behavior, 55*, 76–86. doi:10.1016/j.chb.2015.08.042

Wekerle, C. (1999). Dating violence in mid-adolescence theory, significance, and emerging prevention initiatives. *Clinical Psychology Review, 19*(4), 435–456. doi:10.1016/S0272–7358(98)00091–9

Willard, N. (2006). Cyberbullying and cyberthreats: Effectively managing Internet use risks in schools. Retrieved from http://new.csriu.org/cyberbully/docs/cbctpresentation.pdf

Wozencroft, K., Campbell, M., Orel, A., Kimpton, M., & Leong, E. (2015). University students' intentions to report cyberbullying. *Australian Journal of Educational & Development Psychology, 15*, 1–12.

Ybarra, M. L., & Mitchell, K. J. (2004). Online aggressor/targets, aggressors, and targets: A comparison of associated youth characteristics. *Journal of Child Psychology and Psychiatry, 45*(7), 1308–1316. doi:10.1111/j.1469-7610.2004.00328.x

Yilmaz, H. (2010). An examination of preservice teachers' perception about cyberbullying. *Eurasia Journal of Mathematics, Science & Technology Education, 6*(4), 263–270. doi:10.12973/ejmste/75248

Yubero, S., Larrañaga, E., & Navarro, R. (2017). La continuidad del conflicto en la convivencia escolar: medidas de prevención e intervención del acoso. *Revista de Paz y Conflictos, 10*(2), 89–116.

Yubero, S., Navarro, R., Elche, M., Larrañaga, E., & Ovejero, A. (2017). Cyberbullying victimization in higher education: An exploratory analysis of its association with social and emotional factors among Spanish students. *Computers in Human Behavior, 75*, 439–449. doi:10.1016/j.chb.2017.05.037

Zacchilli, T. L., & Valerio, C.V. (2011). The knowledge and prevalence of cyberbullying in a college simple. *Journal of Scientific Psychology*. Retrieved from www.psyencelab.com/images/The_Knowledge_and_Prevalence_of_Cyberbullying_in_a_College_Sample.pdf

Zalaquett, C. P., & Chatters, S. J. (2014). Cyberbullying in college: Frequency, characteristic, and practical implications. *Sage Open, 4*(1), 1–8. doi:10.1177/2158244014526721

Zweig, J. M., Dank, M., Yahner, J., & Lachman, P. (2013). The rate of cyber dating abuse among teens and how it relates to other forms of teen dating violence. *Journal of Youth and Adolescence, 42*(7), 1063–1077. doi:10.1007/s10964-013-9922-8

8

"YOU NEED A THICK SKIN . . ."

Impacts of cyberbullying at Canadian universities

Wanda Cassidy, Chantal Faucher, and Margaret Jackson

Introduction

The impacts on children and youth who have been the targets of cyberbullying is well documented in the literature. Numerous studies report such impacts as depression, anxiety, low self-esteem, psychosomatic problems including headaches and sleep disruptions, decreased academic achievement, strained interpersonal relationships, withdrawal behaviour, and suicide ideation (Beebe & Robey, 2011; Cassidy, Faucher, & Jackson, 2013; Cassidy, Jackson, & Brown, 2009; Jackson, Cassidy, & Brown, 2009; Kowalski, Limber, & Agatston, 2012; Marczak & Coyne, 2010; Menesini & Nocentini, 2012; Nocentini et al., 2010; Patchin & Hinduja, 2012; Smith, 2012; Sourander et al., 2010; Tokunaga, 2010; von Marées & Petermann, 2012).

One might assume that only youth in their formative years experience negative impacts as a result of being cyberbullied, yet it is apparent from studies with adults in the workplace and at university that the after-effects of being cyberbullied when older are similar. Although fewer studies have been conducted at the post-secondary level compared to K–12, university students report very similar impacts: relationship issues, physical and mental health problems, reduced self-esteem, concentration and academic challenges, decreased motivation, self-blame and even suicide ideation (Arıcak, 2016; Beran, Rinaldi, Bickham, & Rich, 2012; Cowie & Myers, 2016; Cowie et al., 2013; Faucher, Jackson, & Cassidy, 2014; Giovazolias & Malikiosi-Loizos, 2016; Kokkinos, Antoniadou, & Markos, 2014; Larrañaga et al., this volume; Rivers, 2016). University faculty members also report emotional distress, decreased productivity and job satisfaction, absenteeism, avoidance of the bully, and withdrawal behaviour (Blizard, 2016, this volume; Cassidy, Faucher, & Jackson, 2014; Hollis, 2012; Taylor, 2012; Vaughan, 2012). Like children and adolescents in school (Cassidy et al., 2009), university students and faculty members tend to feel powerless to stop the bullying behaviour, further compounding the negative effects (Lampman, 2012; McKay, Arnold, Fratzl, & Thomas, 2008; Minor, Smith, & Brashen, 2013; Taylor, 2012).

The workplace is also a site for bullying behaviour online and in person, with similar consequences reported by those on the receiving end, as well as by those who witness the behaviour: increased stress, lower job satisfaction, absenteeism, reduced productivity, disengagement, mental and physical health impacts, greater job turnover, and suicide ideation (Coyne & Farley, this volume; Duffy & Sperry, 2014; Keashly, this volume; Lutgen-Sandvik & Tracy, 2012; Sallee & Diaz, 2012).

This chapter adds to the growing body of research examining the impacts students and faculty members experience as a result of being cyberbullied at the post-secondary level, including the impact on the wider university culture.

The study and method

This chapter focuses on the self-reported impacts of student-to-student, student-to-faculty, and faculty-to-faculty cyberbullying at four universities in Canada. Students (n = 1925) completed an anonymous online survey with 100 closed and open-ended questions, examining their information and communication technology (ICT) usage patterns, their experiences with online bullying behaviours, and their opinions and proposed solutions. Ten audio-taped focus groups with students were also held at the participating universities, primarily addressing solutions. Faculty members (n = 331) completed a similar online survey with 111 closed and open-ended questions, with 14 also volunteering to participate in a one-on-one anonymous audio-taped interview. Twenty-one university administrators were also interviewed as to their experiences with cyberbullying, reporting issues and policies, adding insight to the researchers' earlier policy scan involving 74 Canadian universities.

Results from the wider study are reported elsewhere (Cassidy et al., 2014; Cassidy, Faucher, & Jackson, 2017; Cassidy, Jackson, & Faucher, 2015; Faucher et al., 2014; Faucher, Cassidy, & Jackson, 2015; Faucher, Jackson, & Cassidy, 2015; Chapters 5 and 16, this volume), while this chapter focuses on the questions in the surveys specifically related to impact: closed dichotomous yes/no questions; open-ended questions where participants were asked to provide an example of when they were cyberbullied, how it made them feel, what they tried to do to stop it, and what happened; and the narratives and insights faculty members shared in their interviews.

Survey, focus group, and interview participants were provided at the outset with a definition of cyberbullying, along with examples, to avoid misinterpretation of the concept. The definition is similar to the one outlined in the Introduction to this volume. Following the prompt, "If you were a victim of cyberbullying

TABLE 8.1 Cyberbullying Impacts as Reported by Victims

IMPACT	*% Student to Student CB*	*% Student to Faculty CB*	*% Faculty to Faculty CB*
Ability to do work	41	64	73
Wanted to quit	14	30	49
Relationships at University	27	62	49
Relationships outside University	41	19	39
Mental health	42	30	39
Physical health	26	28	29
Feeling unsafe	39	34	46

in the last 12 months," respondents were asked whether they had experienced effects related to emotional security and physical safety, ability to do work, desire to remain at the university, personal relationships inside and outside the university, physical and mental health issues, suicidal ideation, and feelings of revenge.

Students' and faculty members' survey responses to closed, dichotomous questions were analysed using SPSS and Excel. Open-ended responses and transcribed interviews were coded using NVivo software as well as hand-coded independently and collaboratively by three researchers (the authors), using a grounded theory process (Merriam & Tisdale, 2016) in order to determine the major themes and sub-themes based on the frequency and/or strength of the response (Miles & Huberman, 1994). Since the major themes related to impacts identified in the qualitative analysis supported the primary impacts identified in the quantitative analysis of the closed questions (see Table 8.1), this chapter discusses the impacts using the Table 8.1 categories. The quotations selected as exemplars from the open-ended responses and interviews are representative of the responses given by participants for each of the seven identified impact categories.

Extent, venues, and rationale

Analysis of respondents' answers to the survey questions revealed that 24% of students said that they had been cyberbullied in the last 12 months, 12% by a friend or acquaintance at the university, 14% by a stranger, and 2% by a faculty member, with 5% admitting to cyberbullying others at university. Twenty-five percent of participating faculty members ranging from instructors just beginning their career to senior tenured professors, and from departments across the universities, had experienced cyberbullying in the past 12 months, 15% by students and 12% by colleagues.

Although the percentages of cyberbullying towards students and faculty represent only a small proportion of cases relative to the entire population of the four universities, these percentages fall within the mid-range of frequencies identified in other studies (see Faucher et al., 2014, Table 1, p. 3). One does not know if a larger sample of respondents in our Canadian study would have yielded a similar percentage of victims.

Students who cyberbullied each other primarily used social networking sites, text messaging, email, and non-course-related sites, while they targeted faculty mainly through email, professor-rating sites, and course sites. Faculty members who were cyberbullied by colleagues received their messages overwhelmingly from email, so the perpetrators were known to them. Students who experienced cyberbullying said it was for interpersonal reasons, because of their physical appearance, gender (females), or ethnicity (males), while perpetrators said it was because the target upset them, that person bullied them first, or because "it was fun."

Faculty members were cyberbullied by students and colleagues primarily for work-related reasons: because of their position at the university or their teaching, with female faculty members noting that their gender also played a role. Students said that they targeted faculty members because the instructor had upset them, they did not like their teaching style or them as people, and because they sought to tarnish their reputation. Students' messages were perceived by faculty members as insulting, demanding, and demeaning, and included spreading rumours and harassment. Negative messages from colleagues were described in similar ways, while also adding attempts to exclude, threaten, and/or humiliate.

Findings: impact – dichotomous survey responses

The percentages of students and faculty reporting particular impacts are recorded in Table 8.1. This table lists the most frequent impacts participants selected from a list of 11 options in the dichotomous yes/no questions.

The impact that was selected the most often by students and faculty combined was the ability to do one's work at the university. Being cyberbullied by colleagues affected faculty members' ability to work (73%) even more so than being bullied by students (64%). Almost half (49%) of the faculty members who had been cyberbullied by colleagues wanted to quit, with the same proportion saying that it impacted their relationships at the university. Thirty percent said that they felt like quitting after being cyberbullied by students, and while faculty said that their relationships at university were more affected by students cyberbullying them (62%) than colleagues (49%), their open-ended and interview responses indicated that being bullied by colleagues had a longer-term impact since difficult students left after a semester, while colleagues remained.

Students reported that cyberbullying affected their relationships outside the university (41%) more so than inside (27%), and that their mental health was more at risk (42%) than their physical health (26%). Approximately one-third of students who reported being cyberbullied by other students said that it made them feel unsafe (39%), with a similar percentage reported by faculty (34%) who had been cyberbullied by students, and a much higher percentage reported by faculty who were cyberbullied by colleagues (46%).

Although Table 8.1 does not list the percentages of respondents who indicated suicide ideation, because this was a less frequent response, 14% of students selected this response, very worrisome for any institution concerned about the health and well-being of their students. Only two faculty members selected this response – not a large number, but two too many, and a wake-up call for university administrators and health providers.

Findings – open-ended and interview responses

Overarching finding of negative affect

One overarching finding from the open-ended responses and the interviews was the depth and extent of the negative affect students and faculty members said that they had experienced (or were still experiencing) as a result of being cyberbullied. This negative affect is woven throughout all other impacts identified in Table 8.1.

Participants frequently used words and phrases such as *feeling wounded, sad, hurt, angry, humiliated, betrayed, crushed, choked, embarrassed, scared, alone, shaking, crying, being emotionally raw*, and *vulnerable*. One faculty member broke down and cried during her interview, remembering her experiences of being victimized by a colleague over a two-year period. Many of the respondents, particularly faculty in their interviews, also used violence-based terminology to express the depth of the anger, hurt, and frustration at the aggression they had experienced; words like *poison, attack, enraging, hate, roaring, shouting, horrific, vindictive, backstabbing*, and *disaster* (Cassidy et al., 2017). Some said that the experience made them want to retaliate or take revenge, since they felt like they were in a "battleground," "combat" zone, or "cyber war." Others went inward, blaming themselves and describing how the experience had shaken their self-confidence, self-esteem, and self-efficacy.

Students identified their appearance as one reason for being attacked, as noted in this open-ended comment: "during Minecraft someone lashed out at me and made fun of my appearance. . . . As an adult I was shocked that it would affect me so much! I was seriously embarrassed and depressed as he had somehow hit the right buttons." Relationships were also a focus, with the bullying designed to disrupt a relationship, challenge the target's reputation, or discredit a friend: "they ['friends'] were spreading rumours about me [on Facebook] that [I] had a sex relationship with many guys, they started sending vulgar messages, updating statuses about me. . . . I felt helpless, emotionally distraut (sic), I cried almost every day, my worst life experience till now."

While some female faculty members discussed the upset they felt for being judged for their "Hotness" on the Rate My Professor website, most comments they received related to their teaching ability or the grade they gave a student.

This comment was typical: "Email, text messages making comments that I was incompetent, not accessible, too slow, workload too difficult and the words used were 'useless', 'lousy,' and 'I am reporting you'. Student was not open to feedback. I felt attacked, humiliated." This form of cyberbullying behaviour fits with the literature on student entitlement (Boswell, 2012; Greenberger, Lessard, Chen, & Farruggia, 2008) and incivility (Chowning & Campbell, 2009; Clark, Werth, & Ahten, 2012; Kopp & Finney, 2013; Wildermuth & Davis, 2012), where students believe that they are entitled to certain grades and to be treated in certain ways by their professors, despite their own behaviour.

Faculty members also discussed being humiliated by colleagues, as noted in this open-ended response:

> [A colleague] gave the wrong time and date for a meeting . . . all other faculty had different communication. SKYPE arranged many times, but month after month, the connection would be "lost" on the colleague's side, their cell phone turned off, the laptop closed, making it impossible to reconnect. Then emails and text messages sent that I was not performing my duties and would be reported for my lack of professional accountability. . . . Humiliating is not a strong enough word.

One faculty member who had been cyberbullied by a colleague for two years, with little done by her superiors to remedy the situation, talked at length in her interview of the devastating emotional toll it took on her. After a culminating event where she felt "kicked in the stomach," and "cried on my direct boss's desk," she went home: "I felt . . . really shaky in myself, really raw, shaky, everything being magnified. . . . I was irritable, I was super sensitive and defensive . . . the world was this strange place."

Ability to do work

Both students and faculty talked about the effect being cyberbullied had on their ability to do work; for example, "She [a "friend"] spammed my emails and FB with hateful messages of my body and sexuality. She called me things like 'whore' or 'slut' and made rumors of me. . . . After my grades went down [I had been an A/B student] because of stress I was put on academic probation." Another student talked about being "disregarded" and "put down" in group emails, which made the student "angry and upset" and feeling "ganged up on and very distracted from school and my social life." A few students also chose to give examples of the demeaning comments made online by a teacher, for example:

> I asked my professor a question [in a course chat] and she belittled me with her response. She essentially told me that I was asking her a stupid

> question . . . like I was wasting her time. I felt invalidated. I was afraid to ask her questions after that. I started skipping classes.

After reading negative comments on the Rate My Professor website, which one professor labelled as "defamation of character," she did not "really feel good about going to that class knowing that someone was hating [her]. . . . It was pretty depressing and unmotivating." Being cyberbullied by colleagues was discussed more often and in greater detail than by students, and with greater impact on their ability to do their work.

> [T]he immediacy of it [cyberbullying incident] has . . . a real . . . emotional dimension which occupies a lot of my time. I think about it all day long . . . or many days on end, like what could I do or how could I respond. . . . So the first impact is that emotional gut – like, oh shit, this is happening, what am I gonna do? I think that this is gonna not turn out well. And the second impact . . . is depending on what kind of a decision I've made, so if I'm going to engage and defend myself or defend the position, um, you have to kind of psych yourself up for that. . . . Yeah, the next wave to come and hit you . . . it's gonna come again and every time you turn on the computer . . . the anxiety of that builds. And if I've decided to disengage then there's the guilt of that. . . . I let the bully win and it also makes me withdraw . . . from my professional position as a member of the community.

Wanting to quit

While some faculty members expressed concern about losing their job "[since] I think I have no power to intervene or do something," others wanted to withdraw from their responsibilities, particularly when they were targeted by colleagues: "I was always on edge . . . like walking on egg shells. . . . I'm quite an open verbal person. I had to actually . . . physically force myself not to be involved in staff meetings because I didn't want to be put down again."

One of the 14 faculty members being interviewed actually did quit her job and moved to a different institution.

> I mean, they [the university department] just kept having people leaving and leaving and leaving but there was no a-ha moment, maybe it has to do . . . [with the situation]. . . . I heard via the grapevine that they were really angry with me after because I left in the middle of the year . . . but I couldn't stand it anymore so I quit . . . and to my knowledge it stayed exactly the same. I've heard via the grapevine that nothing's changed. . . . I mean it just has such a detrimental effect . . . you know on a person's life, on a person's home life, on their job satisfaction, I mean the reason that I didn't leave long

> before I did is I actually enjoyed what I was doing. . . . I love my students, I love the program, I enjoyed teaching the courses that I did teach.

Impact on relationships inside and outside the university

Both students and faculty members said that being cyberbullied impacted their relationships at the university and with friends and partners away from campus. Faculty members talked about cyberbullying impacting their reputation; here are two examples:

> I was (I believe) deliberately excluded by a senior colleague from a series of exchanges related to a project a group of about 15 colleagues were working on. When I stopped showing up to meetings (I wasn't aware had been scheduled), a fellow pre-tenure colleague asked if I wasn't getting the email messages. I said I wasn't. When the coordinating (full prof bully) was asked about it, she apologized and said she thought I was no longer interested. . . . I had never said so, but I had been critical of a decision taken by the full prof bully in prior exchanges . . . my colleagues, at least some, must have believed I was unprofessional if not unresponsive.

A few faculty members also talked about becoming less vulnerable with students – "more strict about rules with students and more standoffish in general" – as a way to protect themselves from negative comments from students. While only a few faculty members discussed the impact cyberbullying at university had on their friendships and partners, one discussed at length the impact on her marriage, concluding with: "I was in a horrible mood and state all the time."

Students mainly talked about how cyberbullying impacted their friendships, as indicated by this example: "A student at another university sent me really rude, hurtful messages. I felt really bad about myself and it really has ruined not just that friendship but almost all my friendships. To stop it I just removed myself from that group of friends."

Mental and physical health impacts

Both students and faculty members talked about the impacts on their health, listing symptoms like depression, anxiety, panic attacks, stomach upset, and sleeplessness. In one faculty interview, the participant discussed having to take "sleeping medication . . . when I couldn't sleep in the middle of the night . . . [a colleague's] angry behaviours towards me . . . yeah, your stomach would go into knots . . . you know the physical signs of stress."

Some students said that they received messages saying that they should kill themselves, with some admitting that the messages "DID make me feel suicidal, depressed, like it was ruining my friendships inside and outside of school."

Feeling unsafe emotionally and physically

Some messages were threatening or so worrisome that the recipients felt unsafe. One student reported: "Over Facebook I was sent a personal message from a bully. Disclosed within this message was a death threat. They threatened that if I didn't stop coming to school and being who I was that they were going to kill me. It was the scariest time of my entire life."

A faculty member reported threatening comments made by a student during a live online tutorial: "I temporarily banned the student in the E-Live classroom, which led to further threats. I was actually frightened that this student would show up at my place of work and physically threaten me." Another faculty member said:

> Over the past week a male student from a seminar class has sent me several demanding, angry and belittling emails. . . . I feel strongly that such behaviour would not occur were I older, and/or male . . . it certainly made me feel unsafe working in the evening in my office when no other faculty members are around.

Faculty also talked about being worried that the office staff in their department may also be a target, if the student, who had been spewing out angry messages, arrived at the office seeking to find the faculty member.

Reporting

Compounding the impacts that students and faculty were experiencing was the fact that those who tried to stop the cyberbullying, whether by themselves or with the help of their superiors, were generally unsuccessful. Approximately two-thirds of faculty members said they tried to address the problem, but less than half said that it worked. Students were less likely than faculty to report their situation to a university authority or counsellor, and more likely to tell a friend. Those who chose not to report the behaviour said that they remained silent out of fear of reprisals, because they believed that nothing would change, and/or because they would be perceived as weak and this would negatively affect their reputation.

Theoretical frameworks

In other publications (Cassidy et al., 2014, 2017; Faucher, Jackson et al., 2014, 2015) we discuss in greater length the theoretical frameworks we use to help understand the dynamics of cyberbullying at the university. Earlier in this chapter, we briefly referred to the student entitlement and student incivility literature. Another literature that is helpful in understanding cyberbullying is contrapower harassment, where students, who normally have less power than their teachers, seek to wield power through student evaluations and assessments, and other course sites, aimed at damaging a professor's reputation or ability to obtain tenure or promotion (Bjorklund & Rehling, 2011; Blizard, 2016, this volume; DeSouza, 2011; McKay et al., 2008).

We also draw on the relational aggression literature (Crick & Nelson, 2002; Jackson et al., 2009), particularly when examining the jockeying of power within female so-called friendship groups. Of particular import is the power and control model (Pence & Paymar, 1993), adapted from the domestic violence literature, where one party seeks to exert power over another through intimidation, isolation, emotional abuse, blaming, and/or privilege. We see evidence of these dynamics being played out in the findings we have discussed in this chapter.

Impact on university culture as a whole

What should also be considered when seeking to understand and curtail cyberbullying at post-secondary is that cyberbullying not only affects individuals and bystanders, but it also has a negative impact on the wider culture of the university. Although only a small proportion of students and faculty at the four universities studied completed the surveys, approximately one-quarter of those who did respond reported being cyberbullied in the last 12 months. More importantly, each target reported negative impacts, which affected their health and well-being, their relationships, their ability to work effectively, and even their safety. As one faculty member noted in her interview, if someone requires a medical leave due to cyberbullying, "it's gonna cost [the university] a lot more money doing that than it is to help keep me healthy in the first place."

Others talked about how tension, stress, and dysfunction spreads and can affect a whole department:

> the culture of the community is not respectful and so people then just disengage. I think that's what happens in the university more often than not. People aren't held accountable for the behaviours so other people just disengage and then issues never get resolved.

Solutions and action points

The solutions the participants recommended in the surveys stressed developing a kinder university culture, better reporting measures, stronger anti-cyberbullying policies that are understood and communicated, more support for victims, as well as increased opportunities for dialogue, awareness, and education. The recommendations made by the 10 student focus groups related to solutions are too extensive to report here (separate paper in progress), other than to mention that students highlighted the importance of modelling, dialogue, engaging bystanders, being proactive in building relationships, fostering a caring community, and "having a collective conscience." Punishment was not widely advocated, as it was deemed ineffective. Both students and faculty seemed attuned to the fact that the wider campus culture can either facilitate positive behaviours, or the opposite can be fostered, especially if the environment is strongly hierarchical or competitive and/ or if negative behaviour is modelled or practised at senior levels (see Crookston, 2012; Driver, this volume).

In their interviews, faculty members stressed that denial of the problem is not a solution; rather, it is important to create spaces where the university community can come together and discuss cyberbullying and its impacts, because "then you create that opportunity for other people to come forward . . . to know that they're not alone." If no one talks about it, "that becomes the power of silence," and nothing is done. While one faculty member said in the aftermath of being cyberbullied, "**you need a thick skin**," others sought to re-direct their attention to appreciative students and supportive colleagues, while others said that they are using their anger to conduct research into bullying with an aim to change the system. Attention was also placed on the university's responsibility to raise important and difficult issues facing society: "I believe that universities are designed to serve communities, not the other way around, and that we really have an obligation to use our privilege to advance social dialogue and to lead those tough conversations in our society."

None of the participants regarded the solutions as easy – a quick fix is unrealistic. What is needed, rather, is a willingness and intentionality to address the problem; collaboration with all stakeholder groups; dialogue, education, and awareness; self-reflection and modelling at all levels; using research to inform policy and practice; and taking action wherever possible.

References

Arıcak, O. T. (2016). The relationship between mental health and bullying. In H. Cowie & C.-A. Myers (Eds.), *Bullying among university students: Cross-national perspectives* (pp. 76–90). London: Routledge.

Beebe, J. E., & Robey, P. A. (2011). The prevalence and psychological impact of bullying on adolescents: An application of choice theory and reality therapy. *International Journal of Choice Theory & Reality Therapy, 30*(2), 33–44.

Beran, T. N., Rinaldi, C., Bickham, D. S., & Rich, M. (2012). Evidence for the need to support adolescents dealing with harassment and cyber-harassment: Prevalence, progression, and impact. *School Psychology International, 33*(5), 562–576.

Bjorklund, W. L., & Rehling, D. L. (2011). Incivility beyond the classroom. *InSight: A Journal of Scholarly Teaching, 6*, 28–36.

Blizard, L. M. (2016). Faculty members' experiences of cyberbullying by students at one Canadian university: Impact and recommendations. *International Research in Higher Education, 1*(1), 107–124.

Blizard, L. (this volume). Student-to-faculty targeted cyberbullying: The impact on faculty. In W. Cassidy, C. Faucher, & M. Jackson (Eds.), *Cyberbullying at university in international contexts* (pp. 126–138). Oxford, UK: Routledge.

Boswell, S. S. (2012). "I *deserve* success": Academic entitlement attitudes and their relationships with course self-efficacy, social networking, and demographic variables. *Social Psychology of Education, 15*, 353–365.

Cassidy, W., Faucher, C., & Jackson, M. (2013). Cyberbullying among youth: A comprehensive review of current international research and its implications and application to policy and practice. *School Psychology International, 34*(6), 575–612.

Cassidy, W., Faucher, C., & Jackson, M. (2014). The dark side of the ivory tower: Cyberbullying of university faculty and teaching personnel. *Alberta Journal of Educational Research, 60*(2), 279–299.

Cassidy, W., Faucher, C., & Jackson, M. (2017). Adversity in university: Cyberbullying and its impacts on students, faculty and administrators. *International Journal of Environmental Research and Public Health, 14*, 888–906.

Cassidy, W., Faucher, C., & Jackson, M. (this volume). Introduction: Context, framework, and perspective. In W. Cassidy, C. Faucher, & M. Jackson (Eds.), *Cyberbullying at university in international contexts* (pp. 1–6). Oxford, UK: Routledge.

Cassidy, W., Jackson, M., & Faucher, C. (2015). Gender differences and cyberbullying towards faculty members in higher education. In R. Navarro, S. Yubero, & E. Larrañaga (Eds.), *Cyberbullying across the globe: Gender, family, and mental health* (pp. 79–98). Basel, Switzerland: Springer.

Cassidy, W., Jackson, M., & Brown, K. (2009). Sticks and stones can break my bones, but how can pixels hurt me? Students' experiences with cyber-bullying. *School Psychology International, 30*(4), 383–402.

Chowning, K., & Campbell, N. J. (2009). Development and validation of a measure of academic entitlement: Individual differences in students' externalized responsibility and entitled expectations. *Journal of Educational Psychology, 101*(4), 982–997.

Clark, C. M., Werth, L., & Ahten, S. (2012). Cyber-bullying and incivility in the online learning environment, Part 1: Addressing faculty and student perceptions. *Nurse Educator, 37(4)*, 150–156.

Coyne, I., & Farley, S. (this volume). Cyberbullying within working contexts. In W. Cassidy, C. Faucher, & M. Jackson (Eds.), *Cyberbullying at university in international contexts* (pp. 80–96). Oxford, UK: Routledge.

Cowie, H., Bauman, S., Coyne, I., Myers, C.-A., Pörhölä, M., & Almeida, A. (2013). Cyberbullying amongst university students: An emergent cause for concern? In P. K. Smith & G. Steffgen (Eds.), *Cyberbullying through the new media: Findings from an international network* (pp. 165–177). London: Psychology Press.

Cowie, H., & Myers, C.-A. (2016). What we know to date about bullying and cyberbullying among university students. In H. Cowie & C.-A. Myers (Eds.), *Bullying among university students: Cross-national perspectives* (pp. 3–14). London: Routledge.

Crick, N. R., & Nelson, D. A. (2002). Relational and physical victimization within friendships: Nobody told me there'd be friends like these. *Journal of Abnormal Child Psychology, 30*(6), 599–607.

Crookston, R. K. (2012). *Working with problem faculty: A 6-step guide for department chairs.* San Francisco, CA: Jossey-Bass.

DeSouza, E. R. (2011). Frequency rates and correlates of contrapower harassment in higher education. *Journal of Interpersonal Violence, 26*(1), 158–188.

Driver, J. (this volume). Faculty members who are bullies. In W. Cassidy, C. Faucher, & M. Jackson (Eds.), *Cyberbullying at university in international contexts* (pp. 212–214). Oxford, UK: Routledge.

Duffy, M., & Sperry, L. (2014). *Overcoming mobbing: A recovery guide for workplace aggression and bullying*. New York: Oxford University Press.

Faucher, C., Cassidy, W., & Jackson, M. (2015). From the sandbox to the inbox: Comparing the acts, impacts, and solutions of bullying in K-12, higher education, and the workplace. *Journal of Education and Training Studies*, *3*(6), 111–125.

Faucher, C., Cassidy, W., & Jackson, M. (this volume). Power in the tower: The gendered nature of cyberbullying among students and faculty at Canadian universities. In W. Cassidy, C. Faucher, & M. Jackson (Eds.), *Cyberbullying at university in international contexts* (pp. 66–79). Oxford, UK: Routledge.

Faucher, C., Jackson, M., & Cassidy, W. (2014). Cyberbullying among university students: Gendered experiences, impacts, and perspectives. *Education Research International*, *2014*, 1–10.

Faucher, C., Jackson, M., & Cassidy, W. (2015). When on-line exchanges byte: An examination of the policy environment governing cyberbullying at the university level. *Canadian Journal of Higher Education*, *45*(1), 102–121.

Giovazolias, T., & Malikiosi-Loizos, M. (2016). Bullying at Greek universities: An empirical study. In H. Cowie & C.-A. Myers (Eds.), *Bullying among university students: Cross-national perspectives* (pp. 110–126). London: Routledge.

Greenberger, E., Lessard, J., Chen, C., & Farruggia, S. P. (2008). Self-entitled college students: Contributions of personality, parenting, and motivational factors. *Journal of Youth and Adolescence*, *37*, 1193–1204.

Hollis, L. P. (2012). *Bully in the ivory tower: How aggression and incivility erode American higher education*. Wilmington, DE: Patricia Berkly LCC.

Jackson, M., Cassidy, W., & Brown, K. (2009). "you were born ugly and youl die ugly too": Cyber-bullying as relational aggression. *In Education: Special Issue on Technology and Social Media, Part 1*, *15*(2), 68–82.

Jackson, M., Faucher, C., & Cassidy, W. (this volume). What's policy got to do with it? The focus on cyberbullying policy at the university level. In W. Cassidy, C. Faucher, & M. Jackson (Eds.), *Cyberbullying at university in international contexts* (pp. 198–211). Oxford, UK: Routledge.

Keashly, L. (this volume). In the e-presence of others: Understanding and developing constructive cyber-bystander action. In W. Cassidy, C. Faucher, & M. Jackson (Eds.), *Cyberbullying at university in international contexts* (pp. 141–156). Oxford, UK: Routledge.

Kokkinos, C. M., Antoniadou, N., & Markos, A. (2014). Cyber-bullying: An investigation of the psychological profile of university student participants. *Journal of Applied Developmental Psychology*, *35*, 204–214.

Kopp, J. P., & Finney, S. J. (2013). Linking academic entitlement and student incivility using latent means modeling. *Journal of Experimental Education*, *81*(3), 322–336.

Kowalski, R. M., Limber, S. P., & Agatston, P. W. (2012). *Cyberbullying: Bullying in the digital age* (2nd ed.). Malden, MA: Wiley-Blackwell.

Lampman, C. (2012). Women faculty at risk: U.S. professors report on their experiences with student incivility, bullying, aggression, and sexual attention. *NASPA Journal About Women in Higher Education*, *5*(2), 184–208.

Larrañaga, E., Yubero, S., Navarro, R., & Ovejero, A. (this volume). From traditional bullying to cyberbullying: Cybervictimization among higher education students. In W. Cassidy, C. Faucher, & M. Jackson (Eds.), *Cyberbullying at university in international contexts* (pp. 99–111). Oxford, UK: Routledge.

Lutgen-Sandvik, P., & Tracy, S. J. (2012). Answering five key questions about workplace bullying: How communication scholarship provides thought leadership for transforming abuse at work. *Management Communication Quarterly*, *26*, 3–47.

Marczak, M., & Coyne, I. (2010). Cyberbullying at school: Good practice and legal aspects in the United Kingdom. *Australian Journal of Guidance and Counselling, 20*, 182–193.

McKay, R., Arnold, D. H., Fratzl, J., & Thomas, R. (2008). Workplace bullying in academia: A Canadian study. *Employee Responsibility and Rights Journal, 20*, 77–100.

Menesini, E., & Nocentini, A. (2012). Peer education intervention: Face-to-face versus online. In A. Costabile & B. A. Spears (Eds.), *The impact of technology on relationships in educational settings* (pp. 139–150). New York, NY: Routledge.

Merriam, S. B., & Tisdale, E. J. (2016). *Qualitative research: A guide to design and implementation* (4th ed.). San Franscisco, CA: Jossey-Bass.

Miles, B., & Huberman, A. (1994). *Qualitative data analysis*. Thousand Oaks, CA: Sage Publications.

Minor, M. A., Smith, G. S., & Brashen, H. (2013). Cyberbullying in higher education. *Journal of Educational Research and Practice, 3*(1), 15–29.

Nocentini, A., Calmaestra, J., Schultze-Krumboltz, A., Scheithauer, H., Ortega, R., & Menesini, E. (2010). Cyberbullying: Labels, behaviours and definition in three European countries. *Australian Journal of Guidance and Counselling, 20*, 129–142.

Patchin, J. W., & Hinduja, S. (2012). Cyberbullying: An update and synthesis of the research. In J. W. Patchin & S. Hinduja (Eds.), *Cyberbullying prevention and response: Expert perspectives* (pp. 13–35). New York, NY: Routledge.

Pence, E., & Paymar, M. (1993). *Education groups for men who batter: The Duluth Model*. New York: Springer.

Rivers, I. (2016). Homophobic and transphobic bullying in universities. In H. Cowie & C.-A. Myers (Eds.), *Bullying among university students: Cross-national perspectives* (pp. 48–60). London: Routledge.

Sallee, M., & Diaz, C. (2012). Sexual harassment, racist jokes, and homophobic slurs: When bullies target identity groups. In J. Lester (Ed.), *Workplace bullying in higher education* (pp. 41–59). New York: Routledge.

Sourander, A., Klomek, A. B., Ikonen, M., Lindroos, J., Luntamo, T., & Koskelainen, M. (2010). Psychosocial risk factors associated with cyberbullying among adolescents: A population-based study. *Archives of General Psychiatry, 67*, 720–728.

Smith, P. K. (2012). Cyberbullying and cyber aggression. In S. R. Jimerson, A. B. Nickerson, M. J. Mayer, & M. J. Furlong (Eds.), *Handbook of school violence and school safety: International research and practice* (2nd ed., pp. 93–103). New York: Routledge.

Taylor, S. (2012). Workplace bullying: Does tenure change anything? The example of a midwestern research university. In J. Lester (Ed.), *Workplace bullying in higher education* (pp. 23–40). New York: Routledge.

Tokunaga, R. S. (2010). Following you home from school: A critical review and synthesis of research on cyberbullying victimization. *Computers in Human Behavior, 26*, 277–287.

Vaughan, S. (2012). *Ya'makasi* or the art of displacement in the corporate world: A target's perspective on the impact of workplace bullying. In N. Tehrani (Ed.), *Workplace bullying: Symptoms and solutions* (pp. 51–66). London: Routledge.

von Marées, N., & Petermann, F. (2012). Cyberbullying: An increasing challenge for schools. *School Psychology International, 33*, 467–476.

Wildermuth, S., & Davis, C. B. (2012). Flaming the faculty: Exploring root causes, consequences, and potential remedies to the problem of instructor-focused uncivil online student discourse in higher education. In L. A. Wankel & C. Wankel (Eds.), *Misbehavior online in higher education: Cutting-edge technologies in higher education* (pp. 379–404). Bingley: Emerald.

9

STUDENT-TO-FACULTY TARGETED CYBERBULLYING

The impact on faculty

Lida Blizard

Introduction

This chapter explores the impact that student-to-faculty targeted cyberbullying can have on faculty members. These findings were captured in a mixed-methods study conducted at one Canadian university in 2012. The study found that targeted faculty members experienced negative physical, emotional, relational, and occupational effects in the aftermath of being cyberbullied by students. The classroom constitutes the *workplace*: in which faculty members are responsible to uphold institutional policy, engage students in meaningful learning experiences, and manage tensions that arise in the process. While teaching is a rewarding experience, student-faculty conflicts are inevitable given that faculty members' decision-making can have an effect on students' academic outcomes. While some students may choose to collaborate with faculty in resolving these differences, others may retaliate by posting about their teachers online.

Some scholars argue that cyberbullying can be motivated by a perceived injustice or for simple entertainment (Hinduja & Patchin, 2010; McKay, Arnold, Fratzl, & Thomas, 2008). In a landmark Canadian court case (*Prigden v. University of Calgary*, 2012), two undergraduate students were expelled for creating a Facebook polling site that rewarded peers for posting slanderous comments about a targeted instructor. Remarkably, whether enticed by peer pressure or the notoriety of posting harmful remarks (e.g., allegations of incompetence, defamatory comments), students engaged in the contagion of vengeful activity for several weeks. Although 10 students were prosecuted and found guilty of non-academic misconduct, two students appealed to the higher courts arguing that the university was not exempt from the standards set by the country's *Charter of Rights and Freedoms*. Ultimately, the courts sided with the students, and their perceived constitutional right to freedom of expression prevailed (see also Jackson, Faucher, & Cassidy, this volume). The targeted faculty member later resigned from the university and relocated to another country.

Literature

In terms of workplace safety for faculty, at the time of this study, the academic bullying literature reported that between 18% and 32% of post-secondary faculty members had been bullied (Keashly & Neuman, 2010; McKay et al., 2008); yet, minimal research had explored cyberbullying within the tertiary sector (Baldridge, 2008; DeSouza, 2010; Lampman, 2012), with even fewer studies focused on a student-to-faculty cyberbullying trajectory (Eskey, Taylor, & Eskey, 2014; Minor, Smith, & Brashen, 2013). Even so, student-faculty cyberbullying research reported relatively high prevalence rates, ranging between 12% (Faucher, Jackson, & Cassidy, 2014) and 17%, to 45% (Eskey et al., 2014; Minor et al., 2013; Smith, 2007; Vance, 2010).

The detrimental impact of cyberbullying on targeted individuals has been well-documented across the workplace bullying, K–12 bullying, and, to some extent, in the post-secondary face-to-face bullying literature (Beran, Rinaldi, Bickham, & Rich, 2012; Cassidy, Jackson, & Brown, 2009; Eskey et al., 2014; Na, Dancy, & Park, 2015; Patchin & Hinduja, 2010; Schenk & Fremouw, 2012; Shariff, 2008). Additionally, on the academic front, studies on faculty-targeted incivility (Lampman, 2012; Luparell, 2004) and cyberbullying directed toward faculty members (Blizard, 2014; Clark, Werth, & Ahten, 2012; Eskey et al., 2014; Faucher et al., 2014; Minor et al., 2013) have exposed the detrimental impact of bullying on teachers. Yet, despite the harm endured by the target, the literature confirms that victims (whether adolescents or adults) tend to avoid reporting the incident, believing either that it will not solve the problem, or else may result in further retaliation (Agatston, Kowalski, & Limber, 2012; Blizard, 2014). Furthermore, research conveys that student-faculty conflict can be pervasive – placing students, faculty members, and the overall learning community at risk of harm (Clark et al., 2012; Frey Knepp, 2012; Luparell, 2004; Twale & DeLuca, 2008).

Purpose

This study was undertaken to develop a greater understanding of this phenomenon – that is, evaluating the extent to which student-to-faculty cyberbullying takes place – including the nature of the experience, the impact on targets, and the support measures needed to cope with cyberbullying incidents. The importance of addressing this issue is two-fold: first, in terms of the individual welfare of faculty members, who may inadvertently be placed at risk while fulfilling their roles; and, second, in how this may affect the occupational health and safety of the overall campus community.

Method

This two-phase mixed-methods study employed online survey and individual interview methods to capture faculty members' experiences of cyberbullying by students. Purposeful convenience sampling was used to survey approximately 1,040 faculty members from within one Canadian university. Both the online survey and interview questions were adopted, and then modified, from previously validated research instruments. The online survey included both closed and open-ended responses. Throughout this study, *cyberbullying* was defined as an electronically mediated message(s) perceived by the targeted individual as containing aggressive, intimidating, derogatory, defamatory, sexist, harassing, or bullying language (Blizard, 2014).

Results

Study participants

From the 36 survey respondents (3.5% of total surveyed), 22 faculty members declared having experienced student-to-faculty cyberbullying at least once in their teaching career, 19 of whom endured at least one "serious" incident that had a negative effect on them. Four of these respondents (three females, one male) volunteered to participate in a one-on-one individual audio-taped interview, which ranged in length from 60 to 90 minutes. Recognizing that interviewees were taking a risk in disclosing, and potentially reliving, painful memories of their cyberbullying experiences, great care was taken to provide a safe, comfortable, supportive environment during the interview process. The recordings were transcribed, member-checked with participants to verify credibility and trustworthiness of the transcript text, then coded using a descriptive coding process (Saldaña, 2009). Pseudonym codes were used to preserve anonymity and confidentiality of the participants' information.

Although this study assessed various aspects of faculty members' cyberbullying experiences (e.g., message content, prevalence, impact, support needed, recommendations), this discussion focuses on the self-declared impact of cyberbullying on targeted individuals. Notably, cyberbullied faculty members (n = 22) were primarily female (68%), over 40 years of age (84%), held Canadian citizenship by birth (72%), spoke English as their first language (97%), held full-time status, and had greater than 10 years' teaching experience within the post-secondary sector. That targeted instructors were predominantly female converges with prior studies of cyberbullying and workplace bullying (Cassidy, Faucher, & Jackson, 2014; Lampman, 2012), post-secondary bullying (Keashly & Neuman, 2010), and post-secondary cyber-harassment (Vance, 2010). The findings diverge, however, from studies of student incivility (Alberts, Hazen, & Teobald, 2010; Alexander-Snow, 2004), whereby young, low-rank, non-white faculty members were more likely to be targeted.

Additionally, "student dissatisfaction with grades" (79%, n = 19) and "student misconduct issues" (32%, n = 19) served as the most common precursors to cyberbullying, while email and online evaluation sites were the most prevalent platforms utilized by students to target faculty members. From a list of options, respondents most commonly described the cyberbullying messages they received as "disrespectful", "aggressive or rude", "defamatory", and "demeaning". The nature of the messages parallel findings from prior studies of post-secondary incivility (Alberts et al., 2010; Clark et al., 2012; DeSouza, 2010) and cyberbullying (Eskey et al., 2014; Minor et al., 2013). Knowing the precursors, the platforms, and the content of cyberbullying messages contributed to developing greater understanding of the impact that cyberbullying had on targeted faculty members, findings which were enriched by affording respondents the opportunity to describe and elaborate on their experiences in open-ended responses and in the interviews.

Impact of cyberbullying

Physical and emotional impact

The following discussion focuses on the data obtained from respondents (n = 19) who declared having a "serious" cyberbullying incident that resulted in detrimental effects. Of this group of respondents, most (80%) were cyberbullied "once or twice", and suffered detrimental physical and emotional effects (e.g., difficulty sleeping, significant anxiety or distress, felt depressed, increased irritability, sudden emotional responses, difficulty concentrating) following the incident. In addition, approximately 50% of the respondents reported fear and avoidance symptoms (e.g., fear of the aggressor, fear of being alone with the aggressor, tried to avoid thinking about it), which is understandable considering the profane, aggressive content of some messages received. Both the survey respondents (hereafter referred to as SR) and the interview participants (hereafter referred to as IP) articulated the inflammatory nature of such messages:

> An anonymous email was sent . . . address line was "fuk (my first and last names) @yahoo.ca" . . . claiming I marked students too hard . . . threatening how students would treat me if they found me walking alone down the street. . . . I was extremely shaken by this email.
>
> *(SR 8)*

> I received several messages referring to me as a bitch.
>
> *(SR 9)*

> Angry email messages . . . it was very upsetting. . . . [I] felt threatened . . . shocked . . . didn't know what to do. . . . I was just trying to help the student.
>
> *(IP Andrew)*

> The email messages . . . threatened to call the press, threatened to file a legal complaint . . . tried to intimidate me into changing the grade . . . to me that is bullying.
>
> *(IP Carol)*

Furthermore, even a single egregious comment posted to a faculty polling site (e.g., accessible to the public) or an online faculty evaluation site (e.g., accessible to administrators) was deemed harmful to those who were targeted:

> I was away on vacation . . . sitting in a coffee shop . . . opened the online evaluation . . . read one of the comments and I was shocked. . . . I really felt physically ill . . . I felt the tears coming. A woman sitting across from me leaned over [said]. "Oh no . . . you've just received some really bad news". . . . I just got up and left . . . couldn't stop thinking about it . . . lost sleep over it . . . bothered me . . . tremendously.
>
> *(IP Debbie)*

> The online faculty evaluation comments were mean . . . unsubstantiated . . . intended to hurt . . . and they did.
>
> *(IP Debbie)*

> "Rateyourprofessor.com" . . . if a student wants to get back at a faculty member they can write a horrible review . . . on the site for everyone to see . . . it can be psychologically damaging.
>
> *(IP Andrew)*

This study also found that student aggression can transcend online platforms and escalate to in-person altercations. For instance, both Andrew and Barbara were recipients of numerous "angry email messages" that escalated to incidents of "shouting and berating" them in-person. Whether male or female, the emotional toll of cyberbullying on targeted faculty members became vividly clear during the individual interviews. Physical and emotional responses varied among participants, and, while most appeared calm at the onset of the interview, some individuals became more emotional and anxious (e.g., fidgeting, struggling to speak, tearful) while sharing their stories:

> (Crying) I was fine until this interview and now all of those emotions came back up. . . . I'm reliving it again as I talk about it.
>
> *(IP Debbie)*

> (Fidgeting, looking at the floor) It was very upsetting. . . . I felt threatened . . . shocked.
>
> *(IP Andrew)*

> (Crying) . . . one bad comment after so many years of positive feedback had such an effect on me.
>
> *(IP Debbie)*

Interestingly, some respondents attempted to minimize or normalize their cyberbullying experience, even while describing the harm inflicted upon them:

> I thought I was over-reacting . . . it wasn't as bad as what happens to other people. . . . I didn't think I was affected, but I was affected (tearful). . . . I have a lot of experience. . . . I should be able to handle it.
>
> *(IP Debbie)*

Compelling findings from this study emerged when participants were asked to identify, from a checklist, the type and duration of negative effects (e.g., physical, emotional, relational, and occupational) that occurred from their cyberbullying experience. The study found that one cyberbullying incident can be highly detrimental to targeted individuals such that some faculty members reported multiple negative effects (five or more) that persisted from "a few days" to "more than one year" (e.g., "sleep disturbances", "felt significantly anxious or distressed", "felt depressed", "increased irritability", "sudden emotional responses when reminded of the event", "had difficulty concentrating", "stress-related illnesses", "tried not to think about the incident", "avoided making contact with the aggressor", "afraid to be alone with the aggressor"). More disturbingly, others experienced greater than nine of the aforementioned negative effects for longer than one year, including thoughts of retaliation (21%) and thoughts of self-harm (5%). These findings pose concern, since some participants would have been experiencing these detrimental effects while attempting to fulfill their teaching role, as well as the unfavorable consequences for the campus community should thoughts of retaliation or self-harm be acted upon.

Notably – while this was not a psychological focused study – upon further review of the literature, similarities were noticed between the study's findings and the *American Psychiatric Association: Diagnostic and Statistical Manual of Mental Disorders* (DSM-5) criteria for Acute Stress Disorder (ASD) and Post-Traumatic Stress Disorder (PTSD). According to the DSM-5 criteria, ASD occurs when an individual has been directly exposed to a stressful or traumatic experience with a pattern of symptoms that persist for three days to one month following the event, whereas symptoms that last beyond one month constitute PTSD (American Psychiatric Association, 2013). As such, faculty members who reported more than nine negative effects that persisted for one week to one month may have experienced ASD-like effects. Likewise, participants who reported multiple negative effects that lasted longer than one month in the form of: intrusion (e.g., "I couldn't stop thinking about it", "I'm reliving it again as I talk about it"), avoidance (e.g., "I tried not to think about it"), alterations in mood or cognition (e.g., "I was very bothered by it", "I felt threatened . . . shocked"), and arousal (e.g., "I lost sleep over it"), bear similarities with the DSM-5 criteria for PTSD. In light of these findings, it is important to consider how targeted faculty members, afflicted with such effects, were able to cope with the experience or interact with students thereafter.

Relational and occupational effects

In addition to the emotional and physical effects discussed, this study found that cyberbullied faculty members (n = 19) predominantly encountered detrimental effects in their relationships with students (74%), followed by colleagues (37%), and Deans or administrators (37%). For example, Andrew stated: "I was unsure how to interact with that student and other students after the [email] incident", while Carol explained: "My encounters with cyberbullying tell me that getting involved too close with students can work against you". Professional ramifications included loss of desire to go to work (68%), loss of productivity (53%), and where victims felt like quitting (53%). Likewise, some participants lost confidence in their ability to: manage student conflict (47%), work with students (42%), or continue teaching students (37%). Respondents explained the perplexity of being cyberbullied while fulfilling one's teaching responsibilities:

> I doubted my ability as a teacher . . . lost confidence . . . it was really upsetting . . . didn't know what to think at the time . . . trying to make decisions and you don't know what to do.
>
> *(IP Andrew)*

> The first time . . . I didn't know what to do . . . felt a tremendous amount of emotions . . . thought I had to reply . . . they just came back with more aggressive emails.
>
> *(IP Carol)*

The adverse relational and occupational effects reported in this study are not new, as similar findings have been reported in former academic and workplace bullying research (Celep & Konalki, 2013; Lampman, 2012; Lampman, Phelps, Bancroft, & Beneke, 2009; Luparell, 2004; Lutgen-Sandvik, Tracy, & Alberts, 2007; McKay et al., 2008; Namie, 2003).

Interview testimonials illuminated the value participants placed on building a positive, supportive relationship with students to help them succeed. Emotions surfaced (e.g., tears, raised voices, trembling) as interviewees explained how invested they were in providing feedback to assist students in learning, as well as how "surprised", "shocked", "shattered", "threatened", or "defenseless" they felt upon discovering that they had been cyberbullied:

> I meet with the students . . . discuss their marks . . . give constructive feedback to prepare them for . . . their upcoming semester. . . . The student wrote

> that I was the worst teacher they ever had . . . I was lazy. . . . I was shocked . . . my confidence was shattered.
>
> *(IP Debbie)*

> Just because you have a good thing with a student doesn't mean they won't come back on you. . . . I decided to keep distance. . . . I don't want to be hurt.
>
> *(IP Carol)*

Although one interviewee was targeted with very angry email messages from a student, she was able to put it in perspective of a learning experience for the student, while maintaining a distance emotionally:

> I received some angry, angry, angry email messages from the student . . . believing that it is not about me is my survival mechanism . . . students' attempts to bully are just opportunities for them to learn . . . if they bully they haven't learned.
>
> *(IP Barbara)*

Implications of reporting cyberbullying incidents

In this study, cyberbullied faculty members predominantly consulted with colleagues (84%), an immediate supervisor (74%), or friends (74%), while fewer reported the incident to an administrator (37%). Furthermore, most respondents (79%) held the opinion that students at their institution can cyberbully faculty members with impunity. When faculty members are unsure of what constitutes cyberbullying – or whether it will be beneficial to report such incidents – they may choose to suffer in silence. Those who chose not to report their cyberbullying experience reasoned that complaints would not be taken seriously; targets would be viewed as incompetent; or, worse, may result in further retaliation by students or administrators:

> I didn't report it . . . didn't know who to report it to . . . or if there was any point.
>
> *(SR 19)*

> I did not report it . . . had fear of further victimization. Administrators may not act on it, or if they do . . . may be detrimental to the faculty member who reports it.
>
> *(SR 23)*

> You just can't tell people about these kinds of incidents . . . you have to be really careful about who you tell and what you say.
>
> *(SR 22)*

Regardless of whether cyberbullying incidents are reported, participants were clear that faculty members should be supported in their ability to manage conflict with students. They should not feel at fault when targeted by students:

> When teachers are hired they should have training . . . it is important to know that faculty members are supported when they feel threatened . . . they shouldn't feel as though they have done something wrong.
>
> *(IP Andrew)*

Discussion

Limitations

The first limitation of this study pertains to the low response rate (N = 1040) from the online survey (3.5%, n = 36) and the interviews (.38%, n = 4), which could be attributed to the narrow 30-day implementation period imposed by the university, the sensitive subject matter, faculty members' uncertainty of what constitutes cyberbullying, or faculty members' concern with what might be done with the findings. Yet, while some faculty members may have been wary about sharing (and potentially reliving) intimate details of their cyberbullying experience, others chose to participate as an opportunity to effect change:

> I realized in reading your research proposal that I too had been a victim of cyberbullying and that this was a great opportunity to participate.
>
> *(IP Carol)*

Second, due to the unique focus – a limited number of faculty members at one institution – the findings are not generalizable across the institution (nor to other institutions). However, despite the low response rate to the online survey, the research process was enriched during the interviews by hearing the intimate details and observing the emotional impact of faculty members' cyberbullying experiences. Participants' testimonials gave voice to the detrimental impact of student-to-faculty targeted cyberbullying, advancing the literature in this way.

Implications and recommendations

The negative impacts of cyberbullying reported in this study parallel former studies of workplace bullying (Hoel & Einarsen, 2011; Namie, 2003), post-secondary bullying (Lampman, 2012; McKay et al., 2008), and cyberbullying (Beran et al., 2012; Cassidy, Faucher, & Jackson, 2014). For example, fear of the aggressor (Beran et al., 2012; Lampman et al., 2009; Lampman, 2012), loss of concentration, increased anxiety, stress-related illnesses, depression (Lutgen-Sandvik et al., 2007; Namie, 2003), and suicidal ideation (Hinduja & Patchin, 2010) have been reported in the bullying and cyberbullying literature. Participants' reluctance to take action may be intertwined with the complexity of detrimental effects being processed, the level of confidence in pursuing administrative or legal action, and the trepidation of revisiting painful memories.

The type and duration of detrimental effects reported by study participants that resemble the DSM-5 criteria for ASD and PTSD suggests that some participants may have experienced ASD- and PTSD-like effects in the aftermath of being cyberbullied. Although the survey instrument was not designed to capture ASD or PTSD effects – nor pose a question to establish whether ASD or PTSD symptoms existed prior to the study – these findings warrant further investigation in future research. Furthermore, it is important to consider how targeted faculty members process or heal from the aforementioned negative effects, given the plausibility that left untreated, and with repeated exposure, detrimental effects may worsen (Namie, 2003). Of equal consideration is the question of how faculty members who reported symptoms of fear and avoidance toward the aggressor might interact with students thereafter, especially when under stress. For instance, the communications literature informs us that teachers who exhibit positive mannerisms toward students (e.g., smiling, calmness, warmth) can positively influence students' attitudes toward their instructors and the tone of civility within the classroom (Kearney, Plax, & Wendt-Wasco, 1985; Klebig, Goldonowicz, Mendes, Neville Miller, & Katt, 2016; Miller, Katt, Brown, & Sivo, 2014).

Student-teacher interactions are further compounded by the element of grading and the power that faculty have to impact students' success in both the short and long term. Knowing that students' dissatisfaction with grades was a leading precursor to cyberbullying affords the opportunity for faculty to discuss grading practices. This also connects students with support services upon notice of academic or personal struggles. When tensions arise, it may be beneficial to acknowledge students' distress, as well as equipping students with skills to better cope with their stressors.

Based on this study's findings, it is not surprising that the participants (n = 22) decided that the top-three priority measures needed to address this issue were: (1) cyberbullying education for faculty (75%); (2) followed by clearly written, well-communicated cyberbullying policies (65%) including sanctions to deter cyberbullying (43%); and (3) support for targeted individuals such as counseling and focus groups (30%). Cyberbullying education for students was also stressed by interviewees, to ensure students would be able to recognize and understand the ramifications of cyberbullying. At the time of this study (2012), the gaps in post-secondary cyberbullying research, institutional policy, and cyberbullying education programs left faculty members to manage cyberbullying incidents on their own. In the absence of knowledge on how to recognize, prevent, or manage cyberbullying, targeted individuals were left exposed and vulnerable to harm. The importance of further research was aptly captured in the following excerpts:

> This is really important research . . . needs to get out in the open to assist faculty members in how to manage it when it happens.
>
> *(IP Debbie)*

> Your study is long overdue. It will improve this institution and the practice for faculty for years to come.
>
> *(IP Carol)*

As a result of the findings from this study, the institution advanced their development of cyberbullying policies and procedures, provided education for faculty members and students (e.g., embedding cyberbullying into curriculum), and increased support services (e.g., cyberbullying focus groups) to assist targeted individuals in their pathway to healing. Furthermore, the institution also enhanced opportunities for students to engage in activities that promote self-care (e.g., yoga, meditation, mindfulness) designed to optimize students' resilience and their ability to cope with academic stressors.

Significance

This study provided a platform for cyberbullied faculty members to give voice, reflect upon, and be acknowledged for their individual cyberbullying experiences – knowing that their testimonials could generate evidence to effect change. Consistent with prior bullying and cyberbullying literature, this study found that cyberbullied faculty members who encountered at least one incident of bullying via electronic media experienced detrimental physical, emotional, relational, and occupational effects. With the growing number of cyberbullying cases that have come before the courts, the proliferation of online platforms to engage in such behaviors, and the damage that can be inflicted upon targeted individuals, a greater body of cyberbullying research is needed. Further exploration into the impact on victims, as well as refinements to survey instruments that capture psychological effects, could illuminate the extent of harm and the support measures most imperative to healing. Finally, the voice of students in this trajectory cannot be understated, as this would broaden the scope of understanding student-to-faculty targeted cyberbullying for students and faculty members alike.

References

American Psychiatric Association. (2013). *Diagnostic and statistical manual of mental disorders* (5th ed.). Arlington, VA: American Psychiatric Association.

Alberts, H. C., Hazen, H. D., & Teobald, R. B. (2010). Classroom incivilities: The challenge of interactions between college students and instructors in the US. *Journal of Geography in Higher Education, 34*, 439–462.

Alexander-Snow, M. (2004). Dynamics of gender, ethnicity, and race in understanding classroom incivility. *New Directions for Teaching & Learning, 99*, 21–31.

Baldridge, J.V. (2008). Civility, incivility, bullying, and mobbing in academe. In D. J. Twale & B. M. DeLuca (Eds.), *Faculty incivility: The rise of the academic bully culture and what to do about it* (pp. 3–31). San Francisco: Jossey-Bass.

Beran, T., Rinaldi, C., Bickham, D., & Rich, M. (2012). Evidence for the need to support adolescents dealing with harassment and cyber-harassment: Prevalence, progression, and impact. *School Psychology International, 33*(5), 562–576.

Blizard, L. M. (2014). *Faculty members' perceived experiences and impact of cyberbullying from students at a Canadian university: A mixed methods study*. Ed.D. Dissertation, Simon Fraser University, Burnaby, B.C. Retrieved from http://summit.sfu.ca/item/13897

Cassidy, W., Faucher, C., & Jackson, M. (2014). The dark side of the ivory tower: Cyberbullying of university faculty and teaching personnel. *Alberta Journal of Educational Research, 60*(2), 279–299.

Cassidy, W., Jackson, M., & Brown, K. (2009). Sticks and stones can break my bones, but how can pixels hurt me? Students' experiences with cyber-bullying. *School Psychology International, 30*, 383–401.

Celep, C., & Konalki, T. (2013). Mobbing experiences of instructors: Causes, results, and solutions suggestions. *Educational Sciences: Theory and Practice, 13*(1), 193–199.

Clark, C. M., Werth, L., & Ahten, S. (2012). Cyber-bullying and incivility in the online learning environment, Part 1: Addressing faculty and student perceptions. *Nurse Educator, 37*(4), 150–156.

Daniloff, D. (2009). Cyberbullying goes to college. *Bostonia*. Boston University. Retrieved from www.bu.edu/today/2009/cyberbullying-goes-to-college/

DeSouza, E. R. (2010). Frequency rates and correlates of contrapower harassment in higher education. *Journal of Interpersonal Violence, 48*(11), 1–27.

Eskey, M., Taylor, C., & Eskey, M. (2014). Cyberbullying in the online classroom: Faculty as the targets. *Proceedings of TCC Worldwide Online Conference, 17*, 30–41.

Faucher, C., Jackson, M., & Cassidy, W. (2014). Cyberbullying among university students: Gendered experiences, impacts, and perspectives. *Education Research International, 2014*, 1–10.

Frey Knepp, K. A. (2012). Understanding student and faculty incivility in higher education. *The Journal of Effective Teaching, 12*(1), 32–45.

Hinduja, S., & Patchin, J. W. (2010). Bullying, cyberbullying, and suicide. *Archives of Suicide Research, 14*(3), 206–221.

Hoel, H., & Einarsen, S. (2011). Investigating complaints of bullying and harassment. In S. Einarsen, H. Hoel, D. Zapf, & C. L. Cooper (Eds.), *Bullying and harassment in the workplace: Developments in theory, research, and practice* (2nd ed., pp. 341–358). Boca Raton, FL: CRC Press.

Kearney, P., Plax, T. G., & Wendt-Wasco, N. (1985). Teacher immediacy for affective learning in divergent classes. *Communication Quarterly, 33*, 61–74.

Keashly, L., & Neuman, J. (2010). Faculty experience with bullying in higher education. *Administrative Theory & Praxis, 32*(1), 48–70.

Klebig, B., Goldonowicz, J., Mendes, E., Neville Miller, A., & Katt, J. (2016). The combined effects of instructor communicative behaviors, instructor credibility, and student personality traits on civility in the college classroom. *Communication Research Reports, 33*(2), 152–158.

Lampman, C., Phelps, A., Bancroft, S., & Beneke, M. (2009). Contrapower harassment in academia: A survey of faculty experience with student incivility, bullying, and sexual attention. *Sex Roles, 60*, 331–346.

Lampman, C. (2012). Women faculty at risk: U.S. professors report on their experiences with student incivility, bullying, aggression, and sexual attention. *NASPA Journal About Women in Higher Education, 5*(2), 184–208.

Luparell, S. (2004). Faculty encounters with uncivil nursing students: An overview. *Journal of Professional Nursing, 20*, 59–67.

Lutgen-Sandvik, P., Tracy, S. J., & Alberts, J. K. (2007). Burned by bullying in the American workplace: Prevalence, perception, degree, and impact. *Journal of Management Studies, 44*(6), 838–857.

McKay, R., Arnold, D., Fratzl, J., & Thomas, R. (2008). Workplace bullying in academia: A Canadian study. *Employee Responsibility and Human Rights Journal, 20*, 77–100.

Miller, A., Katt, J. A., Brown, T., & Sivo, S. A. (2014). The relationship of instructor self-disclosure, non-verbal immediacy, and credibility to student incivility in the college classroom. *Communication Education, 63*, 1–16.

Minor, M., Smith, G., & Brashen, H. (2013). Cyberbullying in higher education. *Journal of Educational Research and Practice, 3*(1), 15–29.

Na, H., Dancy, B. L., & Park, C. (2015). College student engaging in cyberbullying victimization: Cognitive appraisals, coping strategies, and psychological adjustments. *Archives of Psychiatric Nursing, 29*(3), 155–161.

Namie, G. (2003). *The WBI 2003 report on abusive workplaces*. Bellingham, WA: Workplace Bullying Institute.

Neville Miller, A., Katt, J. A., Brown, T., & Sivo, S. A. (2014). The relationship of instructor self-disclosure, nonverbal immediacy, and credibility to student incivility in the classroom. *Communication Education, 63*(1), 1–16.

Patchin, J. W., & Hinduja, S. (2010). Cyberbullying and self-esteem. *Journal of School Health, 80*(12), 614–620.

Prigden v. University of Calgary. (2012). *ABCA 139*. Canadian Legal Information Institute. Retrieved from www.canlii.org/en/ab/abca/doc/2012/2012abca139/2012abca139.html

Saldaña, J. (2009). *The coding manual for qualitative research*. Thousand Oaks: Sage Publications.

Schenk, A., & Fremouw, W. (2012). Prevalence, psychological impact, and coping of cyberbully victims among college students. *Journal of School Violence, 11*(1), 21–37.

Shariff, S. (2008). *Cyber-bullying: Issues and solutions for the school, the classroom and the home*. Abingdon, UK: Routledge.

Smith, A. (2007, January 19). Cyber-bullying affecting 17% of teachers, poll finds. *The Guardian*. Retrieved from www.theguardian.com

Twale, D., & DeLuca, B. (2008). *Faculty incivility: The rise of the academic bully culture and what to do about it*. San Francisco, CA: Jossey-Bass.

Vance, J. W. (2010). *Cyber-harassment in higher education: Online learning environments*. Ed.D. dissertation. Retrieved from University of Southern California Digital Library (usctheses-m2954).

PART III

Solutions

10

IN THE E-PRESENCE OF OTHERS

Understanding and developing constructive cyber-bystander action

Loraleigh Keashly

As this volume illustrates, e-communication has become the latest (and arguably the most virulent) means through which bullying can occur, and academe is particularly vulnerable. I am interested in faculty experiences with cyberbullying because of a faculty's central role in the governance and manifestation of the university's educational and research missions, as well as its students' successes (Keashly & Wajngurt, 2016). Bullying and cyberbullying undermine faculty well-being and, if left unaddressed, will undermine students, the institution, and higher education in general (Black, this volume).

In this chapter, I explore the role of bystanders in the context of faculty experiences, with a particular focus on the interactions through e-communication. The nature of faculty as a self-regulating profession – and the resultant importance of peer review – draws attention to faculty colleagues as particularly influential bystanders whose (in)actions have profound implications for specific cyberbullying situations, and the department and university climate more broadly (Keashly & Neuman, 2010). To that end, I briefly highlight what the research tells us about faculty experiences with cyberbullying. I then discuss what we know about bystander behaviour and decision-making, with respect to engaging in these situations. Within this broader discussion of bystanding, I explore the current thinking as to how bystanding occurs and is shaped in the electronic environment: highlighting what remains the same as in regular bullying, and what unique influences and opportunities these e-media have for bystanders. I then conclude with potential action points for universities to consider.

Nature and prevalence of cyberbullying

The majority of research on cyberbullying has focused on adolescents, with an increasing attention to adults' experience in a variety of contexts (Wingate,

Minney, & Guadagno, 2013). The Pew Research Center (2014) reports that 40% of adults identify as victims of cyberbullying, with 73% indicating they have witnessed others being cyberbullied. This statistic is compelling from a bystander intervention perspective, as it shows that what happens is often in the presence of others and, thus, these people have the opportunity to take action. In work environments, cyberbullying victimization rates range from 10% to 20%, with email as the primary medium of harassment (Coyne et al., 2016; Forssell, 2016; Heatherington & Coyne, 2014; Privitera & Campbell, 2009).

In terms of faculty experience as targets, the prevalence and nature varies by context and actor. Cassidy, Faucher, and Jackson (2014) found that 17% of faculty respondents reported experiencing cyberbullying from students (12%) and colleagues (9%) in the previous 12 months. Email was the primary means of cyberbullying. Rates of students cyberbullying faculty are higher when the focus is on online educational environments, wherein e-communication is the primary means of interaction (Wankel & Wankel, 2012). Specifically, one-third to one-half of faculty in online educational environments perceive themselves as having been cyberbullied by students (Eskey & Eskey, 2014; Minor, Smith, & Brashen, 2013; Vance, 2010). Cyberbullying in online education environments occurs through a variety of mechanisms, including email, phone calls, and posting in public forums (such as the course discussion boards).

Websites and social networking apps focused on campus life and permitting anonymous postings, such as RateMyProfessor (Daniloff, 2009) and Yik Yak (Mahler, 2015), are other e-forums where faculty may be vulnerable to hostility and cyberbullying from students and others. Beyond campus boundaries, posting of faculty thoughts and actions (by themselves or by others) to social media sites such as Facebook, Twitter, and YouTube can result in vigorous discussion and, in some instances, vicious e-firestorms that can have profound implications for the faculty member and for the university (Flaherty, 2017). These publicly available sites are interesting for cyber-bystanding because of the potential for an unlimited audience, which magnifies impact but also provides an enormous pool of bystanders with the opportunity to engage. These public venues also show the range of bystander activities: from bystanders who "joined in" with critique, even attacking and threatening (bullying), to bystanders who challenged these hostile actions and interpretations, and many who – both online and offline – sent support to the faculty who were targets.

Faculty also engage in cyberbullying and aggression. Students identify faculty as engaging in incivility and bullying in online educational environments, primarily through email, class chat, and discussion boards (e.g., Clark, Werth, & Ahten, 2012). Consistent with research on "traditional" faculty bullying (Keashly & Neuman, 2013), colleagues are also a source of cyberbullying and aggression, which is predominantly done through email (Cassidy et al., 2014).

In sum, faculty experience cyberbullying and – more broadly – hostile and aggressive communication from a variety of actors, in a variety of contexts, and through a variety of media. The e-medium used is important, as it determines the opportunity for the presence of bystanders, shaping the types of responses available for them to enact (Bastiaensens et al., 2014; Heatherington & Coyne, 2014). From the research reviewed here, email is the most frequent medium for the cyberbullying of faculty. Media, like email and text messaging, are often one-on-one in their communications (private). Bystander engagement with these media is dependent upon those actions being deliberately shared; it requires another step by the sender or the receiver (e.g., forwarding or copying on a message) (Cassidy et al., 2014; D'Cruz & Noronha, 2013; Eskey & Eskey, 2014; Minor et al., 2013). In the case of more public media – such as social networking sites, listservs or public websites, and blogs – once the message is posted, the audience becomes whoever has access to those forums (i.e., unconfined) (D'Cruz & Noronha, 2013).

What is bystanding?

A typical definition of a bystander is a person who, although "present" at some event or situation, does not take part in it ("Bystander", 2017). Inherent in this definition is an assumption of passivity, specifically that bystanders do nothing (i.e., the nonresponsive bystander) (Latané & Darley, 1970). There is also a presumption that any actions will be pro-social. Those who are present and aware, however, often engage in a variety of actions: pro-social (helpful) and anti-social (harming) (Allison & Bussey, 2016), direct and indirect (Dooley, Pyżalski, & Cross, 2009), and through more active or passive engagement. Paull, Omari, and Standen (2012) articulate 12 constructive and destructive roles that bystanders can play. Examples of destructive roles include actively joining in or assisting the actor, passively succumbing by becoming another victim, or abdicating opportunities to engage. The constructive roles tend to involve active engagement such as intervening, defending or defusing, and the more behind-the-scenes/screens work of sympathizing and empathizing. While developed in on-site situations, these roles also manifest in cyber-contexts as well. Thus, to understand bystanding generally, and cyber-bystanding more specifically, we need to consider all the ways (good or ill) that bystanders can engage. This consideration helps us to identify ways in which bystanders might move in more constructive directions.

Bystander intervention model

Bystander intervention research has a long and rich history reflected in a variety of literatures, including specific types of bystanders, such as whistleblower (Miceli, Near, & Dworkin, 2013), ally (Nelson, Dunn, & Paradies, 2011), and in third-party conflict intervention (Ury, 2000). In response to the 1964 murder of Kitty Genovese in New York City (and the case's presumed bystander inaction), Latané and Darley (1970) undertook a robust program of research to understand when bystanders would – or rather, would not – take action to help another. Based on their work, Latané and Darley developed a five-stage model of bystander decision-making regarding intervention. The first stage is *noticing* that something has happened; the second is *assessing* whether it is a problem requiring action; the third is *acknowledging responsibility* for taking action; the fourth is *choosing* the action(s); and the last is *taking* the action(s). This model has formed the basis of training to build bystander efficacy in a variety of contexts (Swan, 2015), including university campuses – particularly for addressing high-risk and discriminatory student behaviour (e.g., Ashburn-Nardo, Blanchar, Petersson, Morris, & Goodwin, 2014; Banyard, 2015; Nelson et al., 2011). While this model and much subsequent work have focused on face-to-face situations, it is also being examined for the insight it can provide regarding bystanding in the cyber-context (e.g., Dillon, 2014; Dillon & Bushman, 2015). I use this model as a framework for exploring the nature of, as well as influences on, cyber-bystanding decision-making and behaviour in the context of faculty experiences with cyberbullying.

Notice: did something happen? what do I "see" and "what" am I seeing?

Before a bystander can take action, they must be aware of the situation or behaviour taking place. Awareness requires that (a) the potential bystander is "present" and (b) they detect the behaviour or interaction.

At its most basic requirement, the potential bystander needs to be "present" or have the opportunity to be "present" (Allison & Bussey, 2016; Dillon & Bushman, 2015). If they are not there when or shortly after the behaviour or event occurs, they have no opportunity to "notice" what has taken place. In the case of email or texting, potential bystanders – such as other students or colleagues – are not "present". They can become present if the event is shared by the sender or receiver. This could occur through being cc'd or bcc'd on the email or text, or by having the message forwarded after the initial interaction. For example, in studies of online class environments, faculty have shared the event with a program director or chair, as well as with family, friends, and colleagues to gain support or in seeking out a reality check (e.g., Eskey & Eskey, 2014). If the event has occurred in shared space – such as a listserv for department e-communication or a discussion board for class – anyone visiting the space becomes "present".

Being present, however, is not enough to "notice". To be "noticed", the behaviour must also be "out of the ordinary" (Latané & Darley, 1970). Behaviours become "visible" or "noticeable" in several ways: (1) when they contravene expected behaviour; (2) when someone flags it; and/or (3) when the interaction involves someone connected to the bystander in a meaningful way.

Behaviour is noticeable when it violates relational or interactional norms (Dillon, 2014). In terms of emails from students or faculty colleagues, the use of capital letters, swearing, or name-calling are considered violations of netiquette and, thus, will draw the attention of potential bystanders (Shea, 1994).

Related specifically to content, delivering a critique of someone's idea or request may or may not be viewed as a violation. In the academic environment, the culture of debate and critique is valued as an important way to help others hone their ideas and arguments. A potential bystander, particularly if they are a faculty member, may not see critique – even harsh critique – as out of the ordinary. As such, they may not notice it or consider it worthy of further attention. For students (staff and administrators, too), contrastingly, this manner of critique may be viewed as harsh and perceived as an attack, as their relational norms are different (Christy, 2010). To them, the behaviour is "noticed".

For faculty, messages from a student threatening to tell the chair or launch a lawsuit may be considered worthy of attention. These messages are viewed by faculty as a violation of the norms of appropriate conduct regarding disagreement (Clark et al., 2012). For student bystanders, these messages may be noticed because they violate norms of addressing authority (the professor). However, if the bystander subscribes to the notion of student as consumer and faculty as service provider, such messages may not be viewed as "out of line". In more public online environments – particularly social media forums such as Twitter – the boundaries of "appropriate" behaviour may be much broader, with rules of politeness attenuated (Dillon, 2014; Madan, 2014). A cursory review of the comment section of news sites, and even higher education publications, reveals the broad range of behaviours that occur. As a result, what in other contexts (such as in face-to-face communication or in private messaging) would be viewed as "out of the ordinary" – and, thus, worthy of attention – may not be viewed as unexpected. Therefore, the behaviour or event is not "noticed".

Yet, even if the behaviour or incident is considered normative, if someone else flags it as an issue, it becomes noticed. In terms of social networking sites, this may occur by others flagging a post or comment as abusive, or using dislike and other emoticons to express the intensity of disapproval. In email or text situations, the forwarding of an exchange to others signals that something notable has happened and draws the bystander's attention.

Another influence is the connection between potential bystander and target, or actor, or indeed with other bystanders. We are more likely to be attentive to situations involving those with whom we feel a connection, be it personal or social. A behaviour or event will draw our attention if it involves someone we know or with whom we feel a kinship (e.g., identity group) (Brody & Vangelisti, 2016; Levine & Crowther, 2008).

Assess: is this a problem? is help needed?

Once a bystander has oriented themselves to the behaviour or interaction, they need to discern if the situation is problematic and whether some action is required to address it. In the Latané and Darley (1970) studies, the focus was on whether the situation was perceived to be an "emergency". Interactions or events are more likely to be perceived as an emergency, and in urgent need of action, when negative impact or harm is visible.

Harm can be at the individual and/or group level. For example, the negativity of a post raising questions about a faculty member's reputation can have profound negative implications for an academic. Alternatively, the harm may be more at the group level, in which behaviours contravene appropriate principles of the community (O'Reilly, Aquino, & Skarlicki, 2016) – that is to say, the community is at risk of being harmed should such behaviour be allowed to continue. An example of potential community harm is when a faculty member expresses their thoughts on a controversial issue in social media, facing an e-firestorm of threats and calls for their termination. For many academics, these actions by others contravene academic freedom and freedom of expression, and the academic community is subsequently put at risk (Flaherty, 2017).

The visibility of impact on the target is a challenge for text-only communication – such as email, texts, tweets, and posts – as these media tend to be stripped of key social cues like facial expression, tone of voice, and body language, whereby bystanders interpret the meaning of what has taken place, as well as distinguish the implications for others and the broader community (Dillon, 2014; Heatherington & Coyne, 2014). The resultant situational ambiguity makes it difficult for witnesses to discern what has happened or what is happening. Is this a conflict between equals; rudeness or incivility; or bullying or harassment? The latter is most likely to be viewed as having negative impact and, thus, requiring action (Shultz, Heilman, & Hart, 2014).

Another factor related to the determination of impact, generally and to harm specifically, is whether what a bystander is "seeing" is the actor(s) being reactive (e.g., responding to provocation by the target) or proactive (e.g., deliberately targeting and being provocative) (Law, Shapka, Domene, & Gagne, 2012; Madan, 2014), with the latter perceived as negative and harmful. This assessment requires being privy to the chain of events involved, which may or may not be accessible to the bystander. For example, an email between two faculty members may suggest prior conflict, or a long chain of emails reveal the development of the interaction. If the judgement is that this is a conflict, then the bystanders may not view this as an emergency, or else feel the urgency to do something. Rather, they may continue to observe (i.e., non-action) (Law et al., 2012; Madan, 2014). Alternatively, if they perceive the behaviours as being unfair to the other party, they will perceive harm, and may determine an active response is needed to address the perceived injustice (O'Reilly et al., 2016).

Another influence in assessing impact is the perceived severity of the action, which is linked to the degree of harm to the target or to the community – that is, the bystander can imagine that this would hurt and determine, therefore, that some kind of action is warranted (Skarlicki & Kulik, 2004). For example, research on adolescent cyberbullying (e.g., Allison & Bussey, 2016; Bastiaensens et al., 2014) finds that compromising photos or videos are perceived as more severe than posts and, hence, require action to address. Thus, when the specific behaviours are viewed as severe and capable of harm, bystanders will view them as problematic and be more likely to intervene.

The sense of emergency and subsequent need for action is also affected by the asynchronous nature of much of our media, as media influences our perception as to the immediacy of an event's impact. In the case of being copied on an email, visiting a class discussion board, or viewing a Facebook post, for example, if the event had occurred sometime earlier, a bystander may be unclear as to whether – given the length of time – any urgency to respond remains. Furthermore, the delay may make it difficult to discern the specific impact on the victim. Heatherington and Coyne (2014) argue that asynchrony, in combination with the reduced social cue nature of e-communication, reduces the transmission of the emotional reactions of targets. As a result, bystanders may not develop an empathetic response, detect harm, or perceive the injustice required to call for action. To the extent that the bystander assesses the situation as not requiring action, they will not engage.

Responsibility: should I do something about it?

Having made the discernment that the situation requires action, the bystander has to decide whether it is their responsibility to respond. The bystander's social bond with others, and the associated expectations, provide the basis for discerning responsibility. People are more likely to assume responsibility for taking action if they feel connected to the target or to the actor (Brody & Vangelisti, 2016; Levine & Crowther, 2008). Relational norms may specify such action (e.g., standing up for the other/having the other's back). These norms are closely tied to empathy with, and duty of care for, the other. Thus, bystanders are more likely to intervene if the target is a close friend or colleague and, more broadly, if they socially identify with the target (i.e., shared identity group membership) (Levine & Crowther, 2008). Contrastingly, if the bystander feels a kinship with the actor, they may decide they need to take action regarding the actor (Shultz et al., 2014). Given cyberbullying research involving faculty peers shows how individuals are known to each other, or have relationships with each other, relational expectations may be a particularly powerful influence in assuming responsibility (e.g., faculty defend each other's academic freedom). More pragmatically, if the target or another person asks the bystander specifically to help – thus highlighting their relationship to each other – the bystander is more likely to take responsibility and do so (Markey, 2000). For example, forwarding an email to a colleague asking for advice or intervention is a clear request for involvement. This increases the likelihood the bystander will see that personal action is needed.

Broader values, such as deontic justice or particular religious values, specify that the individual has a moral obligation to intervene in situations where harm/injustice is detected (O'Reilly et al., 2016). The developing literature on moral disengagement, and the cognitive and emotional effort required to override these obligations, speaks to the power of these moral frameworks in guiding behaviour (Dillon & Bushman, 2015; Shultz et al., 2014). These moral frameworks are grounded in a very broad sense of social bonds to the actor and target as human beings (i.e., "decent people help others who need it"). In the broadest sense, the bystander recognizes that their behaviour in this moment has implications. Their behaviour communicates their personal commitment to this broader community and associated expectations, and, perhaps more importantly, their own sense of being a moral individual (Allison & Bussey, 2016; O'Reilly et al., 2016).

In essence, bystanders are looking around to see what others are doing, who these "others" are relative to the bystander, and getting cues as to what they should do. At the most basic level, if there are a number of others present, the individual bystander may assume others will take action and, thus, refrain from taking responsibility (i.e., diffusion of responsibility) (Latané & Darley, 1970). This is a particular risk with specific e-media (Dillon, 2014). The "unconfined" spaces of public postings of social media, such as Twitter and Facebook, have the potential to attract an enormous number of bystanders (D'Cruz & Noronha, 2013). With regard to emails and texts, Allison and Bussey (2016) report that the more people who were visibly copied, the less likely people were to help. This diffusion effect is mitigated when the bystanders have a shared identity or sense of connection to other bystanders (e.g., colleagues or fellow students) (Allison & Bussey, 2016; Brody & Vangelisti, 2016; DeSmet et al., 2016). In this situation, the norms of this "peer" group take precedence (i.e., the individual bystander is more likely to follow the lead of other bystanders). Thus, if a close other has responded (e.g., modelling dissent with the action) (Allison & Bussey, 2016), the individual believes they should, too. This "conformity" can be positive or negative (e.g., ganging up on the target or actor/mobbing).

The individual bystander's visibility to others is also important. If the potential bystander is invisible (anonymous), they realize they are not being seen or judged. Being invisible may reduce their sense of connection and need to adhere to group norms and, thus, their sense of personal responsibility. Alternatively, anonymity can counteract the diffusion of responsibility and group norm effects. Anonymity may encourage the bystander to take responsibility and, thus, to action (Freis & Gurung, 2013).

To the extent that other bystanders' actions are visible, asynchrony of e-communication can be helpful in determining responsibility to respond. By examining the history of responses, the individual bystander can see whether responsibility has been taken and evaluate its impact. If the situation has been ameliorated, then there is no need for response. If the situation has become more difficult or has not been addressed, this may increase the individual's sense of responsibility to respond. Asynchrony may also provide time for the individual bystander to seek out advice from others, and ask whether the person should respond.

Decide action: what can I do? what does "do something, say something" mean?

Once a person has decided it is their responsibility to do something, they need to decide what they can do. This decision involves knowing the actions that are possible in the specific context. Choosing from among these actions is influenced by the goals the bystander wishes to achieve and a consideration of the cost-benefit (risk) of these actions for those involved, including the bystander themself.

Research reveals that while bystanders frequently indicate they do not know what to do, they do, in fact, engage, and often try out a number of different actions (Keashly & Neuman, 2013). The challenge is in determining what actions are possible. Features of e-media actually increase the flexibility and capability for bystanders to respond beyond what is possible in face-to-face situations (Dillon & Bushman, 2015; Gahagan, Vaterlaus, & Frost, 2016). First, the asynchrony of much e-media provides the time for a bystander to think about their options and plan their response. Second, bystanders can choose to respond online or offline. Thus, even if the interaction has unfolded online – for example, in a listserv or a discussion post – the bystander could reach out in a private message or in person to the people involved. This behind-the-scenes and behind-the-screens strategy (Dooley et al., 2009), which has been used by actors to amplify their impact, can also be useful to the bystander. Third, and most broadly, actions can be either direct or indirect (Dillon, 2014; Dillon & Bushman, 2015; Latané & Darley, 1970). For example, rather than confronting the actor or showing visible support for the target, a bystander could seek to engage others in becoming involved, such as a department chair, colleagues, and other students (i.e., rallying others to help) (Eskey & Eskey, 2014). Finally, anonymity – which was highlighted earlier as potentially having a negative impact on bystander responding – can be used to a bystander's advantage to the extent with which they are concerned about how others will respond (e.g., fear of retaliation from the actor) or evaluate their response (e.g., evaluation apprehension) (Allison & Bussey, 2016; Latané & Darley, 1970). Indeed, in some e-environments, the bystander has the option of announcing themself when they intervene, or else remaining hidden behind a screen name or in clicking an abuse button.

A model that is helpful in demonstrating the range of possibilities for bystander action is Bowes-Sperry and O'Leary-Kelly's (2005) characterization of the decision-making of observers of sexual harassment. Briefly, in choosing an action, observers of sexual harassment consider the immediacy of their action (at the moment or after the fact) and the involvement or degree of visibility of their actions (i.e., behind the scenes, low visibility vs. visibly public). The crossing of these two dimensions opens a world of possibilities that may not have been considered by potential bystanders of cyberbullying. While Bowes-Sperry and O'Leary-Kelly's model was developed in responding to face-to-face situations, an examination of the variety of responses shows actions that could be suitable for online environments. For example, actions that are available in the immediate situation that can also be done below detection offline (high immediate, low involvement) include changing the topic, asking clarifying questions (e.g., "what do you mean?"), using nonverbals (emoticons or dislikes, in the case of email and social media) to communicate disapproval or concern, affirming the target by highlighting their strengths, or a process observation about the discussion (Nelson et al., 2011). Involvement could become more direct and visible (high immediate, high involvement) by telling the actor to stop, invoking group norms (e.g., against classroom discussion norms; disruption of free exchange of ideas), letting the target know they should report conduct, or by stating that the bystander is reporting the conduct. Actions that are low involvement and after the event (low immediate) would include not forwarding or sharing the negative image or message; advising the target offline to report; advising the person to stay off the media; getting others involved in the form of active intervention by a chair, program director, or other colleague; or posting positive messages regarding the target.

Bystander choice of action will be influenced by the goals they have for their action (i.e., what is it the bystander wants to have happen?). Table 10.1 includes possible goals or desired outcomes for bystander action.

To illustrate, if the goal is to name an inappropriate behaviour so that it is not ignored, relevant actions include naming the behaviour directly, invoking group norms, calling for civility, and confronting the actor – all of which communicate the unacceptability of the behaviour and affirm the group norms. The goal of preventing or stopping harm can be accomplished in a number of ways. Immediate

TABLE 10.1 Goals for Bystander Action

- Name/identify inappropriate behaviour, so it is not ignored or glossed over
- Uphold a community norm/value: making clear that this behaviour is not supported in this space
- Communicate that the behaviour is unacceptable without embarrassing the offending person; save face
- Phrase concern/give feedback in a way that the offending person is able to hear without being defensive
- Create an opening for discussion
- Protect someone from being hurt/offended or prevent further injury
- Protect someone else from causing harm – something they may regret!
- Create an open dialogue to eliminate misunderstanding; tension between people may be due to miscommunication
- Surface a concern that has been festering to prevent escalation into conflict or violence
- Express personal values of the bystander
- Enable an upset person to take a rational view of the situation
- Get help from someone who is better placed to intervene or who has the skill or capacity to handle it
- Make those responsible for the unit know what is going on

and visible action (direct) includes confronting the actor and telling them to stop, which can be done online (public or private) and offline (public or private). Regarding faculty experiences of cyberbullying, given that much of it occurs through email and those involved are known to each other, this makes one-on-one action more possible. For example, if a colleague shares an email from a student threatening to go to the chair, the colleague bystander could help reframe this as an anxiety response on the part of the student. They could explain that it is nothing to fear and, thus, that no response, or else a more tempered response, may be most appropriate.

Multiple actions are often needed to achieve the bystander's desired goal(s). These could occur simultaneously or sequentially. For example, in the situation of a hostile email from one colleague to another, the bystander may take action and disrupt the interaction, preventing or reducing harm (e.g., suggest that this is not the forum for these discussions). They could then follow up with the actor and/or target regarding what happened, thereby exploring alternative strategies to address the situation moving forward.

While the desired goals or outcomes for the action help narrow the focus to particular actions, these actions need to be considered in light of the cost/risk and benefits for those involved. The virality or immortality of the action is an important influence. Virality, which is an aspect that makes cyberbullying potent in terms of its harm and the powerlessness of the target to manage, has implications for the bystander as well. By being visible/public, the bystander needs to consider that their response, and they themselves, can be immortalized and become part of the overall narrative (Dillon, 2014; Dillon & Bushman, 2015). This carries with it a certain amount of risk, both personally and socially, for the bystander (Banyard, 2015; Dillon, 2014). Personal risk includes retaliation and becoming a target themselves. Social risk includes evaluation apprehension (fear of embarrassment; DeSmet et al., 2016); creating disharmony in relationship with the actor, target, or others (Brody & Vangelisti, 2016); and the potential stigma of being associated with a disliked target (Mulder, Pouwelse, Lodewijkx, & Bolman, 2014; Nelson et al., 2011).

Pending the bystander's risk assessment and their evaluation of their own capacity to handle possible blowback, they may choose to go ahead with a visible action and publicly identify themselves. The bystander's power relative to the actor and target is influential in this calculus, with higher-power bystanders assessing less personal and social risk – they are, therefore, more likely to engage directly (Banyard, 2015). Alternatively, and often more frequently, bystanders may choose more low-involvement action. This includes going private or one-on-one with the actor, target, or other bystanders (Dillon, 2014), thereby allowing the bystander to shield themself from unwanted attention. Such indirect action tends to be favoured in cyberbullying situations for these reasons (Freis & Gurung, 2013). While appearing "safe", going behind the scenes or being indirect does involve risk. Because these actions are not visible, they may appear as inaction to others. For example, not forwarding the negative email or image to others is a way of disrupting the negative action. However, the invisibility and ambiguity of this action may be perceived as not providing support for the target; the actor may perceive this "inaction" as consent to continue. For other bystanders who are seeking cues on how to respond, the lack of visibility (and, thus, the perceived inaction) may increase their reluctance to engage.

An important analysis for potential bystanders to undertake is the cost of taking no action (Skarlicki & Kulik, 2004). The potential cost includes the individual's sense of self as a caring person (asking themselves, "would a caring person choose not to do something?"), their relationship with the target (e.g., sense of betrayal), the potential for de-sensitization to harmful actions, and contributing to the development of tolerance for such actions in the e-community and the on-site community. Inaction is a particular challenge in cyberbullying situations involving faculty colleagues, when there are connections to both the actor and the target. The spillover effects of both action and inaction to personal relationships, as well as to department and university climate, can be profound.

Taking action: how do I do it?

Once the bystander has decided the action(s) they will take, they need to enact them. Enactment is dependent upon the bystander's skills and knowledge and, even more importantly, their sense of efficacy that they can apply these skills effectively in the situation (Allison & Bussey, 2016; DeSmet et al., 2016).

What skills are needed is dependent upon the action chosen. Some actions are relatively simple. For example, forwarding the email to the chair with a request for action, or letting the target know that the bystander values or supports them. Some actions can be implemented through the use of mini-scripts or "backpocket phrases". For example, if the goal is to clarify the situation, a handy phrase is: "What do you mean by that?". When problematic situations can be anticipated due to their recurring nature (which is often the case with cyberbullying, particularly involving faculty colleagues or "typical" situations with students), there is an opportunity to develop mini-scripts and backpocket phrases that can be easily accessed when the situation arises again.

Other actions are more complex in terms of skills required and the sequencing of these actions. A complex and particularly challenging action is confronting the actor about the behaviour. This action is complex because the enactment needs to convey a clear message, while also anticipating and mitigating possible negative impact, such as defensiveness and retaliation. If the bystander has a connection to the actor, the confrontation also needs to be enacted in a way that preserves their relationship (Ashburn-Nardo et al., 2014; Nelson et al., 2011). The confrontation action is often not a single statement. Frequently, it involves responding to the actor's reaction and working to manage that. These complex (indeed all) actions benefit from practice. A key focus of bystander training is to have people try out actions in specific situations and to receive feedback to fine-tune their response (Ashburn-Nardo et al., 2014; Nelson et al., 2011). Bystanders can also gain practice with trusted others. As noted earlier, the nature of some e-media provide the bystander with the space and time to seek advice, plan, and practice potential actions (Dillon & Bushman, 2015; Gahagan et al., 2016). Practice builds a sense of efficacy to enact the chosen actions as intended.

Action steps

What is clear from bullying and cyberbullying research is that these behaviours occur in the presence of others. The question this chapter sought to answer was the how and why of cyber-bystanding, considering the decisions an observer makes along the path to take action. Universities can influence community members' decisions to take constructive action to address cyberbullying and, more broadly, bullying incidents, as well. It is critical, however, that whatever policy, education, and training efforts are undertaken, they be developed *with* campus members, and must be grounded in a deep understanding of the character and profile of the institution and its members. The issue of cyberbullying, bullying, and the actions taken to address them create opportunities for sustained meaningful engagement with all campus members. This process of engagement is a living embodiment of the values of the institution, and, in and of itself, has profound implications for the development of a university culture and climate that is antithetical to bullying and cyberbullying (Keashly & Neuman, 2018).

Specific actions are presented using the framework of the bystander intervention model:

- **Notice and Assess**: Education about what cyberbullying is, the types of behaviours involved in cyberbullying, how it is different from behaviours such as constructive critique and debate, and the impact of these interactions is vital. More broadly, this education needs to be embedded in a value-driven discussion about what kind of learning and working environment the university is committed to, and how actions like cyberbullying contravene those values. These discussions need to be grounded in a deep appreciation of, and commitment to, academic freedom. These visions and discussions provide the normative guidelines for community member behaviour.
- **Responsibility**: The discussion of normative guidelines should include articulation of the roles and responsibility of community members in achieving and maintaining this environment (i.e., the learning and working climate is jointly determined). This articulation includes members' responsibility and duty of care vis-à-vis others, particularly when the actions of others can/may negatively affect the working and learning environment. Alongside these policies and codes, there need to be mechanisms that support bystander action by reducing the risk of retaliation (e.g., secure reporting mechanisms).

- **Deciding and taking action**: University community members need to have clear ideas about what actions are possible and supported by the institution. This chapter has provided a framework and other resources for considering a variety of actions. University members need specific and structured opportunities to practice these actions in the context of specific scenarios in order to build up their skills and their confidence, knowing they can take effective action when faced with problematic behaviours (Banyard, 2015; Swan, 2015). Skill development and efficacy can be most effectively accomplished through more broad-based bystander action training, with specific modules focused on cyberbullying.

References

Allison, K. R., & Bussey, K. (2016). Cyber-bystanding in context: A review of the literature on witnesses' responses to cyberbullying. *Children and Youth Services Review, 65*, 183–194.

Ashburn-Nardo, L., Blanchar, J. C., Petersson, J., Morris, K. A., & Goodwin, S. A. (2014). Do you say something when it's your boss? The role of perpetrator power in prejudice confrontation. *Journal of Social Issues, 70*(4), 615–636.

Banyard, V. L. (2015). *Toward the next generation of bystander prevention of sexual and relationship violence: Action coils to engage communities*. New York: Springer.

Bastiaensens, S., Vandebosch, H., Poels, K., Van Cleemput, K., DeSmet, A., & De Bourdeaudhuij, I. (2014). Cyberbullying on social network sites: An experimental study into bystanders' behavioural intentions to help the victim or reinforce the bully. *Computers in Human Behaviour, 31*, 259–271.

Black, T. (this volume). Designing healthy and supportive campus communities: An example from Simon Fraser University. In W. Cassidy, C. Faucher, & M. Jackson (Eds.), *Cyberbullying at university in international contexts* (pp. 162–167). Oxford, UK: Routledge.

Bowes-Sperry, L., & O'Leary-Kelly, A. M. (2005). To act or not to act: The dilemma faced by sexual harassment observers. *Academy of Management Review, 30*(2), 288–306.

Brody, N., & Vangelisti, A. L. (2016). Bystander intervention in cyberbullying. *Communication Monographs, 83*(1), 94–119.

Bystander. (2017). *Wiktionary: The free dictionary*. Retrieved from https://en.wiktionary.org/wiki/bystander

Cassidy, W., Faucher, C., & Jackson, M. (2014). The dark side of the Ivory Tower: Cyberbullying of university faculty and teaching personnel. *Alberta Journal of Educational Research, 60*(2), 279–299.

Christy, S. C. (2010). *Working effectively with faculty: Guidebook for higher education staff and managers*. Berkeley, CA: University Resources Press.

Clark, C. M., Werth, L., & Ahten, S. (2012). Cyber-bullying and incivility in the online learning environment, Part 1: Addressing faculty and student perceptions. *Nurse Educator, 37*(4), 150–156.

Coyne, I., Farley, S., Axtell, C., Sprigg, C., Best, L., & Kwok, O. (2016). Understanding the relationship between experiencing workplace cyberbullying, employee mental strain and job satisfaction: A dysempowerment approach. *The International Journal of Human Resource Management, 28*(7), 945–972.

Daniloff, C. (2009). Cyberbullying goes to college. *Bostonia, Spring*. Retrieved from www.bu.edu/bostonia/spring09/bully/

D'Cruz, P., & Noronha, E. (2013). Navigating the extended reach: Target experiences of cyberbullying at work. *Information and Organization, 23*(4), 324–343.
DeSmet, A., Bastiaensens, S., Van Cleemput, K., Poels, K., Vandebosch, H., Cardon, G., & De Bourdeaudhuij, I. (2016). Deciding whether to look after them, to like it, or leave it: A multidimensional analysis of predictors of positive and negative bystander behaviour in cyberbullying among adolescents. *Computers in Human Behaviour, 57*, 398–415.
Dillon, K. P. (2014). *The unresponsive cyberbystander: A proposed cyberbystander intervention model of the mediated social forces inhibiting intervention online.* Paper presented at the meeting of the Annual National Communication Association, Chicago, IL.
Dillon, K. P., & Bushman, B. J. (2015). Unresponsive or un-noticed? Cyberbystander intervention in an experimental cyberbullying context. *Computers in Human Behaviour, 45*, 144–150.
Dooley, J. J., Pyżalski, J., & Cross, D. (2009). Cyberbullying versus face-to-face bullying: A theoretical and conceptual review. *Journal of Psychology, 217*(4), 182–188.
Eskey, M. T. Sr., & Eskey, M. T. Jr. (2014). Cyberbullying in the online classroom: Faculty as the targets. In *Proceedings of TCC Worldwide Online Conference 2014* (pp. 30–41). Hawaii: TCC. Retrieved June 27, 2018 from https:www.learntechlib.org/p/149826/
Flaherty, C. (2017, June 26). Old criticisms, new threats. *Inside Higher Ed.* Retrieved from www.insidehighered.com/news/2017/06/26/professors-are-often-political-lightning-rods-now-are-facing-new-threats-over-their
Forssell, R. (2016). Exploring cyberbullying and face-to-face bullying in working life – Prevalence, targets and expressions. *Computers in Human Behaviour, 58*, 454–460.
Freis, S. D., & Gurung, R. A. (2013). A Facebook analysis of helping behaviour in online bullying. *Psychology of Popular Media Culture, 2*(1), 11–19.
Gahagan, K., Vaterlaus, J. M., & Frost, L. R. (2016). College student cyberbullying on social networking sites: Conceptualization, prevalence and perceived bystander responsibility. *Computers in Human Behaviour, 55*, 1097–1105.
Heatherington, W., & Coyne, I. (2014). Understanding individual experiences of cyberbullying encountered through work. *International Journal of Organization Theory and Behaviour, 17*(2), 163–192.
Keashly, L., & Neuman, J. H. (2013). Bullying in academia: What does current theorizing and research tell us? In J. Lester (Ed.), *Workplace bullying in higher education* (pp. 1–22). London: Routledge.
Keashly, L., & Neuman, J. H. (2018). Workplace bullying and mobbing in U.S. higher education. In M. Duffy & D. Yamada (Eds.), *Workplace bullying and mobbing in the U.S.* (pp. 507–538). Santa Barbara, CA: Praeger.
Keashly, L., & Wajngurt, C. (2016). Faculty bullying in higher education. *Psychology and Education: An Interdisciplinary Journal, 53*(1/2), 79–90.
Latané, B., & Darley, J. M. (1970). *The unresponsive bystander: Why doesn't he help?* New York: Appleton-Century Crofts.
Law, D. M., Shapka, J. D., Domene, J. F., & Gagne, M. H. (2012). Are cyberbullies really bullies? An investigation of reactive and proactive online aggression. *Computers in Human Behaviour, 28*, 664–672.
Levine, M., & Crowther, S. (2008). The responsive bystander: How social group membership and group size can encourage as well as inhibit bystander intervention. *Journal of Personality and Social Psychology, 95*(6), 1429–1439.
Madan, A. O. (2014). Cyber aggression/cyber bullying and the dark triad: Effect on workplace behaviour/performance. *International Journal of Social, Management, Economics and Business Engineering, 8*(6), 1725–1730.

Mahler, J. (2015, March 8). Who spewed that abuse? Anonymous Yik Yak app isn't telling. *New York Times.*

Markey, P. M. (2000). Bystander intervention in computer-mediated communication. *Computers in Human Behaviour, 16*(2), 183–188.

Miceli, M. P., Near, J. P., & Dworkin, T. M. (2013). *Whistle-blowing in organizations.* London: Psychology Press.

Minor, M. A., Smith, G. S., & Brashen, H. (2013). Cyberbullying in higher education. *Journal of Educational Research and Practice, 3*(1), 15–29.

MIT Ombuds Office. (2004). *Active bystander program and mediation@MIT.* Retrieved from http://web.mit.edu/bystanders/strategies/index.html

Mulder, R., Pouwelse, M., Lodewijkx, H., & Bolman, C. (2014). Workplace mobbing and bystanders' helping behaviour towards victims: The role of gender, perceived responsibility and anticipated stigma by association. *International Journal of Psychology, 49*(4), 304–312.

Nelson, J. K., Dunn, K. M., & Paradies, Y. (2011). Bystander anti-racism: A review of the literature. *Analyses of Social Issues and Public Policy, 11*(1), 263–284.

O'Reilly, J., Aquino, K., & Skarlicki, D. (2016). The lives of others: Third parties' responses to others' injustice. *Journal of Applied Psychology, 101*, 171–189.

Paull, M., Omari, M., & Standen, P. (2012). When is a bystander not a bystander? A typology of the roles of bystanders in workplace bullying. *Asia Pacific Journal of Human Resources, 50*(3), 351–366.

Pew Research Center. (2014, October). *Online harassment.* Retrieved from www.pewinternet.org/2014/10/22/online-harassment/

Privitera, C., & Campbell, M. A. (2009). Cyberbullying: The new face of workplace bullying? *CyberPsychology & Behaviour, 12*(4), 395–400.

Shea, V. (1994). *Netiquette.* San Francisco, CA: Albion.

Shultz, E., Heilman, R., & Hart, K. J. (2014). Cyber-bullying: An exploration of bystander behaviour and motivation. *Cyberpsychology: Journal of Psychosocial Research on Cyberspace, 8*(4) article 3.

Skarlicki, D., & Kulik, C. T. (2004). Third party reactions to employee (mis)treatment: A justice perspective. *Research in Organizational Behaviour, 26*, 183–229.

Swan, S. L. (2015). Bystander interventions. *Wisconsin Law Review, 2015*(6), 975–1047.

Ury, W. (2000). *The third side: Why we fight and how we can stop.* London: Penguin Books.

Vance, J. W. (2010). *Cyber-harassment in higher education: Online learning environments.* Ed.D. dissertation. Retrieved from University of Southern California Digital Library (usctheses-m2954).

Wankel, L., & Wankel, C. (Eds.). (2012). *Cutting-edge technologies in higher education, Volume 5: Misbehaviour online in higher education.* Bingley, UK: Emerald Group Publishing Limited.

White, C. H., & Malkowski, J. (2014). Communicative challenges of bystander intervention: Impact of goals and message design logic on strategies college students use to intervene in drinking situations. *Health Communication, 29*(1), 93–104.

Wingate, S. V., Minney, J. A., & Guadagno, R. E. (2013). Sticks and stones may break your bones, but words will always hurt you: A review of cyberbullying. *Social Influence, 8*, 87–106.

11

THE FAIRNESS LENS

A university ombudsperson's perspective on building a kinder online culture on campus

Natalie Sharpe

Ombudspersons (also known as ombuds) in higher education appeared in North America in the mid-1960s in response to various social and civil rights movements, which led to student unrest and campus conflict. Since then, the role of ombudspersons in higher education has proliferated in other parts of the world: Australia in the 1970s; areas of Europe, Mexico, and Central and South America in the 1980s; with post-secondary student representatives from Africa, Asia, Australia, Europe, and North America also advocating for a global ombudsperson in higher education to UNESCO in 2009 (*Europe: Students call*, 2009, 15 Feb.). Globally, associations of ombudspersons in post-secondary settings have established linkages to promote the growth of the ombuds's role in higher education since the 1980s (Behrens, 2017), meeting at various national and international conferences and establishing journals to promote the exchange of ideas.

Ombudspersons play a critical role on campuses. They respond to complaints related to almost every academic and social aspect of university life, and they are expected to do so in an unbiased, safe, and confidential manner. They examine and recommend policies and procedures for administrative and procedural fairness, and note where there are gaps, delays, and outdated practices within the university system. They help the client, whether that person is a student, staff, or faculty member, to holistically examine the situation, review available options, and develop empowerment skills to voice their concerns. Those who come to the Ombuds Office for help are often from marginalized or vulnerable populations and have experienced bullying from those in more privileged positions.

The ombudsperson also works with the institution to reveal the implications of a policy or decision (or lack thereof), such as the short- and long-term impact of cyberbullying on the complainant, the classroom, the faculty/administrative unit, and the reputation of the university. Unveiling the damage cyberbullying causes to these different stakeholders can prompt a university-wide dialogue on how to foster a healthier work culture – one that is proactive rather than reactive. Hollis (2016, p. 24) describes the ombudsperson as an "early alert figure" to toxic work and study environments, like the canary in a coal mine, warning of impending problems that may harm already marginalized populations within a university, or else ruin a university's reputation of institutional fairness and integrity.

This chapter explores one ombudsperson's views on ways to prevent and curtail cyberbullying on university campuses. The ombudsperson is ideally situated to address cyberbullying and its repercussions, since they are perceived as being a fair and impartial arbitrator of faculty, staff, and student issues.

Fairness as a working principle

Ombudspersons use the principle of multi-partiality when working with various university populations: the ombudsperson is not an advocate for one party in a given conflict, but rather an advocate for fairness. Working with fairness as the underlying principle, the ombuds strives to ensure that all perspectives are heard, particularly from those who are more vulnerable and, therefore, more likely to experience hardship and inequitable treatment.

The lens of fairness that guides the ombudsperson in formal and informal redress processes demands consideration of four points: procedural, substantive, relational, and equitable fairness. *Procedural fairness* asks whether the person was given timely notice and sufficient information to know the case before them; whether they were given an appropriate forum, with sufficient amount of time to be heard; and whether they were provided with reasons for the decision in a timely manner by an unbiased decision-maker (Ombudsman Saskatchewan, 2016, p. 1). *Substantive fairness* focuses on the decision-maker and whether they had the authority or jurisdiction to make the decision, and whether all relevant information was considered in order to reach a just decision (Ombudsman Saskatchewan, 2016, p. 1). *Relational fairness* examines how the party was treated, and whether the authority was approachable and respected confidentiality: was the decision-maker "honest and forthright [and] was an apology offered if a mistake was made?" (Ombudsman Saskatchewan, 2016, p. 1). According to Crean (2016), *equitable fairness* acknowledges the uniqueness of individual experiences and the importance of recognizing marginalization and inequities, meaning that treating parties with different backgrounds and histories in the same way may not be the best strategy to ensure fairness. In fact, in none of the cyberbullying cases I have heard during my many years as an ombudsperson has the harmed party been a member of a dominant group or someone in a position of power.

An ombudsperson must operationalize all four aspects of fairness (procedural, substantive, relational, and equitable) when developing policies, protocols, and best practices to ensure fair treatment of all parties. Cyberbullying cases often involve heightened emotionality and tensions, making it all the more important for parties to feel like they have been treated fairly. Adopting this fairness lens allows the ombudsperson to work towards transforming campus culture by addressing the often-tacit condoning of cyberbullying and, instead, fostering more respectful online behaviour. Campuses can only begin to cultivate a safer and kinder online culture when the university administration acknowledges addressing cyberbullying as a priority. Such top-down proposals can be complemented – indeed magnified – by collaborative initiatives from students, staff, faculty, and student and staff associations and unions.

Two cyberbullying examples

The first example involves a conflict between students who were assigned a group project as part of their coursework. Because the students all had different schedules, they divided up the tasks, with the intention of communicating through Facebook as there was no online class forum to exchange views. When some team members failed to complete their parts on time, one team member expressed frustration and concern for the project's successful completion and its academic quality. This angered those members who were behind in their contributions, with these students voicing their outrage at the suggestion that the quality of their work was being questioned. That night, the female student who had initially expressed concern received multiple online threats mainly from other students who were not participating in the project, but who were upset for their friends. They used strong language that escalated in threats to: "find her on campus, isolate her, and beat her up."

The following day, the targeted student approached the professor, who minimized her complaint, and refused to intervene. When the student's family approached the department chair, her complaint was taken seriously. The chair met with the ombudsperson (myself) to come to a solution that met the student's needs, but also would help the bullies to understand the harm they had caused. For the student this meant a safe place: a speedy resolution that would allow her to finish the project and an end to the threats to her safety. After meeting with those who were bullying, no sanctions were imposed on those who threatened her, although they were aware that further actions would be taken if the behaviour continued. As a result, the group was able to complete the project without further interference.

Unfortunately, despite the resolution in this particular case, there were no plans to incorporate guidelines for respectful online behaviour or information about redress procedures for cyberbullying in the course syllabus, nor were there initiatives for a dialogue around these issues with students in the current or subsequent class. The professor remained adamant that online behaviours were outside the classroom code of conduct and did not want to discuss it any further. As final exams approached, the bullying momentum abated as quickly as it had started. The "friends" who had offered negative commentary simultaneously stopped sending it, but without any direct intervention taking place with others beyond the members of the group. On-going restorative practices could have provided an important learning opportunity about respectful online behaviour.

The second example involves a request from one of the professional faculties for an intervention to address the targeting of a student with disabilities. Other students in the faculty had been gossiping about this student on Instagram and Facebook, leading the latter to feel that his confidentiality had been breached and his professional reputation tarnished. The incident raised broader concerns for the faculty because it called into question the effectiveness of its code of ethics, to which students were required to adhere in their classes and professional clinical placements. Rather than sanction the perpetrators individually, the faculty decided to ask the ombudsperson to facilitate educational sessions that would engage the students in discussions on professionalism and appropriate use of social media. As the ombudsperson, I worked with the students to review common myths about personal gossip and its potential impact on their professional lives. For the session, I designed three classroom case studies based on the following scenarios: (1) a student breaching a client's confidentiality on social media; (2) a student making unprofessional comments about a worker during a clinical placement; and (3) students gossiping about a classmate with special needs. The students discussed the harm caused by each of these breaches, as well as more professional alternative approaches in these situations. Finally, they explored positive options to use social media for professional connections. As a follow-up to the session, the students, faculty, and ombudsperson decided to collaborate to create best practices guidelines that can offer support in the future.

Action items

While developing protocols and intervening in cases of cyberbullying and other unfair treatment are important aspects of the ombudsperson's role, the function also focuses on prevention through initiatives that actively cultivate healthy online communication. In our annual report for 2016–2017, the Office of the Student Ombuds (OSO) at the University of Alberta made the following recommendation, which has been endorsed by our Senate:

> As the number of cyberbullying incidents increases on postsecondary campuses, the OSO recommends that faculty and student groups explore informal modes of conflict resolution to respond to conflicts and restore relationships. The digital citizenship approach to healthy use of social media can serve as a model to mitigate conflicts and teach students ways to defuse conflict in social media discourse.

Furthermore, the OSO has developed A Guide to Healthy Social Media Usage, delivers workshops on best practices in social media usage, and offered a summary presentation of the guide at a recent Student Advisors' Conference.

Some additional practical suggestions are outlined as follows (see also Hoover, 2003; Jones & Scott, 2012; UNESCO, 2014; Walker, 2014):

1 Include a section on civility, social media (mis)use, and sanctions in course syllabi;
2 Hold seminars with undergraduate and graduate students to discuss cyberbullying and encourage positive online behaviour;
3 Establish opportunities for faculty and staff to engage in discussions and develop protocols for addressing cyberbullying;
4 Invite an ombudsperson to class and to faculty and staff meetings to present case scenarios and provide opportunities for participants to engage with issues of fairness and due process, and to develop measures for promoting and modelling digital citizenship;
5 Develop ways to better involve vulnerable student populations in policy and practice – listen to their needs, provide safe spaces to address their issues, and provide support;
6 Work collaboratively across all stakeholder groups (ombudsperson, Human Rights Office, student groups, faculty associations, unions, etc.) to develop codes of conduct, harassment and anti-bullying/cyberbullying policies, and communicate these policies effectively through various media.

References

Behrens, R. (2017). *Being an ombudsman in higher education: A comparative study*. Vienna, Austria: European Network of Ombudsmen in Higher Education.

Crean, F. (2016). The fairness lens in a changing landscape. Retrieved from www.oct.ca//media/PDF/College%20Conference%202016%20Workshop%20PDF/Series%202/The%20Fairness%20Lens%20in%20a%20Changing%20Landscape.pdf

Europe: Students call for a global ombudsman. (2009, February 15). *University World News, 63* [online edition].

Hollis, L. (2016). Canary in the mine: Ombuds as first alerts for workplace bullying on campus. *Journal of the International Ombudsman Association, 9*(1), 23–31.

Hoover, L. (2003). Developing a communication protocol. *University of California David Developing Departmental Protocols, 4*(1). Retrieved from www.campus-adr.org/CMHER/print/hoover4_1.pdf

Jones, J. C., & Scott, S. (2012). Cyberbullying in the university classroom: A multiplicity of issues. In L. A. Wankel & C. Wankel (Eds.), *Misbehavior online in higher education: Cutting-edge Technologies in Higher Education* (Volume 5, pp. 157–182). Bingley, UK: Emerald Group Publishing Limited.

Ombudsman Saskatchewan. (2016). What is fairness? Retrieved from www.ombudsman.sk.ca/uploads/document/files/what-is-fairness-feb-2016-en.pdf

UNESCO. (2014). Paris Declaration calls for renewed emphasis on media and information literacy in the digital age. *In Focus*. [online article].

Walker, C. (2014). Cyberbullying redefined: An analysis of intent and repetition. *International Journal of Education and Social Science, 1*(5), 59.

12

DESIGNING HEALTHY AND SUPPORTIVE CAMPUS COMMUNITIES

An example from Simon Fraser University

Tara Black

In recent years, there has been a growing movement among Canadian higher education institutions to enhance students' and faculty's state of well-being – since well-being is unquestionably impacted by the settings in which people learn, work, and live. The release of the *Okanagan Charter: An International Charter for Health Promoting Universities and Colleges* (2015) provides further impetus for universities to focus on this settings-based approach, calling on higher education institutions to embed health into all aspects of campus culture: across administration, operations, and academic mandates. Consistent with that rationale, Simon Fraser University (SFU)[1] has focused on executing forward-thinking, healthy, campus community efforts. These efforts are worth highlighting, given their potential links with (and opportunity for the development of) upstream anti-bullying strategies nationwide.

In first designing healthy and supportive campus communities, the *Okanagan Charter* recommends creating supportive environments and generating thriving communities to promote a culture of well-being. As the Charter points out, higher education institutions are uniquely positioned to develop and model thriving communities. They can cultivate an individual's well-being through their transformational teaching and learning environments: inspiring students, staff, and faculty to become healthier and more engaged citizens and leaders. A number of Canadian institutions, including SFU, have formally adopted the Charter, therefore, at the Presidential level.

SFU, specifically, has implemented a whole-campus settings approach and successfully created a more healthy and supportive community on site. The Healthy Campus Community (HCC) initiative at SFU has focused on facilitating collective, systemic, and innovative action for well-being to improve its campus culture and environments. This goal has been addressed through action areas, including:

policies and processes, learning and working environments, physical spaces, and services. The vision behind the initiative is as follows: "Simon Fraser University is a healthy campus community where the people, programs, practices, policies and spaces foster well-being, supporting campus members to thrive and succeed at SFU and beyond" (SFU Healthy Campus Community, 2014). The HCC initiative is facilitated by SFU's Health Promotion team and, ultimately, aims to impact prescribed student and faculty health outcomes, such as: thriving, sense of community, social connection, resilience, and social, physical, and emotional health. This has all been, or sought to be, achieved through the settings and systems-defined approaches.

While no one-size-fits-all intervention can effectively lead to more supportive campus communities – given the complex nature of higher education institutions – it is through such comprehensive and innovative projects that real differences have been shown to be enacted in a system. SFU's whole-campus emphasis has catalysed comprehensive action through the engagement of diverse campus stakeholders outside of traditional health fields, drawing attention to the role that all departments and faculties have in impacting both individual and community well-being. Its project engagement has intentionally focused on building relationships and gaining individual and institutional commitment from all levels of the university (from students up to SFU's President and executive team). Additionally, in order to develop targeted action on key elements of the campus setting, strategic partnerships have been established with key campus stakeholders, such as the Teaching and Learning Centre, Senate and Academic Services, Simon Fraser Student Society, and Facilities Services.

SFU's HCC initiative has already resulted in the development of a number of programs that contribute to a supportive campus culture. The learning environment, for example, was affected, as it was identified early on by the university as having a central role in students' experiences, with a powerful ability to impact their well-being (either positively or negatively). Two examples of such potential negative impacts are stress and isolation – and the prevalence of both stress and isolation in higher education has been increasing among higher education students (Robotham & Julian, 2006). In the most recent National College of Health Assessment Data (ACHA, 2016), 63% of SFU students reported feeling exhausted (with a national average of 65%), 81% felt overwhelmed by all they had to do (with the national average at 89%), over 63% reported overwhelming anxiety at least once in the last 12 months (compared to a national average of 65%), and 64% felt lonely (vs. the national average of 67%). Therefore, much like other Canadian universities, SFU does manifest similar issues, although at consistently lower averages than at a national level.

One source of such stress (anxiety) and isolation can be caused by student, staff, and faculty experiences with bullying and cyberbullying on campus, both of which can have similar effects to mental and emotional health (Blizard, 2014; Cassidy, Faucher, & Jackson, 2014, this volume; Celep & Konalki, 2013; Clark,

Werth, & Ahten, 2012; Faucher, Cassidy, & Jackson, 2015; Faucher, Jackson, & Cassidy, 2014; Hollis, 2012). A way to generate more positive effects, as exemplified by SFU, was through the provision of supportive environments. In that regard, university professors had the opportunity to create supportive classroom conditions by building a positive, inclusive, and welcoming classroom culture by establishing a tone of respect. They also contributed to building social connections among students through team and group-based activities, assignments, and grading. This learning environment focus evolved through a partnership established between SFU's Health Promotion Team and the Teaching and Learning Centre, in which professors were involved in the development of the *Well-being in Learning Environments* program. The purpose was to engage instructors in creating supportive learning environments through teaching pedagogy, as well as course design and delivery.

The program itself embodies principles of participatory action, collaboration, and asset-based approaches that build on actions and activities (which can create conditions for well-being). A number of conditions for well-being in learning environments were identified through a literature review and stakeholder interviews, with positive examples, tools, and strategies made available on a website. An annual event was developed to create a platform for professors to share strategies and learn from each other's examples.

In addition to increasing awareness and capacity amongst professors, there have also been efforts to engage staff through dialogue sessions about how they, in their various capacities, can contribute to a culture of well-being on campus. For instance, the staff student advisors participated in a session that drew attention to the opportunity they have to create positive, supportive, and respectful environments, and to impact the emotional wellness of the students with whom they interact. Students have also been integrally involved in all aspects of SFU's Healthy Campus Community initiative, and a Student Health Advisory Committee has been working to engage students and student leaders across campus to consider their role in creating a healthier, collaborative community.

A consideration of health in all policies has been established in the health promotion field as a key action area (de Leeuw, Clavier, & Breton, 2014); however, few examples exist as to how this strategy can be applied in the context of higher education. SFU's Health Promotion team formed a partnership with the Associate Registrar, engaging stakeholders, in a collaborative process, to develop a tool by which universities could apply a well-being lens to policy development and review. The tool, *Well-being through SFU Policies & Procedures: A Guide for Action*, provides a framework that intentionally considers how policies and procedures impact campus well-being when reviewing or creating new policies and procedures. Overarching principles were established, suggesting that all aspects of these policies and procedures should embody a culture of respect and support. Guidelines, such as ensuring the tone and content of the university's guidelines are positive, supportive, and respectful, and using inclusive language when writing such documents, are examples of how such a culture may be fostered.

The guide also recommends that the application of policies and procedures should set a positive, respectful, and supportive tone within a learning environment (as opposed to being punitive). This application should be seen as an extension of students' formal education, using discussions with students as teachable moments that contribute to their learning and development.

Despite this positive outreach, there remain many opportunities at SFU to continue to increase institutional will and action, as based on whole-campus methods. It is promising that SFU, however, among other institutions, is beginning to take notice and prioritize Healthy Campus Community efforts. Although more institutions are taking action, published studies are still sparse. To date, minimal focus has been spent on evaluating the impact of bullying/cyberbullying on campus culture/wellness specifically; instead, attention has been given more substantially to overall campus community wellness, wherein "it is widely accepted that health and well-being are essential elements for effective learning" (El Ansari & Stock, 2010, p. 2). Campus communities thrive when attention is paid to the well-being of their students, instructors, staff, and others in a healthy campus culture – what has been missed is that, as a result, bullying/cyberbullying decreases as well (Cassidy et al., 2014; Clark et al., 2012; DeSouza, 2010; Faucher et al., 2014, 2015; Hinduja & Patchin, 2012; Hollis, 2012; Knepp, 2012).

There is still a lot to be learned about systemic and settings approaches to health and well-being in higher education. While one can appreciate that the results of settings approaches are often long-term and challenging to measure (given the complex nature of higher education institutions), at SFU specifically, there are further opportunities for students to engage with these issues. For example, on the SFU Healthy Campus Community website, there are materials and resources which address such matters. Some of these include: the healthy university community; the rationale for well-being in learning communities (Dhaliwal & Stanton, 2014); overcoming university stress and academic pressures; well-being through policies and procedures; and a video, "Designing Healthy Campus Communities: Enhancing Student Well-being & Academic Success." In addition, on the SFU Safety and Risk Services website, other personal safety guides and workshops of relevance to wellness are listed for students, faculty, and staff alike to access (SFU Safety & Risk Services, n.d.).

In conclusion, it has been shown that there is a connection to be made between healthy campus community efforts that aim to create supportive, connected, thriving people and communities – in that they create a culture of campus wellness – and the prevention of bullying/cyberbullying. This link presents an opportunity for shared learning and collaboration for campus anti-bullying and healthy campus community strategies and action.

Note

1 For context, Simon Fraser University is a comprehensive university with 30,000 students, 6,500 staff and faculty, and three campuses, located in British Columbia, Canada.

References

American College Health Association – National College Health Assessment II (ACHA-NACHA II). (2016). *Canadian Reference Group: Executive Summary* [online]. Retrieved from http://www.acha-ncha.org/docs/ncha-ii%20spring%202016%20canadian%20reference%20group%20executive%20summary.pdf

Blizard, L. M. (2014). *Faculty members' perceived experiences and impact of cyberbullying from students at a Canadian university: A mixed methods study*. Ed.D. dissertation, Simon Fraser University: Burnaby, BC.

Cassidy, W., Faucher, C., & Jackson, M. (2014). The dark side of the ivory tower: Cyberbullying of university faculty and teaching personnel. *Alberta Journal of Educational Research, 60*(2), 279–299.

Cassidy, W., Faucher, C., & Jackson, M. (this volume). "You need a thick skin . . .": Impacts of cyberbullying in Canadian universities. In W. Cassidy, C. Faucher, & M. Jackson (Eds.), *Cyberbullying at university in international contexts* (pp. 112–125). Oxford, UK: Routledge.

Celep, C., & Konalki, T. (2013). Mobbing experiences of instructors: Causes, results, and solutions suggestions. *Educational Sciences: Theory & Practice, 13*(1), 193–199.

Clark, C. M., Werth, L., & Ahten, S. (2012). Cyber-bullying and incivility in the online learning environment, Part 1: Addressing faculty and student perceptions. *Nurse Educator, 37*(4), 150–156.

Dhaliwal, R., & Stanton, A. (2014). *SFU health promotion: Well-being in learning environments rationale*. Burnaby, BC: Simon Fraser University [online].

de Leeuw, E., Clavier, C., & Breton, E. (2014). Health policy – Why research it and how: Health political science. *Health Research Policy and Systems, 12*(1), 55–64.

Designing Healthy Campus Communities: Enhancing Student Well-being and Academic Success. (2013). *Canadian Mental Health Association, BC Division, & SFU Health Promotion: BC Healthy Minds/Healthy Campuses*. Burnaby, BC: Simon Fraser University [online].

DeSouza, E. R. (2010). Frequency rates and correlates of contrapower harassment in higher education. *Journal of Interpersonal Violence, 48*(11), 1–27.

El Ansari, W., & Stock, C. (2010). Is the health and wellbeing of university students associated with their academic performance? Cross sectional findings from the United Kingdom. *International Journal of Environmental Research and Public Health*, 7(2), 509–527.

Faucher, C., Cassidy, W., & Jackson, M. (2015). From the sandbox to the inbox: Comparing the acts, impacts, and solutions of bullying in K-12, higher education, and the workplace. *Journal of Education and Training Studies, 3*(6), 111–125.

Faucher, C., Jackson, M., & Cassidy, W. (2014). Cyberbullying among university students: Gendered experiences, impacts, and perspectives. *Education Research International, 2014*, 1–10.

Hinduja, S., & Patchin, J. W. (2012). *School climate 2.0: Preventing cyberbullying and sexting one classroom at a time*. Thousand Oaks, CA: Corwin Press.

Hollis, L. P. (2012). *Bully in the ivory tower: How aggression and incivility erode American higher education*. Wilmington, DE: Patricia Berkly.

Knepp, K. A. F. (2012). Understanding student and faculty incivility in higher education. *The Journal of Effective Teaching, 12*(1), 33–46.

Okanagan Charter: An international charter for health promoting universities and colleges. (2015). *International Conference on Health Promoting Universities & Colleges*. Kelowna, BC [online].

Robotham, D., & Julian, C. (2006). Stress & the higher education student: A critical review. *Journal of Further Higher Education*, *30*(2), 107–117.

SFU Healthy Campus Community. (n.d.). *Well-being through SFU policies & procedures: A guide for action*. Burnaby, BC: Simon Fraser University [online].

SFU Healthy Campus Community. (2014). *SFU vision for a healthy community*. Burnaby, BC: Simon Fraser University [online].

SFU Safety & Risk Services. (n.d.). *Personal safety guides*. Burnaby, BC: Simon Fraser University [online].

13

PREVENTIVE MEASURES AGAINST CYBERBULLYING AT A UNIVERSITY IN JAPAN

Kenichi Kanayama and Shinji Kurihara

Cyberbullying may not appear to be problematic on university campuses. It is more likely, however, that universities have not fully grasped the magnitude of the problem, and therefore, its effects remain undetected. This chapter describes one pioneering model used at "University A" in Japan to detect and tackle cyberbullying among university students. This is a research-based, structured model, designed to support students using a widespread peer-support scheme, specially designed courses and seminars, testing for potential problems, and counselling.

A comprehensive student support system at University A

The following Comprehensive Student Support system provides three levels of support for individual students, extending from matriculation to graduation.

First level of support: a sense of belonging and preventive measures

At the first level of support, University A incorporates peer support programs into its academic programs. Classes encourage peer-to-peer interactions that help to build informed relationships outside of school hours. Students also sign up for seminars over a one- or two-year period – lab-like classes – that foster group discussion among both peers and the designated instructor. These classes are designed to build relationships and create a sense of community on campus, which helps to act as a preventive measure against cyberbullying behaviour.

In addition, every student at the beginning of their first year must complete the UPI (University Personality Inventory), a screening of potential mental health problems. Students in their first year must also complete a course called "Internet morality education," taught by cyberbullying prevention experts. This course provides tips and guidance on preventive measures against cyberbullying. For example, students learn a variety of legal measures that can be taken against those who upload messages that abuse others. Another example is that students are introduced to typical cyberbullying cases and discuss what one could have done to prevent it from happening or to intervene if one similar to the typical case occurs.

Second level of support: team-based support and peer support

Cyberbullying causes distress. Students facing problems like cyberbullying are often absent from school. The second level of support is founded upon the idea that the university supports students as a team. Specifically, it seeks to ensure that faculty, typically seen as merely academic advisors and lecturers to students, attend to the psychological needs of their students. One way this is implemented is through regular communication between the Office of Student Affairs and faculty members. The former regularly shares students' status regarding credit acquisition, tuition payment, student loan and scholarship applications, and class attendance, with the latter, while the latter communicates reports of students' well-being in classes. Each student is assigned to a faculty member as a tutor, who serves not only as a mentor of academic life but also of emotional and social life. Faculty members are required to go through training involving counselling techniques. As part of the tutoring process, faculty members use the information they have learned from their regular meetings with the Office of Student Affairs to help assess their students' well-being. In addition, the peer support system among students (detailed later in this article) and the services offered by the Counselling Room for Students are also available to the identify students with needs.

Third level of support: a close relationship with medical institutions

Distress from problems such as cyberbullying can lead to mental suffering including, but not limited to, cases of depression. As the third level of support, the Counselling Room for Students assists students with mental health problems, offering guidance and care in consultation with hospitals. This counselling service is offered at no cost to any student who requires this service. Occasionally, counsellors accompany students with medical needs to a local hospital.

Counselling services for students at University A

Screening test

Every year, all undergraduate and graduate students participate in the UPI, a mental health screening test for university students, developed by the University of Tokyo and the University of Kyoto. This mandatory system helps University A keep track of its students' mental health status from matriculation to graduation. The test screens for general mental illnesses, depressive states, and suicide ideation/intentions.

Personalized support plan

Based on the UPI results, counsellors devise a personalized mental health plan for each individual student, which includes some or all of the following four types of support: (1) providing them with a tutor, as well as the previously mentioned team-based system of support with faculty and staff; (2) collaborating with the Department of Student Support and School Nurses; (3) having the student participate in the peer-support program; and (4) suggestions to receive medical support.

Educational programs to prevent cyberbullying

"Mobile Phones and the Law" class in the first-year compulsory curriculum

A large number of universities in Japan require the "Internet morality education" class as part of their mandatory first-year curricula. University A also offers a course on "Mobile Phones and the Law," incorporating quiz sessions, for example:

Question 1. What would happen if you spread messages on social media such as "Ms. B works at a brothel" or "C was caught shoplifting"?

Answer: You could be accused of the crime of defamation (libel); up to three years of imprisonment or a fine of up to 500,000 JPY.

Question 2. What would happen if you posted "D is annoying" or "E is disgusting" on a group chat with other students in your seminar?

Answer: You could be accused of the crime of insult; up to 30 days of detention or a fine of up to 10,000 JPY.

This course informs students that posting such abusive comments online can subject them to criminal responsibility. We believe that these educational efforts deter students from posting similar abusive comments, thereby reducing cyberbullying and cybercrime.

"Cyber Police" class (a branch of the police department designated to tackle cyber-crimes)

The "Cyber Police" seminar series, offered at University A, further introduces students to procedures university counsellors may use to report cases of online abuse to the police. This class is a series of five separate 90-minute seminars, offered by faculty and non-faculty lecturers. Procedures such as the following are discussed: when a student receives an abusive post online, he or she will be asked by a counsellor to take a screenshot of the image. The counsellor then presents a photocopy of this saved image to the cyber police as a piece of evidence, so that the police may investigate further, or perhaps take the case to trial. Student feedback following the class reinforces the deterrence factor, as noted by this student: "By trying out what I learned from the class, I was able to stop cyberbullying."

Peer support system at University A

The peer-support system, designed to bring students closer together and help them form social bonds, is helpful in supporting students who use social media but are uncomfortable socializing offline. This system also assists students who have been targets of cyberbullying in that it facilitates help-seeking behaviour among peers.

The peer-support system is open to all who are registered, regardless of whether a student requires mental health assistance or is facing cyberbullying. Research conducted by Kanayama (2014) shows there is no difference in the effectiveness of peer support for students with or without needs for mental health support; rather, it is equally beneficial for all its participants.

For students who do require mental health support, counsellors help them develop and implement small-step goals, enabling them to build on the experience of more minor successes and to gain self-confidence. This approach builds trust among the student body and empowers individual learners to better adapt to life on campus (Kanayama, 2015).

Outside of University A, peer support is becoming more widely utilized across universities in Japan. In 2015, 49.3% of all universities in Japan (83.5% of national universities, 34.9% of other public universities, and 46.4% of private universities) implemented a peer-support system: a dramatic increase from only 12.9% in 2005 (JASSO, 2017).

Based on the success of the program at University A, we suggest that other universities may wish to implement a comprehensive student support system including screening tests, preventive educational programs, and a peer-support system, as a complement to other anti-cyberbullying measures. These measures have been helpful in reducing cyberbullying among the university student population at University A, as well as maintaining and assisting with students' mental health and general well-being.

References

Kanayama, K. (2014). Yōshiengakusei taishō no piasapōto kenshū puroguramukaihatsu no tameno kisotekikenkyū [Basic research for developing peer support training program for students with mental health support needs]. *Japanese Annals of Peer Support, 11*, 1–10.

Kanayama, K. (2015). Yōshiengakusei to ippangakusei no piasapōto ni taisuru PAC bunsekiniyoru taidokouzō no hikaku [Comparison of attitudinal structure toward peer support between students with and without mental health support needs]. *Japanese Annals of Peer Support, 12*, 27–38.

JASSO. (2017). Daigakunado ni okeru gakuseishien no torikumijōkyō ni kansuru 2015 nendo chōsa [Research into student support programs at institutions of higher learning]. Retrieved from www.jasso.go.jp/about/statistics/torikumi_chosa/torikumi_chosa_2015.html

14

INTERVENING AGAINST WORKPLACE CYBERBULLYING

Samuel Farley and Iain Coyne

In an age of technology-imposed challenges – including phishing scams, surveillance monitoring, and social media spill-over – how universities limit the risks of workplace cyberbullying is another difficult question that human resources professionals (HRPs) must consider. Unfortunately, HRPs are not able to draw upon a wealth of evidence-based recommendations that specify how to address this problem. Practitioners seeking inspiration on how to limit cyberbullying within the university context must, therefore, turn to more developed disciplines to identify empirically evaluated intervention methods. This chapter examines studies on youth cyberbullying and traditional workplace bullying interventions, as well as recommendations from the evidence-based practice movement, to highlight sources that can help university practitioners move towards online solutions.

Developing the most effective intervention to address an issue is a complex process. The evidence-based practice (EBP) approach contends that it should be informed by four different sources: (1) practitioner expertise and judgement; (2) evidence from the local context; (3) a critical evaluation of the best available research evidence; and (4) the perspectives of those affected by the problem (Briner, Denyer, & Rousseau, 2009). The consequences of not using different sources of evidence when developing interventions is that the intervention itself may not provide any tangible benefits or, worse, it may harm the intended recipients (Briner, 2012). It seems prudent, therefore, to assess each source of evidence in turn when making a decision on how to intervene against workplace cyberbullying. In this chapter, we limit our discussions to the best available research evidence that can assist university practitioners during the development of cyberbullying interventions.

Pioneers of the EBP approach recommend examining the problem, question, or issue at hand thoroughly before consulting different sources of evidence.

As noted in Chapter 6 (Coyne & Farley, this volume), workplace cyberbullying has been conceptualized in the same manner as traditional workplace bullying. Accordingly, practitioners may feel that the most effective method of intervening would be to reduce bullying at a broad level, without tailored efforts to reduce its online manifestation. At the same time, cyberbullying differs from traditional bullying in notable ways, which may influence intervention strategies. For instance, it is easier for "organizational outsiders" to enact cyberbullying, as the perpetrator and target do not need to occupy the same physical location. Taking the university context as an example, this means that members of the public can abuse academics who use social networking websites to disseminate their research – the methods that practitioners adopt, therefore, will likely be influenced by investigation of cyberbullying at the local level.

In order to coherently explain bullying intervention efforts, researchers have categorized these efforts as being either primary, secondary, or tertiary. Primary interventions focus on preventing bullying before it occurs; secondary interventions focus on providing employees with coping resources, in case bullying does occur; and tertiary interventions aim to reduce the negative consequences of bullying after it has occurred (Hershcovis, Reich, & Niven, 2015). Primary interventions are naturally seen as the most effective, because they address the causes of bullying, rather than reacting once it has become a problem.

In the university context, there is a lack of evidence for primary interventions geared towards preventing bullying and other forms of harassment. Indeed, a systematic review of bullying interventions across working contexts revealed that only one could be considered effective – and this focused on incivility rather than bullying (Hodgins, MacCurtain, & Mannix-McNamara, 2014). Evaluations demonstrate that the civility, respect, and engagement at work (CREW) program can reduce incivility, absenteeism, and burnout (Leiter, Laschinger, Day, & Oore, 2011). CREW involves work units participating in weekly meetings to discuss and model civil ways of interacting. Since some of the beneficial impacts of CREW were sustained over a 12-month period (Leiter, Day, Gilin-Oore, & Laschinger, 2012), it has been suggested that CREW training could be adapted to address cyber-forms of harassment (Park, Fritz, & Jex, 2015).

In the youth context, a few notable primary interventions have been conducted which report efficacy in reducing cyberbullying. These include the ViSC program, an aspect of Austria's national strategy for reducing traditional bullying and aggressive behaviour in secondary schools. During ViSC, teachers encourage students to take responsibility for preventing bullying, as well as giving them an opportunity to practise their social skills. The program also contains secondary intervention elements, as teachers are trained in how to recognize and tackle acute bullying cases (Gradinger, Yanagida, Strohmeier, & Spiel, 2016). A randomized control design showed that an intervention group decreased in self-reported cyberbullying enactment compared to a control group. Interestingly, these effects were observed despite the fact that the program did not contain any specific cyberbullying elements.

In Finland, the KiVa program has also reported success in reducing cyberbullying (Williford et al., 2013). KiVa aims to reduce bullying by promoting empathy, self-efficacy, and anti-bullying attitudes in bystanders. The program involves universal actions (primary intervention): classroom lessons that raise awareness of bullying and promote empathy. These are combined with indicated actions (secondary intervention): guidance on how to react to bullying cases, including peer support for the victim and discussions with bystanders on how to support the target. Evaluation showed that there was significantly less cyber-victimization among an intervention group who received KiVa training compared to a control group (Williford et al., 2013). Specific aspects of the training may have been responsible for this effect, including lessons on respect during cyber-communication and computer-simulated scenarios of cyberbullying events.

Organizational researchers have not yet evaluated secondary interventions on resources that help employees cope when faced with traditional workplace bullying (Hershcovis et al., 2015). However, theoretical frameworks which specify the development of workplace bullying and detrimental computer-mediated communication have both emphasized conflict escalation as an antecedent factor (Friedman & Currall, 2003; Zapf & Gross, 2001). It has been suggested, therefore, that conflict de-escalation could be a valuable skill that allows employees to cope with negative acts before they develop into protracted conflicts (Branch, Ramsay, & Barker, 2013). A component of conflict de-escalation training could involve guidance on informal resolution strategies, as studies have reported that victims may be cautious about reporting through official channels, often preferring to cope informally using their own resources and support networks (D'Cruz & Noronha, 2010; Zapf & Gross, 2001). Yet, the responsibility to resolve conflicts should not lie solely with victims. A recent study exploring leadership behaviour after bullying events suggested that managers could also benefit from conflict management training (Woodrow & Guest, 2017).

At present, we are not aware of tertiary interventions that have been evaluated using quantitative methods. Mediation is often cited as a potential method for addressing traditional workplace bullying (Saam, 2010), although its efficacy is not yet fully understood. Slonje, Smith, and Frisen (2013) state that an important component of youth bullying programs involves helping the bully to understand the consequences of their actions. The authors comment that if this is true, then helping cyberbullies realize the extent of their actions is particularly important, as they appear less remorseful than traditional bullying perpetrators (Slonje, Smith, & Frisen, 2012). Thus, mediation for workplace cyberbullying cases may promote understanding and remorse. Counselling for victims is another method that falls under the bracket of tertiary interventions. Online modes of counselling are used in employee assistance programs and, intuitively, these methods may provide an outlet for cyberbullying victims. One question is whether they can provide the same level of support as face-to-face counselling, however? Yet, meta-analytic evidence suggests little difference in the latter's effectiveness (Barak, Hen, Boniel-Nissim, & Shapira, 2008).

At the start of the chapter, we asked what universities could do to limit the risks of workplace cyberbullying. Given the lack of dedicated research on workplace cyberbullying intervention methods, we sought to provide the best available evidence on methods from related disciplines, providing university employees with an idea of what might work. The most compelling research to date has evaluated primary interventions, which is perhaps unsurprising given their focus on prevention. Policies and legislation are two factors that were outside the scope of this chapter, but they should nonetheless inform intervention efforts alongside the practitioner's own expertise, the views of those affected by cyberbullying and knowledge from the local context. If the local context is the university, practitioners should seek to understand the nature and source of the cyberbullying, as this context may enable a particular form of behaviour such as abuse towards academics via social media. In summary, further empirical research is needed to develop and evaluate cyberbullying interventions within the university context; yet, we hope the ideas presented in this chapter provide an initial starting point for researchers and practitioners to evaluate and implement cyberbullying policies at the university level.

References

Barak, A., Hen, L., Boniel-Nissim, M., & Shapira, N. A. (2008). A comprehensive review and a meta-analysis of the effectiveness of internet-based psychotherapeutic interventions. *Journal of Technology in Human Services*, *26*(2–4), 109–160.

Branch, S., Ramsay, S., & Barker, M. (2013). Workplace bullying, mobbing and general harassment: A review. *International Journal of Management Reviews*, *15*(3), 280–299.

Briner, R. B. (2012). Developing evidence-based occupational health psychology. In J. Houdmont, S. Leka, & R. R. Sinclair (Eds.), *Contemporary occupational health psychology* (pp. 36–56). Chichester, UK: Wiley-Blackwell.

Briner, R. B., Denyer, D., & Rousseau, D. M. (2009). Evidence-based management: Concept cleanup time? *The Academy of Management Perspectives*, *23*(4), 19–32.

Coyne, I., & Farley, S. (this volume). Cyberbullying within working contexts. In W. Cassidy, C. Faucher, & M. Jackson (Eds.), *Cyberbullying at university in international contexts* (pp. 80–96). Oxford, UK: Routledge.

D'Cruz, P., & Noronha, E. (2010). Protecting my interests: HRM and targets' coping with workplace bullying. *The Qualitative Report*, *15*, 507–534.

Friedman, R. A., & Currall, S. C. (2003). Conflict escalation: Dispute exacerbating elements of e-mail communication. *Human Relations*, *56*(11), 1325–1347.

Gradinger, P., Yanagida, T., Strohmeier, D., & Spiel, C. (2016). Effectiveness and sustainability of the ViSC social competence program to prevent cyberbullying and cyber-victimization: Class and individual level moderators. *Aggressive Behavior*, *42*(2), 181–193.

Hershcovis, S. M., Reich, T. C., & Niven, K. (2015). *Workplace bullying: Causes, consequences, and intervention strategies*. SIOP White Paper Series, Society for Industrial and Organizational Psychology, UK, London.

Hodgins, M., MacCurtain, S., & Mannix-McNamara, P. (2014). Workplace bullying and incivility: A systematic review of interventions. *International Journal of Workplace Health Management*, 7(1), 54–72.

Leiter, M. P., Day, A., Gilin-Oore, D., & Laschinger, H. K. (2012). Getting better and staying better: Assessing civility, incivility, distress, and job attitudes one year after a civility intervention. *Journal of Occupational Health Psychology*, *17*(4), 425–434.

Leiter, M. P., Laschinger, H. K., Day, A., & Oore, D. (2011). The impact of civility interventions on employee social behavior, distress, and attitudes. *Journal of Applied Psychology*, *96*(6), 1258–1274.

Park, Y., Fritz, C., & Jex, S. M. (2015). Daily cyber incivility and distress: The moderating roles of resources at work and home. *Journal of Management*, *16*(4), 457–467.

Saam, N. J. (2010). Interventions in workplace bullying: A multilevel approach. *European Journal of Work and Organizational Psychology*, *19*(1), 51–75.

Slonje, R., Smith, P. K., & Frisén, A. (2012). Processes of cyberbullying, and feelings of remorse by bullies: A pilot study. *European Journal of Developmental Psychology*, *9*, 244–259.

Slonje, R., Smith, P. K., & Frisén, A. (2013). The nature of cyberbullying, and strategies for prevention. *Computers in Human Behavior*, *29*(1), 26–32.

Woodrow, C., & Guest, D. E. (2017). Leadership and approaches to the management of workplace bullying. *European Journal of Work and Organizational Psychology*, *26*(2), 221–233.

Williford, A., Elledge, L. C., Boulton, A. J., DePaolis, K. J., Little, T. D., & Salmivalli, C. (2013). Effects of the KiVa antibullying program on cyberbullying and cybervictimization frequency among Finnish youth. *Journal of Clinical Child & Adolescent Psychology*, *42*, 820–833.

Zapf, D., & Gross, C. (2001). Conflict escalation and coping with workplace bullying: A replication and extension. *European Journal of Work and Organizational Psychology*, *10*(4), 497–522.

PART IV
Policy

15

CYBERBULLYING IN THE AUSTRALIAN UNIVERSITY CONTEXT

The shades of harm and implications for law and policy

Colette Langos and Mark Giancaspro

Introduction

Bullying is not a phenomenon limited by age. Although there has been an emphasis on exploring the concept in relation to school-aged children (Cross et al., 2009; Olweus, 1978), studies examining adult bullying in the workplace inform us that such conduct transcends the context of youth (House of Representatives Standing Committee on Education and Employment, Parliament of Australia, 2012; Leymann, 1990). Cyberbullying, too, does not abate when students graduate from high school (Phippen, 2011; Privitera & Campbell, 2009). While less research has focused on cyberbullying in the post-secondary education context, preliminary findings from studies conducted in various countries indicate that it occurs within colleges and universities, as well (Faucher, Jackson, & Cassidy, 2014).

Research examining the incidence of cyberbullying in an Australian university context is in its infancy, however, and – as such – published studies are not generalizable. They do, however, provide us with useful "prevalence snapshots", suggesting that a significant percentage of students studying at Australian universities are exposed to the conduct. A 2010 study surveying 134 students of the University of New South Wales reported that 62% of respondents experienced cyberbullying in the past year, and that 40% of respondents had personally cyberbullied others (Zhang, Land, & Dick, 2010). In 2012, a study surveying 528 undergraduate students from an Australian university reported that 11.6% of participants had been victims of cyberbullying in the preceding 12 months (Wensley & Campbell, 2012). Lack of a uniform definition, standardized measurement techniques, and variance in survey design make it difficult to determine the prevalence of cyberbullying accurately; yet, with 1.4 million students studying at Australian universities nationwide (Norton, 2016), it would be useful to gain greater clarity on the rate of incidence by way of future research.

The question is whether all cyberbullying behaviours are equally harmful or if there are multiple "shades" of cyberbullying, wherein some behaviours have more severe psychological consequences for its victims compared to others. To date, the only Australian research to examine this issue has been based on a theoretical model (Langos, 2015). Research conducted in the UK and Sweden suggests that not all forms of cyberbullying – when compared with traditional bullying – are perceived as being equally harmful, with cyberbullying via video/photograph regarded as being the most damaging (Slonje & Smith, 2008; Smith et al., 2008). Findings from other European countries also suggest that non-consensual public distribution of visual content is considered to be more serious than text-based cyberbullying, given the intense public humiliation associated with the misuse of visual content (Nocentini et al., 2010). However, there is very scant empirical research to inform our understanding of the severity of harm associated, or the "shades" within various manifestations of the conduct, as experienced by victims (Menesini, Nocentini, & Calussi, 2011).

A comprehensive understanding of the nature and implications of these various behaviours (identified as forms of cyberbullying) enables law and policymakers to tailor regulatory measures accordingly. Findings based on lived experience are particularly useful, as they provide an evidence base for designing and implementing strategies (law and policy), which educate and protect against harms that may arise as a result of cyberbullying. This pilot study thus examines:

- The levels of harm Australian university students experienced as victims of various cyberbullying behaviours;
- The levels of harm Australian university students perceive as being associated with various cyberbullying behaviours;
- Australian university students' understanding of existing criminal laws which regulate instances of cyberbullying;
- Australian university students' awareness of university policies governing cyberbullying.

Part 1 of this chapter explains the research method employed in examining these questions and the results obtained. Furthermore, the authors make several suggestions to explain the somewhat paradoxical findings. Part II considers how the findings may impact law and policy reform, and the authors make a series of recommendations in that regard, as well.

Part I. Method

Participants

Participants self-selected to complete an online survey. This survey was distributed through a research panel provider to an enlisted group of student volunteers: randomly selected from a sample of its registered members, as drawn from various

Australian universities. The research panel provider's invitation email contained a link to the online survey. Students were then directed to an information sheet, which described participation criteria and details about the survey. Criteria for participation in the survey included being over the age of 18, studying at an Australian university, and having experienced cyberbullying. Respondents were informed that they were not obliged to complete the survey and were assured that their answers would remain anonymous. A total of 444 students attempted the survey between January and July 2016. The total number of participants who completed the survey was 213 (115 male, 93 female, and two who identified as "other"). Of the 213 respondents, all were between the ages of 18 and 24.

Measures

The authors formulated a 22-item questionnaire consisting of closed-ended questions. The survey provided participants with a description of cyberbullying[1] and a list of various cyberbullying behaviours before respondents were asked preliminary questions relating to age, gender, and frequency of victimization. The next part of the survey required respondents to indicate whether they have experienced any of the 10 different cyberbullying behaviours listed (Table 15.2) and then to rate, on a Likert scale (scale range of 1 to 5, with 1 being not harmful to 5 being the most serious harm), the level of harm they actually experienced as a result of exposure. Information describing each level of harm on the Likert scale was provided.[2] Participants were then asked to consider the same list of cyberbullying behaviours and to rate, on a Likert scale, the level of harm (scale range of 1 to 5, with 1 being not harmful to 5 being the most severe harm), they think would be associated with each of the behaviours. The final part of the survey asked respondents about their awareness and understanding of criminal laws, as well as university policies governing cyberbullying.

Results

Frequency of cyberbullying

Table 15.1 reflects how often respondents were cyberbullied after turning 18 years of age.

TABLE 15.1 Frequency of Cyberbullying

How often have you been cyberbullied since turning 18 years of age?	*Responses*
Once or twice	50.2%
A few times (More than twice, but not frequently)	43.2%
Frequently (monthly)	5.6%
Very frequently (weekly or more often)	0.9%
Never	0%

Not all cyberbullying is equally harmful

Findings reflected in Table 15.2 provide insight into the complex nature of cyberbullying. Its manifestations are varied, as are the consequences of exposure. Table 15.2 captures both the level (extent) of harm actually experienced by respondents as a result of exposure to any of the listed cyberbullying behaviours, as well as the participants' perceptions of harm – that is, the level of harm they think would be associated with each of the behaviours. The number of participants who have been exposed to each behaviour type is shown in the last column (n = actually experienced), as well as the number of respondents who replied to the question about perception (n = perceived harm). For purposes of reporting, this table collapses the first two levels (not harmful and minimal harm momentarily) and the last two levels (harmful for some time and significant harm ongoing). Level 3 is the mid-range – some harm, for some time.

Interestingly, almost all of the respondents commented on the perceived harm associated with exposure to the various cyberbullying behaviours ("n" ranged from 209 to 213), compared to the number of participants who responded to actual harm experienced. The most common forms of cyberbullying experienced by respondents were, in the following order of frequency: sent offensive messages (n = 201), exclusion from online discussion forums (n = 188), and being the subject of a humiliating photo distributed electronically without consent (n = 180). The least commonly experienced behaviour was being the subject of a sexually explicit, nude, or nearly nude photo taken with consent but distributed without consent (n = 155).

Criminal law

Most respondents were not aware of any criminal laws regulating cyberbullying (61.8%). Of those who were aware (38.2%), most were aware that both state and federal laws may regulate instances of cyberbullying. However, half indicated that they were confused about precisely which cyberbullying behaviours were considered "criminal" behaviour. Of the 213 respondents, an overwhelming majority (n = 204) indicated that lawmakers should do more to educate people about laws that apply to instances of cyberbullying. The majority of respondents (n = 180) indicated that there should be one specific cyberbullying offence which governs serious instances of cyberbullying, instead of various laws regulating different kinds of cyberbullying behaviours.

University policy

The majority of participants (57.1%) had no knowledge of a behaviour code or university policy that addresses cyberbullying. Of those who knew of such a policy (n = 92), most indicated that the cyberbullying policy was effective.

TABLE 15.2 The Shades of Harm Associated With Cyberbullying

CB behaviours	*Harm*	*Levels 1–2 Least harmful*	*Level 3*	*Levels 4–5 Most harmful*	*n*
I have been sent offensive messages via electronic technology repeatedly (e.g., social media, SMS, email)	Actually experienced	35.3%	30.4%	34.4%	201
	Perceived	28.2%	30.1%	41.8%	213
I have been the subject of a "rating list" on a website or on social media inviting nasty public comment and remark	Actually experienced	55.8%	24.4%	19.8%	172
	Perceived	28.1%	28.1%	43.8%	210
I have been the subject of a humiliating photo(s) distributed via electronic technology (e.g., posted to social media, websites, YouTube)	Actually experienced	47.7%	23.3%	29%	180
	Perceived	14.1%	22.5%	63.4%	213
I have been the subject of a sexually explicit, nude or nearly nude photo which was taken with my consent but distributed to others without my consent	Actually experienced	69%	10%	21%	155
	Perceived	13.2%	9.5%	77.3%	211
I have been the subject of a humiliating film/video distributed via electronic technology (e.g., posted to social media, websites, YouTube)	Actually experienced	57.6%	20.9%	21.5%	163
	Perceived	10.6%	21.5%	67.9%	209
I have been stalked using electronic technology (someone repeatedly sent me communications which made me fear for my personal safety)	Actually experienced	48%	20.8%	31.2%	173
	Perceived	16.3%	21%	62.7%	209
I have been purposely excluded from online discussion groups/ chat rooms repeatedly	Actually experienced	41%	25%	34%	188
	Perceived	40.2%	32%	27.8%	209
Someone pretended to be me by creating a fake social media profile or website and posted offensive material/messages on the fake profile/website	Actually experienced	55%	18.4%	26.6%	158
	Perceived	26.2%	25.2%	48.6%	210

(*Continued*)

TABLE 15.2 (Continued)

CB behaviours	*Harm*	*Levels 1–2 Least harmful*	*Level 3*	*Levels 4–5 Most harmful*	*n*
Someone threatened to physically harm me using electronic technology via communication tools such as social media, chatrooms, websites, email or SMS where there are multiple recipients	Actually experienced	48.2%	20.4%	31.4%	172
	Perceived	16%	19%	65%	211
Someone tricked me into disclosing personal information and then distributed this information using electronic technology communication tools such as social media, chatrooms, websites, email or SMS where there are multiple recipients	Actually experienced	56%	20.5%	23.5%	166
	Perceived	15.3%	26.7%	58%	210

A large majority of the total number of respondents (66.4%) indicated that a post-secondary education institutional policy can be an effective deterrent to cyberbullying and most (62%) indicated that they would seek help from a post-secondary institution counselling service. Results show that the large majority of respondents (88.2%) consider an anonymous online reporting system a useful way of encouraging students – who are either victims, bystanders, or perpetrators of cyberbullying – to report instances. Two-hundred-and-one of the total number of respondents also indicated that online reporting systems should provide users with a range of self-help resources.

General discussion

Empirical studies examining the implications of cyberbullying provide us with a growing evidence base that exposure can be potentially devastating: that victimization may result in an array of negative health implications for its targets (Faucher et al., 2014). Responses from participants in this survey echo this conclusion, with 95.3% indicating that they consider cyberbullying to be a serious issue. Additionally, in line with scholarship in this field, it was found that almost 86% of respondents were targets of cyberbullying before turning 18. This demonstrates that cyberbullying continues across multiple educational contexts and fields; it does not cease once students leave high school. Moreover, victimization prior to turning 18 may be a determinant of participants' recognition of cyberbullying as being a serious issue.

Frequency of victimization

Most respondents indicated that they experienced cyberbullying "once or twice" or "a few times" (Table 15.1). However, 14 (or 6.6%) of the 213 respondents were victimized on a "monthly" or "weekly or more frequent" basis. This percentage is higher than findings published to date (MacDonald & Roberts-Pittman, 2010) – yet, further cross-cultural research is required to provide us with a more comprehensive understanding as to whether this higher frequency of victimization is unique to the Australian post-secondary context or also persists in other contexts.

Not all cyberbullying is equally harmful

Data reflecting respondents' lived experiences denote that not all cyberbullying behaviours are equally harmful. Disparity as to the severity of harm experienced by respondents is shown by the spread of the data within each behaviour type. Every manifestation of cyberbullying was associated with all five possible shades of harm. For interpretative purposes, it is useful to observe the extent of harm associated with each behaviour type viewed cumulatively – that is, harm falling within the levels 3 to 5 on the Likert scale.[3]

Individual behaviours: harm experienced vs. perceived harm

It is interesting to consider how respondents' perceptions of harm (in relation to each behaviour) compared with the actual harm experienced by victims. Notably, on the whole, respondents tended to overestimate the extent of perceived harm associated with each of the listed cyberbullying behaviours, compared to actual harm experienced. This finding was particularly pronounced in relation to certain behaviours (discussed as follows):

Non-consensual distribution of a humiliating photo: This behaviour occurred frequently, with 85% of all respondents indicating exposure to this manifestation of cyberbullying. The largest percentage of respondents overestimated the extent of harm associated with this behaviour: 63.4% thought that exposure would result in level 4–5 harm, and almost 86% perceived victimization to result in harm between levels 3–5. Notably, nearly half of all respondents victimized in this manner (47.7%) did not regard the behaviour as harmful or experienced minor harm in the form of momentary negative emotional reactions.

Non-consensual distribution of a sexually explicit photo: This form of cyberbullying was also perceived as significantly harmful behaviour. Approximately 77% of all respondents thought that exposure would result in harm in between levels 4–5. In contrast, the data indicate that 69% of respondents targeted in this way reported experiencing harm in the 1–2 category: no subsequent harm or minimal harm (momentary negative emotional reactions). This behaviour was the least common manifestation of cyberbullying, with 73% of respondents reporting exposure.

Non-consensual distribution of humiliating film: Exposure to this behaviour type was perceived as approximately three times more harmful (level 4–5) to victims in general than to those respondents who actually experienced that form of cyberbullying (67.9% vs. 21.5%). Cumulatively, over 89% perceived this form of cyberbullying to result in harm between levels 3–5. In stark contrast to these findings, the data revealed that 57.6% of victims did not experience any resulting harm or experienced minimal harm (momentary negative emotional reactions) as a result of exposure (level 1–2 harm).

Being stalked online: The majority of respondents (62.7%) thought this behaviour would result in significant or ongoing harm (levels 4–5). Again, contrary to perceptions, approximately half of those victimized in this manner (48%) experienced level 1–2 harm (no harm or momentary negative emotional reactions).

Visual forms of cyberbullying: One of the more unanticipated aspects of our findings relates to the level of harm experienced by the majority of respondents' cyberbullied by way of non-consensual distribution of visual content – sexually explicit, nude, or nearly nude photograph(s); or humiliating film or image(s) depicting the victim. The majority of respondents indicated cyberbullying of this kind to be among the least harmful behaviours (Table 15.2). These results lie in contradistinction to research published to date, which suggests that the public humiliation associated with non-consensual distribution of private or embarrassing film or images makes non-consensual distribution of visual content particularly harmful. On this point, we should highlight that previous findings are informed primarily by data obtained from perception-based studies (Nocentini et al., 2010). Interestingly, and in line with existing research, findings from our study suggest non-consensual distribution of visual content – sexually explicit, nude, or nearly nude photograph(s); or humiliating film or image(s) depicting the victim – is perceived to be among the most harmful manifestations of cyberbullying.

The disparity in our findings on harm experienced and perceived harm may be explained on a number of bases. First, it is possible that human error is to blame. Respondents may have misunderstood the survey items. However, the authors consider this unlikely for two reasons: (1) the questions were worded clearly and unambiguously, and there appears to be very little scope for misinterpretation; and (2) the marked inverse trend in survey responses in regards to harm based on lived experience and perceived harm associated with each cyberbullying behaviour. No notable outliers were identified. There is, therefore, nothing suggestive of error in the interpretation of the scoring scale.

Second, the study may have been affected by the social desirability bias: the tendency of respondents to self-report questionnaires to give socially approved answers about oneself (Weiten, 2016, p. 50). The bias is particularly prevalent when a questionnaire canvasses sensitive issues (Weiten, 2016, p. 50). Cyberbullying and its associated harms are certainly sensitive issues, and so respondents may have sought to answer in a manner which made them appear more "resilient". This theory is plausible, although not appropriately convincing, given that the likelihood of socially desirable responding decreases in proportion to the level of anonymity offered (Randall & Fernandes, 1991, p. 813). The online survey in this study was entirely anonymous and administered electronically, such that there was no "human" interaction whatsoever.

It is also of note that there were many more participants who responded to the question asking them to rate the level of harm they perceived would be associated with exposure to each form of cyberbullying vs. respondents who identified as victims having actually experienced any of the listed behaviours. It is possible that those respondents who had not experienced a particular form of cyberbullying overestimated the impact of victimization, therefore skewing the responses to that factor.

Part II. Discussions surrounding criminal law and policy

As a prelude to the following discussion, it is important to consider that the criminalization of conduct deemed harmful to the community is but one tool lawmakers may resort to when harmful behaviour requires proactive management. Any criminal law response to cyberbullying should be only one part of a rounded management effort. To that end, it is imperative that an array of non-penal policy responses – including targeted education campaigns across multiple contexts and the development of self-help resources – be implemented simultaneously.

Criminal law

There is no single body of criminal law governing the whole of Australia (Findlay, Odgers, & Yeo, 2009, p. 7). Australian states and territories are responsible for their own criminal laws. The Commonwealth government may enact federal criminal legislation pursuant to the powers vested in it by virtue of the Commonwealth Constitution (Australian Constitution s 51).

At present, there is no specific cyberbullying offence. Rather, a complex matrix of state and federal laws criminalize cyberbullying behaviours as they fall within the scope of existing offences (Langos, 2014). For example, non-consensual distribution of visual content may be regulated by state "filming offences" (Part 5A Summary Offences Act 1953 (SA)). Equally threatening content may be governed by state offences, such as "unlawful threats" (s 19 Criminal Law Consolidations Act 1935 (SA)), "assault" (s 20 Criminal Law Consolidations Act 1935 (SA)), or "stalking" (s 19AA Criminal Law Consolidations Act 1935 (SA)). Federal law, too, may regulate cyberbullying (Australian Constitution s 51(v)). The provision that has the greatest relevance, so capturing a broad range of cyberbullying behaviours, governs "harassing, menacing, or offensive" material transmitted electronically (s 414.17 Criminal Code Act 1995 (Cth)).

Community education

Interestingly, most of the respondents were not aware of any criminal laws regulating cyberbullying. Of those respondents who were aware of existing cyberbullying laws, half indicated that they were confused about which cyberbullying behaviours amount to criminal conduct. Of the 213 respondents, 204 indicated that lawmakers should do more to educate people about the laws that apply to instances of cyberbullying. This finding suggests that community education surrounding the relationship between cyberbullying and criminal law is warranted.

Cyberbullying as a single offence

It is also of note that findings indicate that 84.9% of respondents believe that there ought to be one single cyberbullying offence that governs serious instances of this misconduct. It may be that this legal response is viewed as a way lawmakers could clarify concerns surrounding the criminalization of cyberbullying. One can safely argue that a benefit of enacting such an offence would be the formulation of a legal cyberbullying definition, which would clarify both the meaning and scope of the phenomenon. However, a specific cyberbullying offence would need to be drafted with extreme care so as to avoid being overly broad and overly inclusive (i.e., capturing behaviours not sufficiently serious to attract criminal penalty) (Langos, 2013).

Harm associated with cyberbullying is complex

Data illuminating the shades of harm associated with cyberbullying may be helpful to lawmakers. It could assist lawmakers postulating law reform, or else reviewing existing laws, ensuring the community is adequately protected from potentially harmful behaviours. Our findings suggest that different behaviours result in varying levels of harm. Furthermore, each cyberbullying behaviour is capable of causing a spectrum of harm; no manifestation is purely one-dimensional. In addition, it is useful to consider that none of the cyberbullying behaviours listed can comfortably be described as resulting in negligible harm. Of the behaviours, being the subject of a rating list on a website or social media inviting nasty public commentary had the least number of respondents indicate that they experienced protracted harm (i.e., of the kind reflected in level 4 or 5 of the harm scale). However, 19.8% of victims experienced harm lasting a few months, ongoing psychological harm, or self-harm. This behaviour cannot be described as resulting in trivial harm. A greater percentage of respondents suffered serious harm of a monthly or ongoing nature for all other behaviours, with the greatest number of respondents (34.3%) indicating that they experienced this extent of harm as a result of being sent offensive messages electronically. Findings may provide lawmakers with an evidence base for investing further in awareness-raising and prevention initiatives, and may also serve as empirical support when justifying comprehensive regulation of cyberbullying behaviours by way of the criminal law.

One aspect of this data – which ought to be treated cautiously by lawmakers, however – relates to the finding that the majority of respondents did not find non-consensual distribution of visual content to be particularly harmful. Possible explanations for this finding have been discussed. It has also been canvassed that this finding should not be considered in isolation, and that a holistic interpretation to this data is preferred – given that the data also inform us that a significant percentage of respondents who experienced this kind of cyberbullying (whether by humiliating film or image(s), or sexually explicit, nude, or nearly nude image(s)) suffered harm lasting a few months, ongoing emotional harm, or self-harm. It is imperative that lawmakers do not treat the data as irrefutable evidence that existing laws criminalizing these behaviours should be repealed, or, where no laws exist, that laws governing such conduct should not be enacted. The data should always be read as a whole.

University policy

The present study also provides an informative basis for cyberbullying policy development in the post-secondary education context.

Awareness of cyberbullying policy

Findings corroborate existing prevalence studies by demonstrating that cyberbullying continues to be a significant issue, affecting a large number of Australian post-secondary students. Furthermore, the results also paint a concerning picture regarding post-secondary student awareness of cyberbullying policies (or related behavioural codes) at their respective institutions. As the data indicate, the majority of respondents had no knowledge of such policies or codes. This finding is perhaps unsurprising given that many universities currently lack these types of preventative or educational measures (Campbell, 2015). A recent study by Campbell sampled 20 Australian universities from New South Wales, Queensland, South Australia, and Victoria, examining the anti-bullying policies each (if any) had in place (Campbell, 2015). The universities were chosen wherein they were the institutions with the highest numbers of student enrolment in each state for the year 2013. Conclusively, it was found that only seven of the policies sourced, from each of the universities, specifically mentioned bullying amongst students.

Perceived efficacy of a cyberbullying policy

Respondents in the present study who did know of existing university cyberbullying policies noted that they were effective and, overall, two-thirds believed that a policy directly addressing cyberbullying would be an effective deterrent. There is empirical support for these sentiments. Several studies speak to the general efficacy of policies in educational institutions as an effective strategy to combat bullying and cyberbullying behaviours amongst students (Cowie, Bauman, Myers, Porhola, & Almeida, 2013; Hatzenbuehler, Schwab-Reese, Ranapurwala, Hertz, & Ramirez, 2015). Given the prevalence and new empirical data (based on victims' lived experiences, which inform us of the potential harms of such behaviours), it is imperative that universities develop specific policies to address bullying and cyberbullying among their student body.

Educating students and staff

The majority of respondents (57.1%) in the present study reported having no knowledge of any behaviour code or other policy at their university that specifically addressed the issue of cyberbullying. According to the literature, this seems to be an endemic problem in higher education institutions (Minor, Smith, & Brashen, 2013; Campbell, 2015). It is essential, once a policy addressing cyberbullying behaviours is generated, that both students and staff at universities are made aware of this policy and given easy access. To this end, ongoing educational campaigns – catered to raising awareness of the issue of cyberbullying, as well as the availability and effect of the university policies addressing it – should be implemented. A university's cyberbullying policies should be prominent and accessible in hard copy, as well as online: not only for convenience, but to demonstrate institutional commitment to addressing a prevalent issue (Jackson, Faucher, & Cassidy, this volume; Marsh, McGee, Hemphill, & Williams, 2011). This exposure is likely to have a destigmatizing effect, encouraging victims to seek support. It is also likely to have a deterrent effect upon actual or potential perpetrators. Reiteration of the message that cyberbullying will not be tolerated is one way to negate the dissuasive influence of Australia's culture of aforementioned "resilience".

It is also essential that university staff, particularly counselling staff, are adequately equipped with the requisite knowledge and skills to support cyberbullying victims. Appropriate and specific procedures (as opposed to vague aspirational directions) should be in place, ensuring that staff are confident in addressing instances of cyberbullying (Campbell, 2015). Such measures would help to foster a "telling culture", in which students are made to feel confident that university staff will understand and accommodate their issues, working constructively and collaboratively to resolve them (Marsh et al., 2011). In particular, Cowie et al. (2013) recommend that university counselling staff be careful not to trivialize student concerns regarding cyberbullying; routinely screen for depression and anxiety; sufficiently familiarize themselves with the appropriate technology, to be able to recommend "technological strategies (e.g., blocking, reporting) that could be helpful to victims" (p. 170); understand the law and inform victims of legal options where necessary; thoroughly understand university cyberbullying policies; and advocate for effective and accessible mechanisms to address such malevolent behaviour (Cowie et al., 2013). A failure to have such adequate procedures in place, and to respond to reported instances of cyberbullying accordingly, may well expose a university to legal liability should a victim initiate an action in negligence.

Anonymous online reporting system

Findings indicate that 88.2% of respondents felt that an anonymous online reporting system would be a useful way of encouraging students – whether victims, bystanders, or perpetrators – to report instances of cyberbullying. Previous research supports this view (Cunningham et al., 2015; Faucher, Cassidy, Jackson, Waterhouse, & MacDonald, 2014). Some possible explanations as to why this initiative is perceived as being so advantageous include that it simplifies reporting procedures; may limit the risk of retaliation; and that it encourages victims, witnesses, and even perpetrators to speak out against cyberbullying anonymously (Cunningham et al., 2015, p. 380). Additionally, it is important that 201 respondents (94.37%) indicated they believed online reporting systems should provide users with a range of self-help resources: including such resources provides victims suffering severe psychological distress, or those who feel at risk of self-harm, with access to immediate assistance.

University counselling services

It is encouraging that most respondents (62%) indicated they would seek help from a post-secondary institution counselling service if necessary. Needless to say, universities should ensure that they are able to adequately assist students victimized by cyberbullies. Yet, having policies prohibiting such behaviour is not enough: these must also be supplemented by effective support (e.g., referral to counselling services) and enforcement (e.g., internal retribution for perpetrator, referral to law enforcement authorities) measures. To encourage victims to speak up, they must have confidence that their grievances will be appropriately dealt with. As Kenworthy's (2010) study revealed, university students affected by cyberbullying were, perhaps unsurprisingly, strongly disinclined to report the behaviour where apprehended perpetrators were perceived not to be adequately reprimanded (Kenworthy, 2010). In that study, a mere 14% of the 452 respondents indicated that their formal complaints had resulted in disciplinary action.

Recommendations

This pioneering research is the first Australian study to explore whether all cyberbullying behaviours are equally harmful. Furthermore, it explores whether university students have knowledge of existing criminal laws which govern cyberbullying, and whether lawmakers ought to implement strategies aimed at better educating the community as to those laws.

Given the scarcity of empirical data surrounding the shades of harm associated with particular forms of cyberbullying, data from this study has the potential to influence law reform in this area. It provides decision-makers with a preliminary evidence base. Based on these discussions, it would be opportune for lawmakers to consider:

- Increasing community education on the legal implications of cyberbullying to raise awareness and clarifying when cyberbullying is unlawful behaviour;
- Enacting a carefully crafted specific federal cyberbullying offence that governs serious instances of cyberbullying;
- In the absence of introducing new uniform federal legislation, conducting regular reviews of criminal laws in all jurisdictions to ensure cyberbullying is governed comprehensively.

The data also provide us with useful information surrounding university students' awareness of institutional policies that prohibit cyberbullying, whether such policies may act as an effective deterrent, and whether implementation of an anonymous online reporting system could encourage reporting by victims, perpetrators, and bystanders. To that end, post-secondary institutions would be prudent to consider:

- Developing and implementing anti-bullying and cyberbullying policies;
- Ensuring university students and staff are aware of anti-bullying and cyberbullying policies;
- Developing an anonymous online reporting system for victims;
- Ensuring students and staff have access to counselling services and other self-help resources.

Limitations

These findings must be considered in light of the limitations of the study. Although the sample of survey participants was drawn randomly from a research panel provider whose membership base comprised university students Australia-wide, data are not generalizable based on the sample size. Further research drawing upon a larger sample is required to provide a more comprehensive data set. Given the lack of Australian research examining the prevalence of cyberbullying in this context, it would be useful to explore the rate of incidence among university students so we can better understand the extent of the problem in university institutions nationwide.

Acknowledgements

The authors would like to acknowledge the Law Foundation of South Australia for providing the authors with funding support for this exploratory study.

Notes

1 Cyberbullying was described as "bullying that takes place using electronic technology such as cell phones, computers, and tablets as well as communication tools including social media sites, text messages, chat and websites".
2 A rating of '1' indicates that the behaviour was not harmful. A rating of '2' indicates that the behaviour resulted in minimal harm (emotional reactions you felt were not long lasting such as *momentary* fear, grief, anger). A rating of '3' indicates that the behaviour resulted in some emotional harm (anger, anxiety, fear, grief, humiliation for *some time* (a few weeks)). A rating of '4' indicates that the behaviour resulted in harm (either emotional harm where you felt negative emotions such as anger, anxiety, fear, grief, humiliation for *some time* (a few months); or where you were physically harmed). A rating of '5' indicates that the behaviour resulted in significant harm (either emotional harm where you felt *ongoing* negative emotions such as anger, anxiety, fear, grief, humiliation; or where you self-harmed as a result of the behaviour).
3 Note, as the harm scale defined a rating of level 1 as 'not harmful' and level 2 as 'minimal harm' akin to fleeting emotional reactions, harm associated with these levels is construed as negligible.

References

Campbell, M. (2015). Policies and procedures to address bullying at Australian universities. In H. Cowie & C. A. Myers (Eds.), *Bullying among university students: Cross-national perspectives* (pp. 157–171). London: Routledge.

Cowie, H., Bauman, S., Myers, C.-A., Porhola, M., & Almeida, A. (2013). Cyberbullying amongst university students: An emergent cause for concern? In P. K. Smith & G. Steffgen (Eds.), *Cyberbullying through the new media: Findings from an international network* (pp. 165–177). East Sussex: Psychology Press.

Cross, D., Shaw, T., Hearn, L., Epstein, M., Monks, H., Lester, L., Thomas, L., & Data Analysis Australia. (2009). *Australian Covert Bullying Prevalence Study*. Joondalup, Australia: Child Health Promotion Research Centre, Edith Cowan University.

Cunningham, C. E., Chen, Y., Vaillancourt, T., Rimas, H., Deal, K., Cunningham, L. J., & Ratcliffe, J. (2015). Modeling the anti-cyberbullying preferences of university students: Adaptive choice-based conjoint analysis. *Aggressive Behavior, 41*(4), 369–385.

Faucher, C., Cassidy, W., Jackson, M., Waterhouse, T., & MacDonald, L. (2014). *Cyberbullying at Canadian universities: Linking research, policy and practice*. Parameters of the Issue: Working Paper 1. Simon Fraser University.

Faucher, C., Jackson, M., & Cassidy, W. (2014). Cyberbullying among university students: Gendered experiences, impacts and perspectives. *Education Research International, 2014*, 1–10.

Findlay, M., Odgers, S., & Yeo, S. (2009). *Australian criminal justice* (4th ed.). South Melbourne: Oxford University Press.

Hatzenbuehler, M. L., Schwab-Reese, L., Ranapurwala, S. I., Hertz, M. F., & Ramirez, M. R. (2015). Associations between antibullying policies and bullying in 25 states. *JAMA Pediatrics, 169*(10), e15241.

House of Representatives Standing Committee on Education and Employment, Parliament of Australia. (2012). *Workplace bullying: We just want it to stop*. Canberra: Parliament of Australia.

Jackson, M., Faucher, C., & Cassidy, W. (this volume). What's policy got to do with it? The focus on cyberbullying policy at the university level. In W. Cassidy, C. Faucher, & M. Jackson (Eds.), *Cyberbullying at university in international contexts* (pp. 198–211). Oxford, UK: Routledge.

Kenworthy, A. (2010). *One goal, one community: Moving beyond bullying and empowering for life*. Bond University Centre for Applied Research in Learning, Engagement, Andragogy and Pedagogy. Retrieved from https://bond.edu.au/intl/news/44434/one-goal-one-community-moving-beyond-bullying-and-empowering-life

Langos, C. (2013). *Cyberbullying, associated harm and the criminal law*. Doctoral thesis, University of South Australia. Retrieved from http://arrow.unisa.edu.au:8081/1959.8/151636

Langos, C. (2014). Regulating cyberbullying: A South Australian perspective. *Flinders Law Journal, 16*(1), 73–109.

Langos, C. (2015). Cyberbullying: The shades of harm. *Psychiatry, Psychology and Law, 22*(1), 106–124.

Leymann, H. (1990). Mobbing and psychological terror at workplaces. *Violence and Victims*, 5, 119–126.

MacDonald, C., & Roberts-Pittman, B. (2010). Cyberbullying among college students: Prevalence and demographic differences. *Procedia Social and Behavioral Sciences, 9*, 2002–2009.

Marsh, L., McGee, R., Hemphill, S. A., & Williams, S. (2011). Content analysis of school anti-bullying policies: A comparison between New Zealand and Victoria. *Health Promotion Journal of Australia, 22*(3), 172–177.

Menesini, E., Nocentini, A., & Calussi, P. (2011). The measurement of cyberbullying: Dimensional structure and relative item severity and discrimination. *Cyberpsychology, Behavior and Social Networking, 14*(5), 267–274.

Minor, M. A., Smith, G. S., & Brashen, H. (2013). Cyberbullying in higher education. *Journal of Educational Research and Practice, 3*(1), 15–29.

Nocentini, A., Juan, C., Schultze-Krumbholz, A., Scheithauer, H., Ortega, R., & Menesini, E. (2010). Cyberbullying: Labels, behaviours and definition in three European countries. *Australian Journal of Guidance & Counselling, 20*(2), 129–142.

Norton, A. (2016). *Mapping Australian higher education*. Victoria, Australia: Grattan Institute.

Olweus, D. (1978). *Aggression in schools: Bullies and whipping boys*. Washington, DC: Hemisphere Publishing.

Ortega, R., Elipe, P., Mora-Merchan, J. A., Genta, M. L., Brighi, A., Smith, P. K., . . . & Tippett, N. (2012). The emotional impact of bullying and cyberbullying on victims: A European cross-national study. *Aggressive Behavior, 38*, 342–356.

Phippen, A. (2011). *The online abuse of professionals-research report from the UK safer internet centre*. Plymouth: University of Plymouth.

Privitera, C., & Campbell, M. (2009). Cyberbullying: The new face of workplace bullying? *CyberPsychology and Behavior, 12*(4), 395–400.

Randall, D., & Fernandes, M. F. (1991). The social desirability bias in ethics research. *Journal of Business Ethics, 10*, 805–817.
Slonje, R., & Smith, P. K. (2008). Cyberbullying: Another main type of bullying? *Scandinavian Journal of Psychology, 49*, 147–154.
Smith, P. K., Mahdavi, J., Carvalho, M., Fisher, S., Russell, S., & Tippett, N. (2008). Cyberbullying: Its nature and impact in secondary school pupils. *Journal of Child Psychology and Psychiatry, 49*(4), 376–385.
Weiten, W. (2016). *Psychology: Themes and variations* (10th ed.). Boston: Cengage Learning.
Wensley, K., & Campbell, M. (2012). Heterosexual and non-heterosexual young university students' involvement in traditional and cyber forms of bullying. *Cyberpsychology, Behavior and Social Networking, 15*(12), 649–654.
Wierzbicka, A. (2003). *Cross-cultural pragmatics: The semantics of human interaction*. Berlin: Mouton de Gruyter.
Zhang, A., Land, A., & Dick, G. (2010, July). *Key influences of cyberbullying for university students*. Paper presented at the Pacific Asia Conference on Information Systems, Taipei, Taiwan.

16

WHAT'S POLICY GOT TO DO WITH IT?

The focus on cyberbullying policy at the university level

Margaret Jackson, Chantal Faucher, and Wanda Cassidy

> Just as it is important in the context of the (lower grades) to address the problems of cyberbullying in an informed way, so it is important to develop research-based policies and programs at the post-secondary level that prevent and/or curtail CB, and also provide victims with clear avenues of reporting, as well as offer support and counselling when harm has occurred.
>
> – (Cassidy, Faucher, & Jackson, 2017, p. 26)

Part I. Introduction – policy foundations

Since educators became concerned with the effects of face-to-face bullying in primary and secondary (K–12, in Canada) school populations many years ago, suggested solutions frequently speak to the need for appropriate policy development or reform to address the concerns. Similarly, as issues with cyberbullying began to emerge in these same school age groups eight years ago in Canada, calls for policy reform were heard once again.

The turning point for Canada in this process can be argued to have occurred beginning with earlier media coverage of high-profile cases involving cyberbullying in the younger-aged student population, such as the 2012 Amanda Todd suicide case in British Columbia, or at the university level, such as with the 2012 University of Calgary Pridgen brothers' case in which it was alleged the brothers' (both students) Facebook bullying of their instructor occurred. The right to freedom of expression held sway over the right to security of person in the court decision, the outcome in favour of the brothers (see also Blizard, this volume). Cyberbullying subsequently began to emerge as a major issue in Canada.

In even more recent times, the same policy approach to solutions as had been proposed for the younger-aged children has been recommended for university-level cyberbullying issues (Campbell, 2016; Cassidy, Faucher, & Jackson, 2017; Langos & Giancaspro, this volume). It is thus worth examining the role that policy responses might reasonably play today when dealing with cyberbullying concerns at the university level. We start first by examining what a policy really is.

Policies are values-based statements. Procedures and actions can be assessed for being effectively derived from policy (or not), if those procedures and actions secure the policy's values-based intent and goals. A policy often even specifies within itself, or in its related procedures, what those actions are. The values to be considered may be in conflict, or a tension may exist between different policies' values. The policy itself establishes the balance between, for example, individual and societal values. When policy sets out the balance between the values in tension, the balance can become incorporated into actions to address the behaviour or problem (Dunn, 2008; Dye, 2017; Faucher, Jackson, & Cassidy, 2015).

Each policy's intent refers to an action which can be set out to secure the stated value balance. So, one set of tensions, for example, in a cyberbullying situation, might be between an individual's right to freedom of expression and another's rights to have security of person, as in the right to freedom from harassment (Brown et al., 2006). For the latter group, the harassment may affect their quality of life, possibly even their safety. If the expression does cause harm, then limits must be placed on the expression to the extent that is reasonable. The right to privacy may hold the key to that balance (Mathiesen, 2014).

Within the context of cyberbullying at the university level, policy refers to institutional protocols and directives governing behaviour within and related to the university. In the first part of the chapter, we attempt to make meaning of having one type of policy or another governing cyberbullying behaviour, whether a student conduct policy, a human rights policy, or an information communications technology (ICT) policy. In the second part, recommendations for values/elements to consider when developing policy to address cyberbullying at the institutional level, as gleaned from the literature, our own studies' findings, and from the reflections of contributors in this volume are discussed.

Rights and intersecting factors in policy for cyberbullying

The Canadian Charter of Rights and Freedoms is a high-level policy document, which clearly sets out rights balances of the type discussed prior. It is therefore appropriate to reference the Charter in terms of the scope of rights which should be considered when developing policy at the university level to address cyberbullying.

In terms of scope, it has been argued that policymakers should consider factors such as gender and sexuality, age, race, ethnicity, socioeconomic status, and disability when developing rights policy solutions; however, other than the first two variables, there is little information about how those factors do interact with cyberbullying behaviours (Faucher, Jackson, & Cassidy, 2015). Even so, authors continue to support the consideration of these factors in developing appropriate cyberbullying policy at the university level; in fact, cultural differences have been thought important to include as well (Kanetsuna, Aoyama, & Toda, this volume). Finally, there are also concerns expressed about the need to address inherent power imbalances, an especially troubling factor often at play with university-level cyberbullying.

Pescitelli (this volume) makes an argument in her chapter on LGBTQ post-secondary students and cyberbullying that is consistent with a rights-based analysis. She indicates there is a need for administrators to consider both gender and sexuality when drafting policies and procedures related to online activities (see also Faucher, Cassidy, & Jackson, this volume). Along with that, there is also the need to pay attention to possible discrimination/possible homophobia and transphobia when creating policy. Since LGBTQ individuals have been shown to experience cyberbullying and harassment more seriously than non-LGBTQ youth, their needs should be addressed. For example, in one study by Cooper and Blumfeld (2012), as cited by Pescitelli, LGBTQ youth were shown to experience much higher levels of depression, and suicidal thoughts and attempts were also higher than for non-LGBTQ individuals. Therefore, their associated needs are higher with respect to responses and support. Finally, more generally, there is a need for sensitivity to overall diversity as well (see also Blizard, this volume).

Overall, then, there are strong arguments made for a rights-based frame to the policies (Faucher et al., 2015) because of the nature and impacts of cyberbullying behaviour. In addition, Campbell (2016) argues that all forms of bullying should be included under the policy frame: physical, verbal, relational, and cyberbullying (p. 163). In her article entitled, "Human Rights for the Digital Age," Mathiesen (2014) argues that there should even be a Declaration of Digital Rights. She suggests that one can use the concept of human rights to provide an ethical framework since ethics are "the well-founded standards of right from wrong" (pp. 2–3), thus forming moral rights. Furthermore, moral rights can be used as a standard against which "legal rights can be evaluated or demanded" (p. 3). She states that "we have human rights because they are needed to protect us from certain kinds of threat; for example, violence [. . .]" (p. 8).

Mathiesen continues by citing Cohen (1993) that humans also have "a fundamental interest in being able to communicate with one another . . . without the right to access such communications, the right to express oneself is meaningless" (p. 10).

Therefore, here again is an occasion in which different values/different rights tend to compete: the right to be protected from violence (or from harm) and the right to freedom of expression, in keeping with Charter rights. The policy's role, through legal interpretation, is to determine the balance between the competing values.

Which is most effective: policy or law?

In order to achieve the desired policy intent of effectively addressing cyberbullying issues at the university level, one question which can emerge is whether using the law instead of policy might prove to be a better approach.

In fact, arguments have been put forward for the value of creating new cyberbullying law at both the provincial (e.g., Cyber-Safety Act of Nova Scotia)[1] and federal levels (e.g., the Protecting Canadians from Online Crime Act) to deal with cyberbullying in the educational context. While other arguments state that such law, as in the case of the federal one, by criminalizing harassing and annoying behaviour via electronic communication, may actually exacerbate the problem of nondisclosure and may unnecessarily involve youth becoming caught up in the criminal justice system (Coburn, Connelly, & Roesch, 2015; in Australia, see Young et al., 2016).

Three recent court decisions in Canada suggest that using the law to regulate this kind of cyber behaviour raises questions about the enforceability of those two specific pieces of legislation. That, in fact, those decisions can be expected to limit the extent to which Canadian legislators and law enforcement agencies can successfully prosecute cyberbullies (Cartwright, 2016).[2] As Cartwright concludes, "(t)he question remains whether it will ever be possible – at least in Canada – to legislate moral and civil behaviour in cyberspace" (p. 6).

Going back then to the original question asking whether law or policy is more effective in addressing cyberbullying at the university level, we juxtapose another study, also from Australia. Young et al. (2016) examined the opinions of 12 influential, authoritative employees from the education and legal systems who were interviewed about their perceptions of the role of law and cyberbullying. The pros for introducing a specific cyberbullying law were seen to be that it can provide a specific deterrent and punishment for the offender. Just as Campbell (2016) argued could be true at the institutional level, Young et al. argue that specific law can set up a norm or standard at the societal level and can provide compensation to targets and provide an imperative for schools to create effective cyberbullying policies. As well, Young et al., quoting Langos (2013), a specific law may lead to increased awareness and understanding more generally around cyberbullying.

However, as mentioned earlier, one major point against such an approach in using law, is the reality that a law with a broad focus and application risks criminalizing young people, who normally would not be, whereas the practice in Australia according to Young et al., referencing Keeley et al. (2014), is that the police only take formal action if the harm resulting is serious, using existing young offender legislation. With regard to the question of which system should manage the issue, the legal or the educational system, Young et al.'s participants were divided in their support for the introduction of a specific cyberbullying law.

Following the policy route

Since, as stated earlier, university policies refer to institutional protocols and directives governing behaviour within and related to the university, what are the needed elements to include in policy to achieve the policy intents of a safe learning environment and the reduction of cyberbullying? Using British Columbia as an example, the Ministry of Education has a Safe and Caring School Communities Policy that basically affirms all students' rights to an education free from discrimination, bullying, intimidation, and other forms of violence – a very clearly stated directive (PREVNet, 2018).

Furthermore, under the British Columbia's School Act, school boards must establish codes of conduct that define what is unacceptable behaviour, including both bullying and cyberbullying, and to identify the consequences of engaging in such behaviour. This follows from a Ministerial Order, the Provincial Standards for Codes of Conduct Order (PREVNet, 2018). Thus, it appears that there are institutional directives that can address these issues.

Policy can become actionable through the creation of practice, procedure, and/or law, but each of those must be consistent with the policy intent (e.g., the reduction of cyberbullying/the safety of victims). Therefore, while policy is not law, it sets the foundational value direction for the creation of law.

We can look for guidance from the earlier literature on cyberbullying in younger school-aged children, in terms of the policy values which informed cyberbullying case outcomes. By comparing values of note in cyberbullying case outcomes emerging at the university level, we can see a notable shift from the protection-from-harm values for the younger school-aged children group case outcomes. At the university level, with an older student population (often young adults), decisions appear to weight and value freedom of expression over protection-from-harm issues. Some authors, on the other hand (Larrañaga, Yubero, Navarro, & Ovejero, this volume), still argue that universities have the responsibility to protect students by providing students with safe physical and digital environments, and that, therefore, the focus should similarly also be on protection from harm and victimization issues.

Just as it has been argued that specific laws be established to address bullying and cyberbullying (Langos & Giancaspro, this volume), it has also been consistently argued that a specific policy should be developed to address bullying and cyberbullying, whether at the younger-aged school level or university level – not just considered in a subsection of another policy such as harassment (Faucher et al., 2015; Langos & Giancaspro, this volume). It should be noted, however, that other recent developments at the university level in Canada have affected how the problem has come to be framed. For example, even in the last year or so, it can be argued that cyberbullying has shifted from being a single-focus behaviour of concern for university administration to being one of a variety of troubling interpersonal behaviours umbrellaed under a harassment, sexual harassment, and/

or sexual misconduct label. Indeed, sexual harassment has become a watershed topic in the news more generally across the globe. Thus, policy reform in these areas has taken on the broader-scope focus – one in which the definition of the various troubling behaviours, and the specification of which of those behaviours fall under the university's jurisdiction for appropriate response, and which of those behaviours are to be streamed to external law enforcement's jurisdiction, become all important. Does it constitute a criminal offence or is it misbehaviour that the university can legitimately respond to within to resolve? Apart from that level of institutional jurisdictional question – that is, is it internal to university governance or external? – another question which remains for the university is under which mandate within the university the cyberbullying problem should fall.

In fact, three years ago, in our scan of 74 Canadian universities' policies directed to cyberbullying behaviours (Faucher et al., 2015), several rather divergent sites in the university portfolio could legitimately be assessed as the most appropriate to handle the problem. Whether the policy is housed in the Human Rights Office, the student conduct office, or the office for regulating appropriate computer usage (ICT), cyberbullying could be framed in several different ways for developing procedures and protocols for responding. But when we finished our policy scan, we found that of the 74 universities' websites examined, few had any specific policies dealing with cyberbullying. As well, even fewer provided a clear, consistent definition of cyberbullying or a description of the process by which one could determine the most appropriate policy to engage, or similarly, even the department or office most appropriate to contact.

Three main types of policies were found in our 2015 policy study, which provided some indication of the directions the universities were taking to determine the most appropriate sites for handling cyberbullying issues. The most common were those categorized as codes of student conduct and discipline; the second most common were those relating to electronic communications (ICT); and the third most frequent were ones dealing with harassment or discrimination (including sexual harassment, racism, hate speech, etc.) (Faucher et al., 2015).

And so the question must be asked, given the differing types of policies found and the differing possible sites from which responses to cyberbullying could be made: what does it mean, first, when differing policies with differing policy intents are employed to respond to the behaviour? Second, and related, how does one determine which lens is the appropriate one to handle a cyberbullying situation? As indicated earlier, rather divergent lenses could be involved. Framing it as a human rights issue, for example, suggests that a foundational right has been broken, while framing it as communications usage violation suggests it might not be as serious an infraction (Faucher et al., 2015). It has been suggested actually that a roadmap of the offices associated with the various lenses (e.g., human rights office, student conduct office, ICT office), along with a procedure explaining each focus, should be helpful in directing students, staff, and faculty to the appropriate office and policy. It was also thought this roadmap exercise could be a most appropriate one to take place near the beginning of an individual's arrival at the university (Jackson, 2015).

A comparison of some of the descriptor findings from examining actual policies from our Canadian study can be made with a similar study conducted in Australia by Campbell in 2016. She did an examination of website policies for universities with the largest enrolments in each state with respect to their listed bullying policies. She referenced the work of Smith and colleagues (2008) as being the first researchers to analyse the content of school anti-bullying policies. They employed four primary categories: the definition of bullying behaviour; reporting/responding to bullying incidents; recording/reporting/responding to bullying incidents; and strategies for preventing bullying.

Only seven of the Australian universities' policies which were examined mentioned bullying specifically. For some of the universities the anti-bullying policy was prominent, clearly set out, and in one place. But for a majority, any mention of student-to-student bullying was hard to find, which the author argued indicated a lack of commitment to "real" prevention and intervention of bullying among the students.

As well, also in Australia, Langos and Giancaspro (this volume) undertook a pilot study using a survey with randomly selected university students. Two of the questions enquired first about the students' understanding of existing criminal law regulating cyberbullying and, second, about their awareness of university policies governing cyberbullying. Similar to our Canadian study findings, a majority of students were unaware of the existence of such university policies. Most were also unaware of any criminal laws regulating cyberbullying and, in fact, for those who were aware, there was confusion about which cyberbullying behaviours were criminal. In that regard, one recommendation emerging from the survey was that there should be one specific criminal offence of cyberbullying, which clearly defines the serious behaviours covered. It was also noted that not all cyberbullying behaviours are equally harmful. Along with that discussion, it was suggested that criminalization was to be seen as only one tool for proactive management of the behaviour.

On the other hand, the argument found for the perceived efficacy of cyberbullying policies came from the students who were aware of existing policies, and they felt they were successful in that policy directly addressing cyberbullying would be an effective deterrent. And there is empirical evidence for this perception, argue Langos and Giancaspro, which emerges from several studies. The recommendation here is that, especially in light of the potential harms of cyberbullying behaviour, specific policies should definitely be developed.

Similarly, it is also argued that one value of having policies specific to anti-bullying itself is they can formalize an institution's social norms and can be used to modify behaviour through the influence of sanctions and punishments as well (Campbell, 2016). The ultimate aim (the policy intent) here is to reduce bullying at the institutional level.

Part II. Cyberbullying policy at the university institutional level: recommendations

From our own studies and from others in this volume and in the literature, a number of recommendations about how policy can best address the issues of cyberbullying at the university level emerged. These are set out in the following paragraphs of Part II. It was first recommended there is a need to have a clear definition of the behaviour of cyberbullying that is under the policy, including its nature and scope. If it is a stand-alone policy, dealing with the behaviour, then it should indicate not only where a concern/complaint should be registered but also what actions might be taken when a breach of policy occurs, and indicate the range of sanctions/penalties as well.

But both definition and actions must be set within the context of the values to be supported. This again raises the important point of the values to be established in the policy. The importance of equality has already been discussed. In addition, as stated earlier, certainly there is an interest in student, faculty, and staff well-being, and that value is supported at our university in the form of health promotion more generally. Broadly speaking, it is felt that health and well-being should be established in all university policies, but it is especially important in having well-being as a value and lens for policy development and review. It should be a guide to the types of actions possible. Along with that, all aspects of policy and procedure should embody a culture of respect and support (Black, this volume).[3]

In addition, as Cassidy and Jackson (2005) argue, expansion of existing policies on harassment and bullying or creation of a new policy specific to cyberbullying should set out the social values underpinning the policy, such as:

1 Caring and respectful behaviours in . . . exchanges;
2 Safe and nurturing environments for healthy development of identity and netizenship, and,
3 The principles of tolerance and impartiality.

Similarly, the value of civility has been mentioned (Keashly, this volume). In the U.S. chapter, Keashly argues that civility is needed not only specific to a particular cyberbullying situation between the victim (target) and the offender, but for the entire campus community more broadly, such that even a bystander will see the need to act civilly and responsibly within that setting. It is also a value that can be "operationalized" when actually developing policy, practice, and procedure as, for example, is appropriate when working collaboratively among all stakeholders (Sharpe, this volume). A related value to civility is cyber-kindness, with the ethic of kindness encouraging moral good behaviour for the whole university learning environment/community (Beck & Cassidy, 2009).

Mentioning practice brings to the fore the next steps to be taken after developing the values-based policy, and that is the need to develop protocols and legislative frameworks (Larrañaga et al., this volume) that are derived from the policy and its intent, and assist in securing that intent. As well, university community members need to have clear ideas about what actions are not only possible in response to the behaviour but are also supported (Keashly, this volume).

Associated with the value of defining the behaviour, Campbell (2016) indicates that one of the first steps toward prevention of bullying behaviour is the articulation of policy, which actually describes the unacceptable behaviours and the values that they offend, such as equity and the safety and security of the learning environment. Interestingly, few of the policies we examined dealt with the issue of prevention (less than one-quarter), but the Université de Montréal harassment policy is one example where prevention is made a priority.

Once a clear cyberbullying policy has been developed for a university (ideally with input from institutional administrators, as well as other key stakeholders, such as students, staff, and faculty), another important consideration noted by a number of authors (Faucher et al., 2015; Jones & Scott, 2012) is the importance of having those same individuals become aware not only of its existence but also of how to apply it. If the policy is disseminated to those in the institution, they become knowledgeable about the unacceptable behaviours and learn of the values the university upholds. If there is no policy, Campbell (2016) argues, it is difficult to establish the mandate of protection of those bullied and to implement change in the organization.

In our study in which university administrators were interviewed, one noted the importance of relevant policies that are also accessible to students and staff, and for immediate supervisors (such as Deans) to effectively address the problems when they first surface, so that the issues do not fester and become even more widespread (Driver, this volume; Cassidy et al., 2017). In order to be truly accessible, there is also the need to provide information on how to navigate the various possible sites in the university for submission of complaints and for receiving support (Driver, this volume). Interestingly, specific to actions to be taken, some policies we examined provided great detail about the complaint procedure and the steps to be taken by various involved parties, including possible sanctions, whereas others did not.

As Larrañaga et al. (this volume) point out, education and training is needed in that regard. Others have commented on this by saying that not only greater awareness and accessibility but also education and information are needed about cyberbullying and available support services (Blaya, this volume; Langos & Giancaspro, this volume; Keashly, this volume).

With respect to the last point about support services, it must be stressed that having policies to prohibit cyberbullying are clearly not enough in and of themselves; these must be supplemented by effective support (e.g., referral to counselling services) and, as mentioned earlier, enforcement measures and sanctions (e.g., internal retribution for perpetrator, referral to law enforcement) (Langos & Giancaspro, this volume).

In the chapter by Faucher et al. (this volume), the authors suggest a complementary set of recommendations: to develop, implement, communicate, enforce, and review university policies that speak to the issue of cyberbullying. They argue that the campus should be held responsible for upholding standards of conduct (including online conduct) that support the well-being of all community members and promote an engaging learning environment. Within educational institutions, policy also can establish the direction for the management of change within the institution. Policy at this level is also more proximal to actual institutional operations.

In addition, more research is needed. As Blizard puts it, more research is needed to actually inform policy development (Blizard, this volume). This is consistent with the Chilean argument (Condeza, Gallardo, & Reyes, this volume) that evidence could promote the development of policies and new practices with proactive approaches at both the university and state levels, to reduce the effects and impacts of cyberbullying (see also Myers & Cowie, 2017; Walker, Sockman, & Koehn, 2011).

Specific to the Chilean context, another educational value of policy, it is argued, is for the (Chilean) government to consider the existence of specific policies and protocols in this area as a requisite for university accreditations, thus stimulating the institutional attention to and awareness of the students' well-being (which includes social relationships) across the country.

Finally, Cassidy and Jackson (2005), in referencing Farrington (2001), discuss the critical need to evaluate the effectiveness of policies in order to determine if they are actually achieving their policy intent and not undermining other relevant policies and systems already in place. In Australia, in the university study (Campbell, 2016), there was no mention of evaluation of policies; however, most policies had a review date. However, in an earlier article, Campbell (2005) emphasized that policies must be in force on a continual basis in order for them to be effective. Brown et al. (2006), in referencing Lewiston and Sutton (2001), also caution that, in order to be effective, the policies need to be locally informed in the making of meaning in practice with reference to their own jurisdictional culture.

Overall, the evaluation component of such policies appears to remain less focused upon in many of the studies reported in this volume. It is often difficult to know how to evaluate such policies, given the often-confounding cause-and-effect challenges, but indicators should be developed. However, it must be acknowledged that another reason for the lack of evaluation of the policies may also be the lack of available funding to do so.

Discussion

While policy exists at a "higher" governmental level (e.g., Canada's Charter of Rights and Freedoms), even with legislation aimed at cyberbullying specifically, that clearly targets misconduct and harmful behaviours, policy at the institutional university level came to be the primary focus of this chapter on cyberbullying behaviour. Nonetheless, the guarantees, rights, and values set out in the higher-level documents must also be compatible with and inherent in the policy intents of the institutional policies developed. There should not be disjunctures between the two in that regard. Rights such as freedom of expression and security of person need to be considered and balanced at the institutional level as well.

It is true that policy at the university level has a more "local" context (the university itself) in which to operate and must be sensitive to the wider needs of that environment, with the values of a civil community profiled in policy. That implies not only participation of the differing and diverse community members in the development and application of the policy, and reflections of that diversity contained within it, but also mechanisms in place to assure awareness of, accessibility to, and education about the policy once placed into force. Whether the site for responses under the policy emerges from the ICT centre, the human rights centre, student conduct centre, etc., it must be clear to the affected persons which site to contact.

Finally, a policy of this nature, even though it targets one particular troubling behaviour, does need to consider the wider context of factors that may be impacting the behaviour for both the affected victim and the offender. Those factors may require attention by way of available support services, such as counselling and even safety measures, in order to assure that the well-being and security of the university is encouraged and sustained.

Notes

1 Nova Scotia's Cyber-Safety Act was struck down as being unconstitutional in December 2015. Bill 27, the Intimate Images and Cyber-Protection Act, is a new bill which was brought forward in October 2017 with the intent of replacing the previous act.
2 *R. v. Spencer*, by the Supreme Court of Canada (2014); *Crouch v. Snell*, by the Supreme Court of Nova Scotia (2015); and *R. v. Elliott*, by the Ontario Court of Justice (2016).
3 But the need for self-care at the individual level is also emphasized (see Blizard, this volume).

References

Beck, K., & Cassidy, W. (2009). Embedding the ethic of care in school policies and practices. In K. Riele (Ed.), *Making schools different: Alternative approaches to educating young people* (pp. 50–64). Thousand Oaks, CA: Sage Publications.

Black, T. (this volume). Designing healthy and supportive campus communities: An example from Simon Fraser University. In W. Cassidy, C. Faucher, & M. Jackson (Eds.), *Cyberbullying at university in international contexts* (pp. 162–167). Oxford, UK: Routledge.

Blaya, C. (this volume). Cyberbullying among university students in France: Prevalence, consequences, coping and interventions strategies. In W. Cassidy, C. Faucher, & M. Jackson (Eds.), *Cyberbullying at university in international contexts* (pp. 9–22). Oxford, UK: Routledge.

Blizard, L. M. (this volume). Student-to-faculty targeted cyberbullying: The impact on faculty. In W. Cassidy, C. Faucher, & M. Jackson (Eds.), *Cyberbullying at university in international contexts* (pp. 126–138). Oxford, UK: Routledge.

Brown, K., Jackson, M., & Cassidy, W. (2006). Cyber-bullying: Developing policy to direct responses that are equitable and effective in addressing this special form of bullying. *Canadian Journal of Educational Administration and Policy, 57*, 1–36.

Campbell, M. (2005). Cyberbullying: An older problem in a new guise? *Australian Journal of Guidance and Counselling, 15*(1), 68–76.

Campbell, M. (2016). Policies and procedures to address bullying at Australian universities. In H. Cowie & C.-A. Myers (Eds.), *Bullying among university students: Cross-national perspectives* (pp. 157–171). London: Routledge.

Cartwright, B. (2016, June 12–14). *Cyberbullying and the law: A Canadian perspective*. Paper presented at IEEE International Conference on Cybercrime and Computer Forensics, Vancouver, BC.

Cassidy, W., Faucher, C., & Jackson, M. (2017). Adversity in university: Cyberbullying and its impacts on students, faculty and administrators. *International Journal of Environmental Research and Public Health, Special issue Cyber Pathology: Cyber Victimization and Cyber Bullying, 14*(8), 888–890.

Cassidy, W., & Jackson, M. (2005). The need for equality in education: An intersectionality examination of labeling and zero tolerance practices. *McGill Journal of Law and Education, 40*(3), 435–456.

Cassidy, W., Jackson, M., & Faucher, C. (2016). Gender differences and cyberbullying towards faculty members in higher education. In R. Navarro, S. Yubero, & E. Larrañaga (Eds.), *Cyberbullying across the globe: Gender, family, and mental health*. Basel, Switzerland: Springer.

Coburn, P., Connelly, D., & Roesch, R. (2015). Cyberbullying: Is federal criminal legislation the solution? *Canadian Journal of Criminology and Criminal Justice, 57*(4), 566–579.

Condeza, R., Gallardo, G., & Reyes, P. (this volume). Experiences of cyberbullying perceived at a Chilean university: The voice of students. In W. Cassidy, C. Faucher, & M. Jackson (Eds.), *Cyberbullying at university in international contexts* (pp. 36–51). Oxford, UK: Routledge.

Coyne, I., & Farley, S. (this volume). Cyberbullying within working contexts. In W. Cassidy, C. Faucher, & M. Jackson (Eds.), *Cyberbullying at university in international contexts* (pp. 80–96). Oxford, UK: Routledge.

Driver, J. (this volume). Faculty members who are bullies. In W. Cassidy, C. Faucher, & M. Jackson (Eds.), *Cyberbullying at university in international contexts* (pp. 212–214). Oxford, UK: Routledge.

Dunn, W. (2008). *Public policy analysis* (5th ed.). Upper Saddle River, NJ: Pearson Publishing.

Dye, T. (2017). *Understanding public policy* (15th ed.). Toronto: Pearson Publishing.

Faucher, C., Cassidy, W., & Jackson. M. (this volume). Power in the tower: The gendered nature of cyberbullying among students and faculty at Canadian universities. In W. Cassidy, C. Faucher, & M. Jackson (Eds.), *Cyberbullying at university in international contexts* (pp. 66–79). Oxford, UK: Routledge.

Faucher, C., Jackson, M., Cassidy, W. (2014). Cyberbullying among university students: Gendered experiences, impacts, and perspectives. *Education Research International, 2014*, 1–10.

Faucher, C., Jackson, M., & Cassidy, W. (2015). When on-line exchanges byte: An examination of the policy environment governing cyberbullying at the university level. *Canadian Journal of Higher Education, 45*(1), 102–121.

Jackson, M. (2015). *Roadmap for the university: How can policy serve as a solution?* Paper presented at the Justice, Law, and Ethics in Education M.Ed. cohort mini-symposium on Bullying, Cyberbullying, and Harassment at the University, Simon Fraser University, Surrey, BC.

Jones, J. C., & Scott, S. (2012). Cyberbullying in the university classroom: A multiplicity of issues. In C. Wankel & L. Wankel (Eds.), *Misbehavior online in higher education* (pp. 157–182). Bingley, UK: Emerald Group Publishing Limited.

Kanetsuna, T., Aoyama, I., & Toda, Y. (this volume). Relationships among university students/faculty and cyberbullying in Japan. In W. Cassidy, C. Faucher, & M. Jackson (Eds.), *Cyberbullying at university in international contexts* (pp. 23–35). Oxford, UK: Routledge.

Keashly, L. (this volume). In the e-presence of others: Understanding and developing constructive cyberbystander action. In W. Cassidy, C. Faucher, & M. Jackson (Eds.), *Cyberbullying at university in international contexts* (pp. 141–156). Oxford, UK: Routledge.

Langos, C., & Giancaspro, M. (this volume). Cyberbullying in the Australian university context: The shades of harm and implications for law and policy. In W. Cassidy, C. Faucher, & M. Jackson (Eds.), *Cyberbullying at university in international contexts* (pp. 181–197). Oxford, UK: Routledge.

Larrañaga, E., Yubero, S., Navarro, R., & Ovejero, A. (this volume). From traditional bullying to cyberbullying: Cybervictimization among higher education students. In W. Cassidy, C. Faucher, & M. Jackson (Eds.), *Cyberbullying at university in international* contexts (pp. 99–111). Oxford, UK: Routledge.

Mathiesen, K. (2014). Human rights in the digital age. *Journal of Mass Media Ethics, 29*(1), 2–18.

Myers, C.-A., & Cowie, H. (2017). Bullying at university: The social and legal contexts of cyberbullying among university students. *Journal of Cross-Cultural Psychology, 48*(8), 1172–1182.

Pescitelli, A. (this volume). MySpace or yours? An exploratory study of homophobic and transphobic cyberbullying of post-secondary students. In W. Cassidy, C. Faucher, & M. Jackson (Eds.), *Cyberbullying at university in international contexts* (pp. 52–65). Oxford, UK: Routledge.

PREVNet (2018). *Policy & legislation (BC): Resources for educators: Promoting relationships & eliminating violence network*. Retrieved from www.prevnet.ca/resources/policy-and-legislation/british-columbia/for-educators

Sharpe, N. (this volume). A university ombudsperson's perspective using a fairness lens to build a kinder online campus culture. In W. Cassidy, C. Faucher, & M. Jackson (Eds.), *Cyberbullying at university in international contexts* (pp. 157–161). Oxford, UK: Routledge.

Walker, C. M., Sockman, B. R., & Koehn, S. (2011). An exploratory study of cyberbullying with undergraduate university students. *Tech Trends, 55*(2), 1–38.

Young, H., Campbell, M., Spears, B., Butler, D., Cross, D., & Slee, P. (2016). Cyberbullying and the role of law in Australian schools: Views of senior officials. *Australian, Journal of Education, 60*(1), 86–101.

Legislation and legal cases

Bill C-13, Protecting Canadians from Online Crime Act, 2nd Sess., 41st Parl. 2015 (Assented to 9 December 2014, into force March 2015 – with Criminal Code amendments).

Charter of Rights and Freedoms, Part I of the Constitution Act, 1982, being Schedule B to the Canada Act 1982 (UK), 1982, c 11. Canada.

Safe and Caring School Communities Policy, BC Ministry of Education (in force, 2005; revised 2017).
School Act [RSBC 1996], Chapter 412, BC Ministry of Education (in force, 1996).
The Provincial Standards for Codes of Conduct Ministerial, School Act, sections 85(1.1) 168 (2) (s.1) (in force, 2007; amended, 2012).
Pridgen v. University of Calgary, ABCA 139 (2012).
R. v. Spencer, SCC 43 (2014).
Crouch v. Snell, NSSC 340 (2015).
R. v. Elliott, ONCJ 35 (2016).

17

FACULTY MEMBERS WHO ARE BULLIES

Jon Driver

I have dealt with faculty bullies throughout my 20 years in university administration – as Faculty Association President, Department Chair, Dean, and Provost. Although faculty bullies are relatively rare, the damage they inflict can be significant. They can poison academic departments and make life miserable for staff and students. Worst of all, they model behaviour that other faculty colleagues come to believe is appropriate or even normal for a university employee.

Most of the faculty bullies that I have encountered share a number of characteristics. First, when someone complains about their behaviour, they use the principle of academic freedom to justify actions that would not be tolerated in most workplaces. Second, they have little experience of the world outside the Ivory Tower; they have never had to be part of a normal workplace or a team, and their performance has never been evaluated on qualities such as empathy, cooperation, or leadership. Third, they are amateur lawyers, in that they delight in intimidating others, but run to the administration or the union when they feel they have been treated unfairly. Fourth, they almost always underperform in service to the institution or the discipline, and not infrequently in other areas as well.

I have learned the following about dealing with bullies:

1 *Nip the problem in the bud.* Whenever a bully acts up, tell them they are out of line. This is particularly important when faculty members bully administrative staff or students. Make it very clear where they have crossed a line, and explain that such behaviour will not be tolerated. Document the warning.
2 *Don't play the email game.* The rest of the world may have moved on to other forms of social media, but (at least in 2017) email still forms the platform

for communication in many institutions. Bullies use email to intimidate colleagues, subordinates, and administrators, and they delight in copying widely. Do not reply to them via this medium (or through other social media) – you need to set the communication process. Use face-to-face meetings and old-fashioned memos. Limit involvement to those who really need to know. Make sure that other people involved understand this tactic and that they also limit their communications.

3 *Ensure that the bully's immediate supervisor deals with the behaviour.* Provide appropriate guidance, support, and backup to the bully's supervisor – but have the problem dealt with locally. It is far more effective for a department chair to rectify the situation than for senior administration to interfere in local governance. Most department chairs have little experience in supervising anyone except graduate students, so they will need training, help, and support.
4 *Get good advice.* Before taking action to deal with a bully, check with legal counsel, or the director of faculty relations, or whomever else can help you navigate policies and collective agreements.
5 *Don't bully the bully.* It is very tempting for administrators to find ways to "punish" bullies – perhaps by denying a sabbatical on a technicality, or else scrutinizing expense claims especially carefully. You have to deal with the bullying behaviour directly. There is no ethical basis for an "eye for an eye" approach. Any perceived unfairness will give the bully the moral high ground (and there is no one more hypocritically virtuous than a bully with a legitimate grievance).
6 *Incentivize the bully's department to behave better collectively.* By the time bullying behaviour reaches the attention of the Dean or Provost, it has usually caused damage within a department, and may have already sparked retaliation that provokes serious divisions between colleagues and further bullying of staff and students (especially graduate students). Deans and Provosts usually have a number of tools to improve such situations. Once administered to one department, word will spread rapidly that unacceptable behaviour is not tolerated. Don't worry that you are "punishing" a department for the misbehaviour of one or two people – it will not make your reputation as an administrator any worse than it already is. While not all institutions will have policies and collective agreements that allow all of the following, I have found them highly effective when bullying behaviour infects a department:

   - If you are a Dean or Provost, refuse to approve or fund any new faculty positions until a more positive atmosphere is created.
   - Work with the Dean of Graduate Studies to suspend graduate admissions to the department, on the grounds that one cannot admit students to such a dysfunctional environment.

- Cut off access to discretionary funding until bullying stops.
- Bring in an experienced department chair from another unit on an interim basis to re-establish a more collegial environment.

Finally, remember that there will be a large silent majority of people who will not stand up to a bully themselves, but they will be very grateful that you have taken action. They may even quietly thank you.

18

CYBERBULLYING IN THE SHELTERING DARKNESS OF DIGITAL ANONYMITY

Dov Schafer

During undergrad, I took a sociolinguistics course. In this class, the teacher would often solicit feedback, stories, and comments. It was a small class of about 17 students. Early on, I emerged as one of the more active participants in discussion. Perhaps I was speaking too often; I must admit I have a clear propensity toward over-contribution. Someone in the class felt that I was negatively affecting their ability to learn, but rather than confronting me about it or going to the professor, they took it upon themselves to cyberbully me. They created a fake Facebook profile and made a page called "Shut Up Dov" and posted a long, scathing criticism of me. They made it look like a few other students had liked the page. I stopped attending class since it was past the withdrawal date.

I caved to the pressure of anonymous criticism because I did not want to have to sit in a class wondering who hated me enough to make a fake Facebook account and a special page to "let [me] know that everyone hates [me] and wants [me] to shut up". That emotional decision earned me a failing grade, 34%. Prior to graduation, I approached the Dean to get the class removed in light of the cyberbullying, but they were not understanding. I ended up taking the class again in my final semester, with a significantly improved grade, just so I could explain the first grade away in future graduate admissions applications. The net effect of the bullying was a drastic reduction in my GPA during that term, loss of honours standing that year, and the time/money to take that course over again. It was a costly incident.

Cyberbullying is not just for kids; research indicates that adults often have to deal with forms of bullying/cyberbullying in the workplace and institutional settings (Faucher, Jackson, & Cassidy, 2015). Jackson, Faucher, and Cassidy (this volume) draw attention to the notion of power imbalance in cyberbullying; they note that this is an especially pressing concern at the university level. My own personal experiences have made me aware of the asymmetrical power relationship at the heart of cyberbullying. Bullies change the rules of the game to benefit themselves. When the bully chooses to move an exchange from the physical realm to an anonymous space, they are emboldening themselves and shifting the balance of power (Faucher et al., 2015; Myers & Cowie, 2017) in order to minimize ego threat and potential reciprocity or punishment.

I hesitate to use the terms *victim* and *offender* to describe the cyberbully/target relationship because it ignores the evolving power dispute between the people involved. The cyberbully is seeking to feel dominant by suppressing the target, and when the bullying is anonymous, they gain power and are strengthened in their malicious intent to berate, humiliate, or criticize another person. Anonymity and the perceived lack of consequences are key issues. I argue that if the target of cyberbullying had a tool to unmask the source of the anonymous digital criticism, and the institutional support to arbitrate that power struggle in person, we would see a reduction in the incidence of cyberbullying. It is the fuzzy embrace of digital anonymity that emboldens the bully.

As a strange twist of fate, another experience of cyberbullying happened as I was writing this essay. While playing an online competitive card game called Hearthstone (Blizzard, 2018) during lunch, I faced an opponent and ended up winning quickly. The opponent added me as a friend so they could type a message to me. I was happy to accept the friend request. Without adding people as friends, they can only use pre-made emotes instead of typing whatever they want to you. Instead of saying "good game, you were really lucky there" or something similar, they were full of profanities and anger. They started off sounding harmless – "you should play the lottery", to which I replied "Yah, that was really lucky . . . good game". Then they came back with "Fuck you faggot" and "I hope your family dies in a car crash and you have to watch". I was really horrified at the rage this person was expressing and the deep level of violent anger they felt towards me, simply for losing a friendly game of Hearthstone.

The ego threat my opponent suffered for that quick loss needed an outlet. The only suitable vent they could release was to spew the most hurtful thing they could muster at a complete stranger on the internet. That person escalated the friendly anonymous interaction we had for the sole purpose of trying to hurt me. My opponent continued to try to insult me, so I removed them from my friends list. I was happy to move on with my day and forget about the whole event but could only imagine how that might have made me feel when I was younger and more easily hurt by strangers' words. I knew how that anonymous hatred would have felt if it was a classmate of mine. I would want the university to be aware of that student's behaviour so they could monitor and take disciplinary action if it proved to be a trend. Additionally, a report button in the game chat interface would have been nice; I want this person to be suspended from playing for a day or two to think about how they are treating others online.

Making people feel like the internet is a public space, rather than a private one, is essential to reducing this sort of behaviour. Along with design features that allow user reporting, I think technologies that actively eliminate anonymity may reduce bullying. One potential solution could be using the power of distributed ledger technology. Essentially, cryptocurrencies are shared digital books which are used to track transactions by recording public records of each trade. This technology can also be used to digitally fingerprint online activity. Some cryptocurrency companies, such as Self-Key and Dock, are already using cryptocurrency (distributed ledgers) that are tied to identity data in order to transmit user information across social networks. It seems reasonable to assume that a lack of systemic anonymity in online interaction would reduce the likelihood that potential bullies would feel emboldened to act maliciously when speaking online to both peers and strangers.

In this chapter I gave two personal examples of cyberbullying: one clear example of student-to-student bullying at the post-secondary level using Facebook and one example of stranger-to-stranger incivility that occurred, ironically, while I was writing this chapter. Both examples show cyberbullying as an asymmetrical power struggle; a sneak attack from bully to target designed to make the bully feel better about themselves at the cost of the target in an anonymous setting with little to no risk for the attacker. I feel that an increased focus on software interface design features that eliminate the anonymity of online behaviour can begin eroding the confidence of would-be bullies. When we feel like we are in public, we tend to act in a more outwardly civil way. Fewer crimes of opportunity are committed in plain sight than in the sheltering darkness.

References

Blizzard Entertainment. (2018). *Hearthstone: Heroes of warcraft* [online game]. Retrieved from http://battle.net/hearthstone/

Faucher, C., Jackson, M., & Cassidy, W. (2015). When on-line exchanges byte: An examination of the policy environment governing cyberbullying at the university level. *Canadian Journal of Higher Education, 45*(1), 102–121.

Jackson, M., Faucher, C., & Cassidy, W. (this volume). What's policy got to do with it? The focus on cyberbullying policy at the university level. In W. Cassidy, C. Faucher, & M. Jackson (Eds.), *Cyberbullying at university in international contexts* (pp. 198–211). Oxford, UK: Routledge.

Myers, C. A., & Cowie, H. (2017). Bullying at university: The social and legal contexts of cyberbullying among university students. *Journal of Cross-Cultural Psychology, 48*(8), 1172–1182.

REFLECTIONS AND CONCLUSIONS

Wanda Cassidy, Chantal Faucher, and Margaret Jackson

In this book, we have endeavoured to bring together a diverse set of perspectives that cross jurisdictional as well as disciplinary lines. Our purpose was twofold. On the one hand, we wanted to offer a wide examination into the ways that cyberbullying manifests itself at the post-secondary level, the forms it takes, how prevalent it is, the reasons why it occurs, the impacts on those who are targeted, as well as the broader effects such incidents have on university life. On the other hand, we also wanted to focus on the development of solutions to the problem and the role that policy can and should play in addressing cyberbullying on university campuses. In this chapter, we review the key points that emerge from the different contributions offered in this book and reflect on areas for future research in order to further what we have learned to date.

Nature, extent, and rationale

Student-to-student cyberbullying

Although the studies described in this book use different instruments, employ slightly different definitions of cyberbullying, and use different methods to examine the phenomenon, the results of these studies indicate that cyberbullying among university students who participated in the studies is occurring at rates varying from 3% (Japan) to 46% (Chile). Since cyberbullying occurs through the venues that students regularly access, it is no surprise to see hurtful messages and unwanted pictures posted on Facebook, YouTube, Instagram, Skype, Snapchat, WhatsApp, chat rooms, gaming sites, email, text messaging, etc. (Chapters 1–8, 15 and 18). Cyberbullying among students who know each other appears to be more common than cyberbullying from strangers. This fits with those authors who discuss relational aggression theory as a way to understand aggression within friendship groups and dating/partner relationships (Chapters 5, 7, and 8). The primary reasons given for the targeting is also relational: the person upset them; they were targeted first and are fighting back; the person is not liked or is "different"; and/or because it is "fun." Pescitelli (Chapter 4) discusses homophobic and transphobic cyberbullying experienced by LGBTQ students, who were targeted because of their "differences," with the perpetrators being strangers, but also members of the LGBTQ community.

While students are more likely to be targeted by someone they know, anonymous cyberbullying is also a factor, particularly towards male students (Chapter 5) and those involved in the gaming community. As noted by Kanetsuna, Aoyama, and Toda in Chapter 2, beliefs about anonymity play a role in aggressive and deviant online behaviour because this perception either weakens personal and collective norms to morally disengage or strengthens students' conformity to a particular group norm. Furthermore, it affects students' perception of risk of victimization and the measures they take to protect themselves. Schafer (Chapter 18) also identifies anonymity as a contributing factor in the cyberbullying he experienced as an undergraduate student, as well as while playing an online game.

University students, like their younger counterparts in school (Cassidy, Jackson, & Brown, 2009), tend to see cyberbullying as a "normal" part of the online world, rather than a problem that can be eliminated (Chapter 3). This perception has implications regarding how we engage youth and young adults in finding solutions.

Cyberbullying of faculty

There are fewer studies examining student-to-faculty and faculty-to-faculty cyberbullying. The authors of Chapters 2, 5, 6, 8, and 9 examine these relationships, using such theoretical constructs as contra-power harassment – where one group, such as students who normally have less power, change the power imbalance through nefarious actions such as ruining a professor's reputation on rating sites or writing negative evaluations. The literature on academic entitlement and on classroom incivility may also factor into students' aggressive behaviour towards their professors, as described in Chapters 5, 8, and 9. Indeed, the reasons students give for cyberbullying faculty primarily relate to the professor's teaching style, the courses they teach, and their grading practices. Students primarily rely on email, online course sites, and professor rating sites to cyberbully their professors.

Faculty members who cyberbully each other, especially those who are in positions of leadership in the academy, may also be seeking greater power and control, lending support to the Power and Control theoretical model discussed by the authors of Chapters 5 and 8. Coyne and Farley (Chapter 6) also identify power imbalance, along with frequency and duration, as characteristics that differentiate workplace cyberbullying from other related aggressive acts.

The studies reported in this book indicate that between 15% and 52% of faculty members who participated in the studies report being cyberbullied by students, with one study (Chapter 8) reporting that 12% of participating faculty were cyberbullied by colleagues, primarily over email and by those known to them. Although fewer studies have been conducted on workplace cyberbullying compared to workplace bullying, Coyne and Farley refer to three university workplace studies in the UK, which show a cyberbullying frequency rate among faculty of between 13.6% and 20.8%.

Gender issues

Gender appears to be a factor in cyberbullying at post-secondary, although the impact is inconsistent across studies. While females tend to participate in greater numbers in surveys and interviews (see Chapters 1, 3, 5, 8, 9, and 15), and report more serious impacts compared to males (Chapter 8), different patterns emerge. In some studies, females are targeted more often, particularly by friends, while males are targeted more by strangers and in online communities. In Blaya's study (Chapter 1), male students declared greater involvement as perpetrators and as victim/authors, but in the study discussed by Faucher, Cassidy, and Jackson (Chapter 5), female and male students were perpetrators in relatively equal numbers.

As noted by Jackson, Faucher, and Cassidy (Chapter 16), gender must also be a factor considered in creating policy at the post-secondary level to address cyberbullying. Policy is needed which is equality-based, in terms of considering power imbalances, in order to develop equitable solutions for both male and female university members.

Impacts and redress

The studies discussed in this volume point to a range of impacts on victims, author/victims, and the wider university culture, discrediting the perception that cyberbullying is a childish phenomenon that does not affect adults (discussed in Chapters 5 and 7). Commonly reported impacts on university students include: mental and physical health effects, declining achievement, disrupted relationships, deteriorating social life, withdrawal behaviour, reduction in self-esteem, as well as a broad range of emotional reactions from anger, hurt, humiliation, shame, and frustration, to shaking and crying, sometimes lasting for months. Suicide ideation is also reported among a minority of respondents across jurisdictions. Perpetrators may also experience victimization, as noted in Blaya (Chapter 1), since authors may become victims, and victims authors.

Faculty report experiencing very similar impacts, after being targeted by students and/or colleagues. Blizard's quotations (Chapter 9) from interviews with faculty members highlight the depth of the impacts on their work and personal lives, particularly because very little was done at the administrative level to address the identified situations. Cassidy, Faucher, and Jackson (Chapter 8) contribute additional open-ended and interview examples to the discussion of impacts. Faculty members in this chapter reported being more upset long-term with being targeted by colleagues than by students, because students generally were gone after a semester, whereas they had to interact with their colleagues on a regular basis.

Kanetsuna, Aoyama, and Toda (Chapter 2) discuss the impact on the university culture as a whole, where collective norms of good behaviour are weakened, and where supportive networks are fractured. A negative tone may pervade the university, compounded by frustration when known problems are not addressed in meaningful ways by those in authority. Larrañaga, Yubero, Navarro, and Ovejero (Chapter 7) discuss the important role that social support systems play in preventing cyberbullying as well as providing a buffer to the consequences.

Students and faculty across the studies reported here consistently mention challenges with reporting mechanisms and the inadequacy of solutions. Those on the receiving end of cyberbullying either ignore the problem, try to solve it themselves, or talk with friends, which usually does not resolve the situation. University policies and procedures generally are either not established, not known, or not acted upon, thus further preventing an effective resolution.

Solutions

Many of the authors of the chapters in this volume stress the importance of education and dialogue across university stakeholder groups, de-naturalizing the acceptance of aggressive actions among students, developing clearly stated and communicated policies, establishing better reporting options – including anonymous reporting, providing greater support for victims, and focusing on relationship-building, as pathways towards solutions.

The section of the book titled "Solutions" brings together chapters specifically geared to solutions that are being tried in institutions. Keashly (Chapter 10) discusses the importance of developing constructive cyber-bystander action since it is often bystanders who, if empowered, can intervene to prevent negative actions, to provide needed support to victims, and/or to change the culture of an institution. Farley and Coyne (Chapter 14) consider the value of evidence-based practices, which might include training staff in such programs as CREW (civility, respect, and engagement at work), and conflict de-escalation. Kanayama and Kurihara (Chapter 13) discuss specific ways that universities in Japan are addressing cyberbullying, by empowering peers to teach each other, requiring students to enrol in seminars on internet morality and criminal behaviour, screening all incoming first-year undergraduates for mental health issues, and providing access to counsellors and health practitioners once a problem is identified.

The two remaining chapters in this section are written by practitioners, each with a wealth of experience fostering more positive campus cultures. Sharpe, a university ombudsperson, discusses the importance of using a fairness lens to address relational conflicts and to prod administrators to act when required. Since the appointment of an ombudsperson is becoming more common at universities globally, those in this position have an opportunity to influence practice and policy. Black's chapter raises the importance of universities prioritizing the health and wellness of their students, staff, and faculty, and taking concrete steps to implement a design that is collaborative and has stakeholder support.

While no one approach represents a panacea, many different approaches, geared to the needs of a particular university and designed to work in sync with each other, represent a step forward. Special considerations in program planning and implementation should also be given to populations with an increased risk of being cyberbullied, such as the LGBTQ students discussed by Pescitelli, and to culturally appropriate practices. For example, some of the interventions used in Japanese universities may not be directly transferable (without modification) to other contexts. Furthermore, since gender surfaces as a factor across many studies, attention should be given to tailoring initiatives to meet identified gender issues, rather than relying on one-size-fits-all initiatives.

What is clear from the discussions in this volume is that universities have a responsibility and an obligation to address the health and well-being of their communities, and not to do so places students, faculty, and staff at risk.

Policy issues

Adherence to equality-based policy principles should assist in meeting that requirement. Those foundational principles can guide the development and implementation of appropriate solutions to cyberbullying problems seen on campuses cross-jurisdictionally. Without the policy component, the policy intents and their associated values, such as civility and wellness, are not clarified for the institutional members. It was argued in Jackson, Faucher, and Cassidy (Chapter 16) that in instances of cyberbullying, the balance between conflicting values, such as freedom of expression and safety of person, is set by policy. In the absence of those values and that balance, prevention and intervention programs may flounder and be directionless because they were not initially grounded in the policy balance and intent. Again, this is true cross-jurisdictionally.

Both chapters by Jackson, Faucher, and Cassidy (Chapter 16) and Langos and Giancaspro (Chapter 15) also identify the importance of higher-level documents such as, for example, the Canadian Charter of Rights and Freedoms, and other overarching legislation that articulates the rights and values of a society, and which institutional policies should reflect and reinforce. Rights such as freedom of expression and security of person need to be considered and balanced at the institutional level as well as in the society at large. Langos and Giancaspro's study demonstrates students' lack of knowledge about online behaviour that is considered criminal, as well as ignorance of university policies related to cyberbullying, if they do exist. Both chapters stress the importance not only of clearly communicated policy that is understood but also policy that is supported by other services, such as counselling and safety measures, to ensure that the well-being and security of the university is encouraged and sustained.

Finally, Driver, University Provost at the time of writing (Chapter 17), notes that policy without action is insufficient; that administrators must take effective and decisive action when they learn that faculty members are being cyberbullied. Graduate student Schafer zeroes in on cyberbullies who hide behind the wall of anonymity, while noting new technological advances that soon may be used to identify all internet users by their unique digital fingerprint, thus exposing anonymous cyberbullies and reducing their negative behaviour. Different kinds of policies and procedures may well be needed to address the latter advances.

Areas for future research

The authors of the chapters in this book are rooted in many different disciplinary perspectives: education, criminology, psychology, law, health sciences, communications, sociology, business, labour studies, humanities, and social work, yet each contribute significantly to our understanding of the problems of cyberbullying at the university level. We suggest that the field would benefit from more cross-disciplinary and multi-disciplinary research within jurisdictions and across jurisdictions. Collaborative international efforts can reap a broader understanding.

We also note the benefits of participatory action research that involves the various stakeholders in the university context, in particular, with populations that have not yet been studied – for example, staff. While research at the university level to date primarily has focused on student-to-student cyberbullying and (to some extent) student-to-faculty cyberbullying, more studies should examine faculty-to-student exchanges, as well as workplace cyberbullying among faculty and staff.

Studies at the university level have tended to employ surveys, whereas other methods, particularly qualitative approaches such as case studies, narrative inquiry, and phenomenological studies, would add a richness to the literature, as would studies that offer a more critical research lens investigating university populations who are marginalized and the intersectionality of their marginalization. As noted in Chapter 16, further studies are needed to examine the factors influencing policy development and implementation, and to evaluate programs and approaches that have proven useful.

Momentum is also needed to move research into practice – to provide opportunities for universities at several different levels to experiment with prevention and intervention measures and to evaluate their effectiveness. Although universities deal with a different age group and have a different mandate than primary and secondary schools, programs that have been shown to be effective in those contexts may have some applicability at the post-secondary level, particularly when it comes to educating and empowering bystanders to take action. These efforts may complement the recommendations made by Keashly in Chapter 10. Universities also can benefit from the expanding research on cyberbullying in the workplace and in other environments, as many of the principles of power and control, relational aggression, and social dominance theory (see Chapter 5) are at work in these settings.

We also acknowledge that cyberbullying is a moral problem, one that is endemic in the wider society: practised in homes, schools, and communities; represented in popular culture; and sometimes applauded. As such, there is no easy fix, although that does not mean that tackling the problem of cyberbullying should not receive our full attention. In our own work, we draw on the ethic of care theoretical framework posed by Noddings (1992, 2002) in considering ways to improve behaviour, foster positive relationships, and build a more respectful and kinder culture. Noddings advocates the importance of modelling, dialogue, practice, and confirmation as ethical teachers. We suggest that more research needs to be done (perhaps as case studies) on applying an ethic of care theoretical approach to improving relationships among university students, staff, and faculty.

Concluding comments

We undertook this book as a way to bring together cyberbullying scholars and practitioners from various geographic locations – North and South America, Europe, the United Kingdom, Asia, and Australia – to share what each has learned from their respective research and practice about the problem of cyberbullying on university campuses and to recommend ways to take action. It is our hope that this book will encourage research-based, creative approaches to the prevention and intervention of cyberbullying at the post-secondary level, locally and globally.

References

Cassidy, W., Jackson, M., Brown, K. (2009). Sticks and stones can break my bones, but how can pixels hurt me? Students experiences with cyber-bullying. *School Psychology International, 30*(4), 383–402.

Noddings, N. (1992). *The challenge to care in schools*. New York, NY: Teachers College Press.

Noddings, N. (2002). *Educating moral people: A caring alternative to character education*. New York, NY: Teachers College Press.

INDEX